Understanding & Paying Less Proper... For Dumm...

C000184258

Income Tax

Payable on income from employment and investment.

Personal allowances	2008–9
Under 65	£5,435
65 to 74	£9,030
75 upwards	£9,180

The taxable income bands are:

Rate	Band
20%	−34,600
40%	£34,601 or more

Stamp Duty

Payable on property transactions.

Property purchase price (disadvantaged areas)	Property purchase price (all other areas)	Rate
Up to £150,000	Up to £125,000	0%
£150,001 to £250,000	£125,001 to £250,000	1%
	£250,001 to £500,000	3%
	£500,001 and over	4%

Tax is paid at the rate applicable to the purchase price on the whole amount.

Capital Gains Tax

Payable on gains in the value of assets, such as on the increase in value of a property.

Flat rate: 18 per cent

Annual exemption: £9,600 per person

For Dummies: Bestselling Book Series for Beginners

Understanding & Paying Less Property Tax For Dummies®

Corporation Tax

Payable by companies on their annual profits.

Rates

Full rate	28 per cent
Small companies rate	21 per cent

The small companies rate is payable by companies with taxable profits up to £300,000. The full rate is payable on taxable profits above £1.5 million. Between £300,000 and £1.5 million a sliding scale applies.

Value Added Tax

Payable on goods and services.

Rates	Payable on
0%	books, newspapers, children's clothes, most food items
5%	domestic gas and electricity/energy-saving materials
17.5%	most items (standard rate)

Traders must register for VAT if their annual sales exceed £67,000 (from April 2008) for the previous 12 months or expect to go over this level within the next 30 days. Traders whose sales fall below £65,000 (from April 2008) may (but aren't obliged to) deregister for VAT.

Inheritance Tax

Payable on the value of your estate after your death.

Nil rate: £300,000 – £312,000

40 per cent rate band: £312,001 or more

For Dummies: Bestselling Book Series for Beginners

Understanding & Paying Less Property Tax

FOR DUMMIES®

by Steve Sims

John Wiley & Sons, Ltd

Understanding & Paying Less Property Tax For Dummies®

Published by
John Wiley & Sons, Ltd
The Atrium
Southern Gate
Chichester
West Sussex
PO19 8SQ
England

E-mail (for orders and customer service enquires): cs-books@wiley.co.uk

Visit our Home Page on www.wiley.com

For general information on our other products and services, please contact our Customer Care Department within the U.S. at 800-762-2974, outside the U.S. at 317-572-3993, or fax 317-572-4002.

For technical support, please visit www.wiley.com/techsupport.

Wiley also publishes its books in a variety of electronic formats. Some content that appears in print may not be available in electronic books.

British Library Cataloguing in Publication Data: A catalogue record for this book is available from the British Library

ISBN: 978-0-470-75872-4

Printed and bound in Great Britain by TJ International, Padstow, Cornwall

10 9 8 7 6 5 4 3 2 1

WILEY

About the Author

Steve Sims is a landlord, property developer, tax consultant, and writer. He has 20 years experience in the property industry, and with his wife, Amanda, runs a property tax advisory company, Property Tax Plus (www.propertytaxplus.co.uk).

Before plunging into the property world, Steve was a journalist working for many years on regional evening newspapers, and as a press officer. Besides writing this book, he writes blogs and articles for several property and tax websites.

Steve lives with Amanda in Harlech, North Wales, and has four grown up sons, Alan, Carl, Peter and Tim. His interests include West Ham United, beer, and music (though not necessarily in that order!).

Dedication

This book is dedicated to Amanda. She was the angel whispering persistent encouragement in one ear, while the devil sat on my other shoulder shouting temptations at me to idle my days away. Without her support and help with research, I am sure this book would not have been written.

Author's Acknowledgments

Whenever I read a book, I feel that this section is like one of those drawn out Oscar acceptance speeches thanking everyone I've known, spoken to or passed in the street at some time or another.

So, I'll keep this short and sweet and just mention the two people who merit most praise in bringing this book in to print other than my wife, Amanda.

The staff at Wiley have been a dream team, especially Sam Spickernell, my Executive Editor, and Simon Bell, my Development Editor. Both have offered invaluable advice and assistance while showing great patience – neither probably realise how much I have appreciated their comments and guidance.

I know they are at the sharp end of a support pyramid and I hope they pass on my personal thanks to all the other 'nameless' ones whose shoulders they stand on.

Publisher's Acknowledgments

We're proud of this book; please send us your comments through our Dummies online registration form located at www.dummies.com/register/.

Some of the people who helped bring this book to market include the following:

Acquisitions, Editorial, and Media Development

Executive Editor: Sam Spickernell.

Development Editor: Simon Bell

Copy Editor: Anne O'Rorke

Technical Editor: Chris Norris, Policy Officer, National Landlords Association (www.landlords.org.uk)

Proofreader: Kim Vernon

Publisher: Jason Dunne

Executive Project Editor: Daniel Mersey

Cover Photos: © Steve Sant/Alamy

Cartoons: Ed McLachlan

Composition Services

Project Coordinator: Lynsey Stanford

Layout and Graphics: Carl Byers

Proofreaders: Melissa Bronnenberg, David Faust, Caitie Kelly, Dwight Ramsey, Amanda Steiner

Indexer: Cheryl Duksta

Contents at a Glance

Table of Contents

Introduction

*I*n the property business, as in life in general, only two things are certain: Death and taxes. Like anyone else, landlords and property developers can't do much about avoiding the Grim Reaper, but tax is a different matter.

Make no mistake about it, tax is compulsory, and rightly so. The economy, and society in general, wouldn't work without it. Unlike only a few generations ago, nowadays practically everyone has to have dealings with the taxman, otherwise known as Her Majesty's Revenue & Customs (HMRC). The fact that everyone has to pay tax, however, doesn't mean that anyone should pay more than they legally have to, and that includes landlords and property developers.

The business of buying and making money from property has become high profile in modern popular culture. No end of television programmes focus on the dramas, triumphs, and pitfalls of buying and 'doing up' houses for profit, while the number of landlords looking to secure long-term investment income from rented property has risen steadily in the last decade or so. That doesn't mean it's an easy option, however, and the tax regime doesn't make it any easier: Good job this book is here to help.

About This Book

Understanding & Paying Less Property Tax For Dummies does what it says on the tin. First, it will help you to understand the fearsomely complicated rules and regulations by which HMRC seek to recover their due. Then, it helps you to realise that perfectly legitimate means exist to pay no more tax than you legally have to.

In summary, this book covers the following:

- ✔ Deciding what sort of property business, or businesses, you're going to run.
- ✔ Understanding the various taxes you can expect to encounter.
- ✔ Coming to terms with your tax obligations.
- ✔ Reducing your property tax burden to the legally required minimum.

You don't need to read this book cover-to-cover. Dip in as you need to, picking out the nuggets of info you require for any particular tax circumstance in which you find yourself.

Conventions Used in This Book

To help you navigate through this book, I set up a few conventions:

- ✔ _Italics_ are used for emphasis and to highlight new words or defined terms.
- ✔ **Bold faced** text indicates the key concept in a list.
- ✔ Monofont is used for website and e-mail addresses.

What You're Not to Read

This book is largely concerned with the nitty-gritty of property tax issues, but every now and then we use sidebars – grey-tinted boxes of text – to give some historical background or a bit of supplementary info. Feel free to skip over these bits if you want to.

Foolish Assumptions

While writing this book I made some assumptions about you:

- ✔ You either are, or want to be, a landlord letting property for rent, or a developer buying property to sell on at a profit.
- ✔ You aren't a tax adviser or accountancy professional. If you are, you've got enough books on tax, and more profitable things to spend your time on than reading a basic guide to the property tax system.
- ✔ You can fill in your annual self-assessment tax return on your own. I don't go through the return form step-by-step because most of it doesn't relate to property, and the guidance that comes with it is comprehensive and straightforward. Instead, I offer what you need to fill in the property sections of the form easily and accurately.
- ✔ You don't get your kicks reading about property tax. You want to know exactly what you need to make sure that you pay the tax you actually owe, and claim what you are entitled to: No more, no less.
- ✔ You want to know both the pitfalls and the high spots when it comes to sorting out your property portfolio to minimise property tax.

How This Book Is Organised

This book has six major parts. Each part is divided into chapters relating to the theme, and each chapter is subdivided into individual sections relating to the chapter topic. Additionally, take a look at the table of contents at the start of this book and the detailed index at the end to help you pinpoint what you particularly need to know about.

Here's an outline of what you can expect to find out about in each part.

Part 1: Property Tax Facts

This part takes you through the ground rules of your relationship with the tax system – what you pay, when you pay it, and what events triggers tax payments. I also give you a rundown on a few people who can help.

Part 11: Balancing the Books

In this part, I look at the fundamentals of accurate, tidy record keeping, the secret of success in running a property business. I also introduce you to the importance of keeping tabs on all your property income, and – just as importantly – your expenses.

Part 111: Property Taxes and How to Slash Them

This part goes into the important detail on which taxes you need to pay, and exactly how much you need to hand over for each. The chapters in this part give you the meat and veg of your tax-saving strategy.

Part 1V: Professional Property Investing

This part covers the serious business of, well, business. Here's where to come if you want the skinny on developing property for sale, running holiday lets, and avoiding all the tax traps that go with them.

Part V: Keeping the Right Company

This is where you need to come if you're thinking about running your property business through a company. I take you through who should be looking to incorporate, and who shouldn't. I also go into the detail of incorporation, the evils of Corporation Tax, and the best ways to deal with both in a stress-free manner.

Part VI: The Part of Tens

This part is an essential ingredient in any *For Dummies* book. Each of the three chapters contains ten succinct, must-know points. The first covers ten must-do tax-saving tips for the savvy property entrepreneur. The second is a guide to potential tax banana skins, the tax disasters that can catch out the unwary. The third is a list of useful online resources that can help keep your tax knowledge at the cutting edge.

Icons Used in This Book

Within each chapter you find the following icons pointing you to particular types of information that you may find immediately useful:

This icon contains true-to-life examples to help illustrate a point. These examples are designed to give you a better understanding of how to put the theory into practice, but if you already have a grasp of the topic, you can skip over them.

This is the stuff you really need to take away with you. Keeping in mind anything this icon highlights can make your tax life easier.

Handy hints and insider wrinkles to give you the edge in your adventures with property tax.

This icon flags up the pitfalls of property tax. If the text with this icon tells you not to do something, don't.

Where you see this icon you know that the accompanying text is a little more complex. If you're struggling to get to grips with the detail, feel free to move on.

Where to Go from Here

You can read this book in several ways. If you want, you can start at the front cover and read all the way through to the end. This way, you get to understand property tax in all its awful glory, and you won't miss a thing about any of the main taxes you have to deal with in whichever type of business you run.

Alternatively, you can pick a topic that you want to know about and dive straight in there. This book is set up so you read the bits that interest you in self-contained sections. Some chapters also apply more to landlords than developers (and vice versa). If you do want to dip in and out of the book, I recommend that you at least read Part I first. This gives you a good foundation for understanding the whole process of property taxation. But of course, you can read it in any way you want – it's your call.

Wherever you go from here, whenever you find a piece of advice or a warning that applies to you, copy it, and then fix it to the fridge with a magnet, or pin it up on your notice board, and then don't forget to act on it. And as you read through this book, why not make pencil notes on your tax form to help you when you come to complete the form for real? Being informed and planning well ahead is the best tax advice anyone can give you.

Part I
Property Tax Facts

'Well, now we're up and running, Miss
Grunblatt, the world will soon be
beating a path to our door.'

In this part . . .

This part, as its title suggests, gives you the basics. Here you can find out your part in the tax regime and your responsibilities to it. I introduce you to the idea that tax doesn't just happen, but is triggered by what you do, and how you need to react in order to manage your property as tax-efficiently as possible.

I also introduce you to the nice people at Her Majesty's Revenue & Customs (HMRC), and to a few people – advisers, accountants, and tax experts – who can help you deal with them.

Chapter 1

You and Property Tax

*T*ax is a good thing. Really. It pays for the state education system, the National Health Service, the police and the armed forces. It's very unlikely you've made it this far in life without benefiting in some way from services funded by the great British taxpayer, and property tax in its many and various forms is a big part of the overall tax picture. Having said all that, no one wants to pay more tax than they have to, whatever it's on. That's why you're reading this right now.

Paying property tax, like paying any other form of tax, is not an opt-in process. You must declare all your income, whether from property or otherwise, to Her Majesty's Revenue and Customs (HMRC), and pay the taxes due by law – or face the consequences. To do that efficiently, you need to have a basic understanding of where your cog fits into the big tax machine.

This chapter provides an overview of the nuts and bolts of property tax. It doesn't tell you a lot about how to save money, but does show you the taxes you have to pay if you want to run a property business and the difference between tax avoidance (legal) and tax evasion (criminal).

Making Tax Law Is One Thing . . .

Let's start with the basics - what is tax law? Like any other law, tax law is a set of rules that everyone must obey.

The three ways of making law are:

- ✔ Statute or Acts of Parliament voted in by MPs and the House of Lords
- ✔ Statutory instruments, bye-laws and the like made under powers delegated by Parliament to ministers and other organisations
- ✔ Statute voted in by the European Assembly

Property tax is not a single tax coming from a set of rules laid out by a particular Act of Parliament. It's a bit of this Act and a bit of another. That's one of the reasons property tax can be difficult to master.

Bringing a law to the statute book

Imagine the tax year is a clock face. Replace the numbers with months – with April as 12 o'clock, May as 1, June as 2 and so on.

Now you have the tax year laid out. The tax year, also called the *fiscal year* or *year of assessment* is right at the heart of the tax machine.

The tax year runs from April 6 of one year until April 5 the following year, including leap years. The current tax year started at 00.01 am last April 6, 2008 and ends at 23.59 p. m. next April 5.

Now, each year the tax clock starts ticking on April 6. The Chancellor makes a Pre-Budget Report sometime around 7 November that announces any intended changes in tax rules, rates and allowances. The Budget proper, around 11 March, confirms the Chancellor's intentions.

The Budget is the basis of tax legislation and lays out any changes for the tax year starting from April 6 following the Budget.

Parliament debates and amends the Budget proposals and then they pass in to law as the Finance Act. Each year has a Finance Act that governs the rates of taxes you are charged and any reliefs and allowances to which you are entitled. The Finance Act can also amend or repeal other tax legislation.

Other Acts in the tax framework give Her Majesty's Revenue and Customs (HMRC) powers to collect your tax or punish you for failing to pay. They also lay out the finer points of the many property taxes, as you will see in more detail later in this chapter.

Who's got jurisdiction?

The United Kingdom has three legal *jurisdictions,* the areas to which tax law applies applies

- England and Wales
- Scotland
- Northern Ireland

Not all laws apply to each jurisdiction, but generally tax law is the same in all of them and the information in this book applies equally to you, wherever you live in the UK. Any legal differences mostly arise in rules governing property ownership rather than the taxes arising from property use.

In this book, the UK means England, Wales, Scotland and Northern Ireland – anywhere else, including the Isle of Man and the Channel Islands, is overseas.

. . . Making Law Work Is Another

Just like anything else, those clever ladies and gentlemen who draft our laws don't always get it right first time. Sometimes the law is famously an ass. At other times ambiguous wording in a statute baffles even the cleverest legal brains. There are even occasions when the interpretation of a tax law can work to your advantage in surprising ways.

Parliament has the authority to make, change and repeal laws, but another important set of cogs in the tax machine are the tax commissioners. These fall into two groups:

- **The General Commissioners of Tax:** An independent tribunal of lay people that hears appeals from taxpayers unhappy with HMRC decisions
- **The Special Commissioners:** Often lawyers with detailed technical knowledge of the tax system, these people determine more complex appeals.

The tax commissioners can tweak the way law works in practice by interpreting the meaning of a statute law. The commissioners give written decisions after hearing evidence from the taxpayer and HMRC, and their opinion comes to form *case law*.

Case law has the same standing as statute law. If you are basing an appeal on the wording of a statute, it is very important that you also bear in mind how later case law or amendments may have changed the original meaning of the legislation.

If you don't agree with the tax commissioners and have enough cash to take the fight on, you can appeal to higher courts and even go all the way to the European Assembly.

Paying Your Property Tax

OK. It's time to get down to the nitty-gritty – what is property tax? Property tax is the product of a mish-mash of different Acts of Parliament thrown together over the years without as much thought or planning as you might expect.

Nevertheless, the law's the law and you have to pay your dues. I cover the main types of tax to which you'll be subject as a property businessperson in the following sections.

Stamp Duty

Stamp Duty Land Tax (SDLT), to give it it's full name, applies to most property transactions involving buying or leasing property. The rate of stamp duty you pay increases with the value of the property you buy, starting at 1 per cent on a property valued at £125,000, and rising to 4 per cent on a property worth more than £500,000, unless the property is in a disadvantaged area, where special rules apply.

Your solicitor should calculate stamp duty and fill in your stamp duty returns when you buy property. Check the figures to make sure he's got it right. See Chapter 8 for more details on how to lick Stamp Duty.

Income Tax

Property investors – people who buy property in order to get a steady income from rent – pay income tax on their rental profits. These profits are the rent they receive minus expenses.

Property developers – people who buy property in order to refurbish it and sell it on at a profit – pay income tax on business profits. These profits are the price of any property sold, less the costs of acquiring and preparing the property for sale, and general business costs.

Property investors pay income tax on rental profits and capital gains tax on profits from selling property. Traders pay income tax on all property profits.

See Chapters 5–7 for more about income, expenses, and working out your profits or losses.

Capital Gains Tax

Capital Gains Tax, or CGT, is a tax payable on the profit you make when you sell assets. It's also the tax beast everyone wants to tame. Planning for CGT is a huge part of tax planning for property investors and developers, and the tax which catches most people in its traps.

Property investors pay CGT on the profits they make on the increase in value of their properties when they sell.

See Chapters 9 and 10 for strategies to slash your CGT bills.

Corporation Tax

Corporation Tax is the tax companies pay on their profits.

Rules for calculating company profits and tax are a little different from those for individuals. Companies pay Corporation Tax both on rental profits and on gains from selling property, instead of paying Income Tax and Capital Gains Tax.

Chapters 18 to 21 cover the advantages and disadvantages of holding property in a company.

Value Added Tax

Value Added Tax (VAT) is a challenge, even to tax inspectors. The rules are so obscure and complicated that even many VAT office staff disagree on how to apply them. In short, VAT is a tax on goods and services. Fortunately for you, VAT is not that big an issue in the property world, though it's as well to know it's out there.

Chapter 12 gives you the inside track on your VAT responsibilities.

PAYE and NIC

After the nightmare of VAT comes the acronym hell of Pay-As-You-Earn (PAYE) and National Insurance Contributions (NIC). PAYE is the system HMRC use to collect Income Tax and National Insurance from the pay of people in employment as they earn it. NIC is a tax on people who work and their employers.

If you are an employee, then your employer deals with your PAYE automatically. If you're an employer, you register with HMRC and run payroll yourself. You will need to run a payroll scheme if you employ people like bookkeepers, gardeners and cleaners full or part time, even if they are family or friends.

As an employer, you must calculate and deduct income tax and NIC from salaries and pay them directly to HMRC by the 19th of each month. You must also account for holiday pay, sick pay, student loans and maternity leave.

For free help with PAYE, go to the HMRC website at www.hmrc. gov.uk/employers/first_steps.htm. In this book, Chapter 12 deals with PAYE and NIC.

Inheritance Tax

Inheritance Tax is the tax payable on your estate when you die. Some tax experts say that estate planning, the business of making a will and sorting out a strategy for handing your assets over to your family when you die, is the cornerstone of tax planning.

This is one of the few taxes that you can eliminate completely by careful tax planning, especially if your estate is valued at more than £312,000, which is the threshold where inheritance tax (IHT) kicks in. Most property owners will easily breach this threshold if they have a main home and two or three investment properties.

Take a look at Chapter 11 to find out how to save IHT.

Tax Avoidance and Tax Evasion

Many people resent paying tax and come up with reasons why they think they shouldn't. They confuse tax avoidance with tax evasion.

Psychiatrists call this *denial*. Tax inspectors call it *crime*.

Arranging your financial affairs to avoid paying tax is perfectly legal: Just plain lying about them, deliberately or by omission, is not.

Know your rights

Property investors and traders have the same rights as any other taxpayer to pay the least amount of tax they possible by knowing the rules and applying them to their own financial circumstances – as long as they break no rules.

These rights are set out in case law.

In one case, rejoicing in the name *Ayrshire Pullman Motor Services & Ritchie v Inland Revenue Commissioners (1929 14TC754),* Lord Clyde said: 'No man in this country is under the smallest obligation, moral or other, so to arrange his legal relations to his business or to his property as to enable the Inland Revenue to put the largest possible shovel in to his stores.

'The Inland Revenue is not slow – and quite rightly – to take every advantage which is open to it under the taxing statutes for depleting the taxpayer's pocket. And the taxpayer, is, in like manner, entitled to be astute to prevent, so far as he honestly can, the depletion of his means by the Revenue.'

This was supported in *Inland Revenue Commissioners v The Duke of Westminster (1936 19TC490),* when Lord Tomlin said: 'Every man is entitled, if he can, to order his affairs so that the tax attaching under the appropriate Acts is less than it otherwise would be.'

Tax avoidance schemes

Many accountants and tax advisors have set up complicated schemes aimed at avoiding tax. If you are a member of any tax avoidance schemes, you must notify HMRC on your tax return.

Before joining, you should consider the Ramsay Principle, which derives from case law: *WT Ramsay Ltd v Inland Revenue Commissioners (1981 STC 174).*

The principle is that where tax is due and a transaction or series of transactions are made with no purpose other than avoiding tax, the transactions should be ignored and the original tax due stands.

This effectively puts the taxpayer back in to the position he was before the scheme started. That's why these schemes don't work and generally only benefit the provider, who profits from charging the taxpayer a fee to join the scheme.

Tax planning key points

Effectively, these three cases sparked eternal conflict between taxpayers and HMRC with one side poring over the minutiae of tax laws trying to poke holes in the legal dyke to save money, while the taxman runs around drafting new regulations to plug the leaks.

The case law highlights the key points to tax planning:

✔ You have a right to avoid tax if you can.

✔ You must exercise that right honestly.

✔ If you act dishonestly, HMRC will rewind your financial affairs back to where you started evading rather than avoiding.

Tax evasion

Tax evasion occurs when a taxpayer deliberately sets out to falsify a tax return in order to reduce the tax due. No reputable tax adviser will knowingly become involved in tax evasion as it is a crime.

Common tax evasion scenarios include:

✔ **The cuckoo syndrome:** Trying to prove a letting property was your home to obtain Capital Gains Tax reliefs when you have never lived there.

✔ **The ostrich syndrome:** Failing to submit tax returns that account for rental income or sales of letting property in the hope the tax man won't notice.

✔ **The headless chicken syndrome:** Running around seeking offshore tax solutions – like owning UK property via an offshore company or having money paid in to an offshore bank and failing to declare the income on a tax return.

✔ **The fly-the-nest syndrome:** Claiming you have left your spouse to claim tax reliefs on two properties – saying you have parted is not enough, you will need to prove you have with at least a deed of separation from a solicitor.

In the end, honesty is the best policy and all these efforts just make the taxman suspicious. After all, what's the point in seeking a solution if you haven't got a tax problem you're trying to hide?

Offshore tax myths

If someone tells you a foreign company can own your UK property so you avoid capital gains tax by having nominee directors meeting in some far off country, don't believe them.

Three simple rules apply to paying tax:

- ✔ If you live in the UK, you must pay tax on your worldwide income and capital gains in the UK

- ✔ Companies resident in the UK must pay tax on their worldwide income and capital gains in the UK

- ✔ A company is resident in the UK in either of two circumstances

  - If it is registered here

  - If it is registered offshore but management and control is exercised from the UK

It's the decisions you make here that count, not those made in your name by some shadowy nominees basking in a sunny tax haven.

Going through your dirty washing

Money-laundering legislation aimed at terrorists is also netting international tax cheats. Anti-terrorist laws oblige banks, solicitors, accountants, financial advisors and estate agents to report 'suspicious' transactions without tipping off their clients.

The courts have also forced UK banks with offshore branches to pass HMRC details of taxpayer's accounts this information can be cross-checked against your tax return.

The odds are stacked against you fooling the tax man, and in these days of digital technology, HMRC links to all sorts of computer databases at home and overseas that track your financial activities.

Double trouble overseas

Owning property overseas often tempts people in to the ostrich syndrome (see the previous section, 'Tax evasion').

Many mistakenly believe they can rent or buy a house overseas, give HMRC an address is some far-flung country and claim they are non-resident for UK tax while still spending most of their time here.

Don't bother, because wherever you go you leave an electronic trail so HMRC can track where you live and where you spend your money from your passport, phone calls, bank statements and credit card statements.

On the other hand, another worry many taxpayers have is double jeopardy on your income. Don't fret. If you pay taxes overseas while working or in connection with property you own, the double taxation agreements the UK has with many other countries mean you credit the tax you pay overseas against tax owed in the UK. This means you are safe from paying tax on the same income twice.

Keep any official documents relating to your overseas property as they are evidence to prove your tax status in the country where you own the property and in the UK.

Chapter 2

Grasping Property Tax Basics

*U*nderstanding property tax is no big deal. You don't need a degree in accountancy, just a clear head and some talent for organisation. Too often, property investors or developers try to plan their tax in reverse. It's too late to try to work out how to save cash when a fat tax demand you can't or don't want to pay thumps onto your doormat. Plan your tax *before* buying property.

Savvy property investors have a tax checklist and tick the boxes off as they go along. That way, they make the right tax decisions at the right time, save the most money and don't have their days spoiled by unexpected tax demands.

Tax planning is like playing a game – the same rules apply to everyone; you find out about them and how to apply them to your best advantage. Like any game, the referee penalises rule breaking. In this case, the ref is Her Majesty's Revenue and Customs (HMRC), who scrutinise your game like football pundits picking over a slow-motion replay, looking at your tax returns in the minutest detail to check for discrepancies.

Understanding What You Want From Your Property

The first box on the tax checklist establishes what sort of property business you run. Once you've decided which it is, your tax planning route rolls out in front of you like a red carpet, and you just follow.

To work out your route, the points to consider include:

- What do you plan to do with the property when you've acquired it? Are you going to keep it for long term investment or sell as soon as possible for a profit?
- Where is the property?
- Who owns the property?

The following sections address these key questions.

Looking at the lie of the land

When this book talks about property, you can take that to mean *residential* property – like flats and houses. Take professional advice if you need information about farms, industrial or commercial buildings, as a lot of other rules may apply to these types of property.

For our purposes, property comes in two types:

- **Residential property for investment**: Property owned to generate long-term income from rents and any capital gain from an increase in the property's value.

- **Residential property for development:** Property bought and sold in the short term for profit, with value added by refurbishment.

A rental property is always an investment property and a property bought for short-term profit is always a trading property, unless (and there's nearly always an 'unless' in tax law) you decide to make the property your home or change the use from development to investment.

As soon as you own a property, your initial business intention for that property fixes your tax route, regardless of whether you own other property or have intentions to acquire any other property.

 Any property business has a basic ingredient – *land*. In fact, the word *property* is not defined in tax law. The term 'land' includes just land, such as a field, or land with buildings and any other structures, land covered with water, and any *interests and rights* in or over land. Interests and rights include issues such as having a right of way over someone else's land.

Different tax for different folks

Tax law defines the following three property businesses, regardless of whether you call yourself a landlord, developer, or trader:

- ✔ Buying to let in the UK
- ✔ Buying to let outside the UK
- ✔ Buying to sell in the UK and overseas

In the following sections I look in detail at each of these options.

Buying to let in the UK

Known popularly as *buy-to-let*, or *property investment*, in UK tax law buy-to-let is called a *UK property business*.

As a landlord, you pay income tax on the profits from letting a property, and *Capital Gains Tax* (CGT) on gains from the sale or disposal of the property. However, if you set yourself up as a company to own letting property, the company pays Corporation Tax on rental profits and gains, instead of Income Tax and CGT. See Chapters 18 to 21 for more about companies and corporation tax.

Completing the land and property supplement of your tax return notifies HMRC of any UK property business profits or losses. For capital gains or losses, you have to complete the capital gains supplement.

Companies have their own tax returns. See Chapters 18 to 21 for more on running a property business through a company.

Also included in a UK property business are cash from lodgers under the Rent-a-Room Scheme (see Chapter 13) and managing UK furnished holiday lets (check out Chapter 16). Both these letting strategies offer tax advantages that aren't available to a residential buy-to-let business.

Fly-to-let: Buying to let overseas

Tax for an overseas property business is handled in more or less the same way as that for a UK property business – except overseas furnished holiday lets come in the same category as any other overseas letting property and don't receive the same tax advantages as those in the UK.

The official term for buying to let overseas is *overseas property business*.

UK resident taxpayers must declare and pay income tax on profits from letting overseas property and pay CGT on gains on sale or disposal of the property. Completing the foreign income supplement of your tax return notifies HMRC of any overseas property business profits or losses.

For capital gains or losses, you need to complete the capital gains supplement.

Buying to sell at home and overseas

Property traders, dealers, developers, and builders all run *buy-to-sell* (BTS) businesses, no matter what they call themselves. Buy-to-sell, or *property development* includes:

- Buying property, refurbishing it, and selling it on.
- Speculating by buying property off-plan and selling on without ever entering the front door.
- Building from the foundations up and selling on.

Buying a property, and refurbishing it with the intention to let it out is not classed as buy-to-sell because the initial purchase intention is investment, not immediate profit.

UK resident taxpayers pay income tax on buy-to-sell profits and no CGT on property at home or overseas. Companies pay Corporation Tax instead of Income Tax and CGT.

Completing the self-employment supplement of your tax return notifies HMRC of any property trading profits or losses.

Letting, selling, or trading property overseas may make you liable for local taxes that lie beyond the scope of this book. You should check with tax authorities in the country where you intend to run a property business to find out more about the financial consequences of investing or trading before you enter in to any binding contracts.

A UK property business lets property in England, Scotland, Wales, or Northern Ireland. Anywhere else is overseas – including the Isle of Man and the Channel Islands.

Taxing ownership

As a general rule, tax follows ownership of an asset. This means that whoever owns a property pays the tax on any income from the property. That's why it's important to establish ownership of a property.

Surrendering your rights without a fight

If you own property jointly, don't leave the management to someone else, however much you trust his or her judgement.

In a well-known case before the Tax Commissioners (*King v King* (2004)), a husband and wife moved out of their home and let the property to tenants. Mr King had the tenancy agreement in his sole name and all the rent received went into his bank account.

The tax commissioner held that Mrs King had surrendered her rights to the rent received and Mr King was taxed on the whole profits.

Had Mr King set up the tenancy in his and his wife's names and paid part of the rent in to her personal bank account, he would have paid less tax, as his wife had unused personal allowances entitling her to pay no tax on some of her income whereas her husband paid tax at the basic rate on all of his.

By ownership, you need to delve in to your files and find out who is entitled to the income from renting a property or the proceeds from any sale. Often, the owner is the person or persons named at the Land Registry or on the property's deed of conveyance. Not always, though. A *beneficial owner* is an owner entitled to the rents and gains from a property, but not necessarily on the deeds or showing at the Land Registry.

The tax man will seek out the beneficial owner and look to charge them any tax arising from rental profits or capital gains.

Appreciating that Investment Isn't Trading

Tax law looks at different types of income and taxes them in different ways:

- ✔ **Trading income:** Money a business receives in return for providing goods or services – like buying something from a shop or paying a plumber for his services. This category includes property development income.

- ✔ **Wages and salary**: Payments employees receive in return for their labour.

- ✔ **Interest**: Money investors receive from savings, like cash in the bank or building society.

- ✔ **Dividends and rents**: Returns on investment. Dividends are a share of a company's profits in return for paying to invest in shares. Rent is a fee a landlord receives in return for allowing someone to occupy property. Buy-to-let businesses fall in to this section.

The important point here is to differentiate between *earnings* and *income*. Trading income and wages are earnings, while interest, dividends, and rent are income.

Developing property for sale generates earnings and letting property for rent generates income. The rules for taxing the profits are similar but don't make them the same.

If you let property and provide extra services to tenants, you need to decide whether:

- ✔ Letting and providing the extra services amounts to generating earnings.

- ✔ The services form part of your property business and generate income

- ✔ The services are a trade separate from your property business and generate earnings

In each case, the tax calculation on any profits is different.

Separating property development earnings from property rental income is a long established tax principle.

Don't confuse the terms *business* and *trade*. The dictionary definitions may be similar, but as tax terms they're poles apart.

Why it's important to show a property business is not a trade

Property transactions come under the HMRC's microscope due to the substantial profits generated from a single sale.

Tax inspectors and property people wage a constant battle – if there's s any doubt as to intention, the taxman infers that the property transaction is a development because the tax treatment often realises more than the sale of an investment.

Conversely, property developers try to show the transaction was an investment to try and pay less tax.

HMRC and the courts test the transaction against a checklist, to establish whether the original purchase intention was investment or development.

When letting property is a trade

Letting property becomes a trade where the owner lives in the property and provides services over and above those usually provided by a landlord.

Providing bed and breakfast, or running a hotel or a camping site, for example, fall into the category of trading.

The difference between letting property as a business and letting property as a trade comes down to the fact that traders retain the right of access and control how and when people can enter and leave their property.

A tenant takes on exclusive possession of a property and the landlord can only enter with permission except under extreme circumstances.

When letting property is not a trade

To establish that letting a property is not a trade, a landlord must show that the services offered do not go beyond those normally provided by a landlord. Examples of services normally provided by a landlord include:

- ✔ Cleaning stairs and passages in multi-unit premises.
- ✔ Providing hot water and heating.
- ✔ Supervising rent collection and arranging new tenancies.
- ✔ Arranging for repairs.

The fact you provide any or all of these services does not mean your letting business is a trade or that any cash from these services are earnings.

If you have a large property investment business, you may need to work full time to manage the properties and tenants. The number of properties owned and the time spent running a property business does not make the activity a trade.

The key tax case, *Salisbury House Estate Ltd v Fry* [1930] 15TC266, held that money from investments and trading generate separate sources of income that are taxed under their own rules.

At the hearing, Lord MacMillan said: 'A landowner may conduct a trade on his premises, but he cannot be represented as carrying on a trade of owning land because he makes an income by letting it.'

This principle is often applied by the courts, so although property income is calculated like trading income, letting your own property is not a trade. It's just convenient to use the same rules to calculate profits.

Getting Ahead of the Taxman

Many landlords think that because they do not make a rental profit, they do not need to declare their rental income. This is a mistake. You must tell the tax man if:

- ✔ You receive any rent – even a single one-off payment and even if your rental business has never made a profit

- ✔ Sell a property you do not live in – even if it was your home for a period during the time you owned it

Understanding why you need a tax strategy

From the day you purchase a property you, as a taxpayer, need to know what tax rules apply to the income you receive. Knowing the tax rules familiarises you with the rules the tax inspectors apply to your property business. You can then maintain the correct financial records, make the appropriate tax returns, and pay the correct tax.

A tax strategy is not a magic solution that means you pay no tax. Avoid advisors who 'reveal property tax secrets' because there are none. What landlords and developers really need to do is take up the challenge and get tax right. This means taking control of your property affairs instead of reacting to them. You need to:

- ✔ Make sure you implement an effective financial record keeping system

- ✔ Keep up with filing your tax returns

- ✔ Weigh your risks. Are you confident you will pass a tax investigation with flying colours or will you be bogged down with red tape?

If you demonstrate to the tax man that you understand the rules that apply to your property business, your life will be easier and you will have more time to devote to making money rather than excuses.

Making your intentions clear: Keeping a property register

Property businesses pay tax based on the initial intention behind the purchase of property, so you need some way to record your intention.

Keeping a file for each property, called a *property register*, helps fireproof you against the taxman by detailing your intentions and decisions. After all, some years down the line, you may have difficulty recalling why some decisions were made, so keeping accurate, written records makes sense.

A property register should contain at least:

- ✔ The statement of purchase from your solicitor showing the buying costs broken down by category, like stamp duty, legal fees and search fees.

- ✔ A note in writing from your buying solicitor clearly showing the completion date – often this is not on the completion statement.

- ✔ If paid separately, statements showing any valuation and mortgage costs like broker feeds.

- ✔ During the period of ownership, receipts for any capital spending like the cost of an extension or garage.

- ✔ The statement of sale from solicitor showing the selling costs like estate agent and legal fees.

- ✔ A list of owners and their percentage share of ownership.

Capital spending can be set off against any gain made when selling a property, so a property register is important for tax saving in years to come.

Property developers do not need to keep property registers because they do not pay CGT, but many of the same costs can be reclaimed through their accounts against profits when selling a property.

Discovering and Applying the Rules: Intentions and Indicators

A property business is *either* a development for sale or an investment. As soon as you understand this, you need to consider how to show how each property you own slots in to the right category.

If you have a well thought out tax strategy, and you know the law and how to apply the tax rules, you're less likely to make costly mistakes.

The law works on a basis of *points to prove*. Circumstances are broken down and analysed against statute law and case law and the evidence is marshalled by you, your advisers, and the taxman to prove or disprove each point.

The taxman has a list of points he tries to prove. These points show whether you're a developer or an investor. If you know what those points include, and their basis in law, you can adapt your tax strategy to show how these points apply – or don't apply – to you.

The taxman's list of points is the insider information you need to know taken from the taxman's own internal guidance detailing the points to prove for property trading and investment.

Showing the best of intentions

Demonstrating your intentions in buying a property is a key indicator of whether your transaction was investment or a devlopment – if your intentions gives a clear indication of which it was, then the other indicators do not necessarily have to be considered. Your intentions can be categorised as follows:

- ✔ If the original intention on purchase was to rent the property, then the intention was probably investment, and therefore forms part of a property business.

- ✔ If it was to profit from selling the property, then the intention was probably property development.

- ✔ If the intention is not obvious, the courts look at the *balance of probabilities*, which means if an ordinary person looked at the evidence, how would they be likely to consider the transaction?

The tax man's word is not the rule of law – it is guidance based on the law and experience of applying the rules and has no more legal force than this book.

If you disagree with his decision, you can appeal to the tax commissioners and keep on going through the courts to the Court of Appeal, the House of Lords and then the European courts.

Considerations involve looking at the other points to prove, apart from intention. The following paragraphs cover these points.

As an investor in property businesses you need to ensure that property transactions receive the most advantageous tax treatment. You therefore need to keep written, dated records detailing why you bought each property, and your intentions. Consider keeping a rental report from a letting agent and calculate the property's rental yield.

If you're investing in a property business, keep your rental report and calculations in your property register as evidence that your intention to invest was as a property business, not as a developer.

As a developer, consider filing a written report from an estate agent showing the likely sale price of a property after the refurbishment, and a calculation of your likely trading profits. Drawing up a *schedule of works* for the agent is also a good idea. A schedule of works is a list of the jobs you or a builder carried out during the refurbishment.

Open your property register before you exchange contracts on a property, and make sure that the documents are dated prior to that. Exchange of contracts is the date on which the contract to buy becomes unconditional. Exchange is the date that counts in tax law, not the date when you acquire the keys.

Make sure that later correspondence does not contradict your original intention, and if you sell, document why you decided to sell. Again, do this before you exchange contracts.

Calculating rental yield

Rental yield is the return on investment received from your property. To calculate rental yield:

1. **Work out the annual rent if the property had 100 per cent occupancy for the year.**

2. **Work out annual expenses, for example mortgage repayments, insurance, repairs, and agent costs.**

3. **Deduct expenses from rent received to leave a profit or loss.**

4. **Add up your cash investment in the property, which is cash deposit plus annual expenses.**

5. Divide the profit or loss by your cash investment.

6. Multiply by 100.

For example, let's say you buy a property for £200,000, with a £30,000 cash deposit. You rent it out at £950 per month.

Annual rent received is £950 × 12 = £11,400

Annual expenses = £10,700

Annual profit = £11,400 – £10,700 = £700

Cash investment = £30,000 + £10,700 = £40,700

700/40700 = 0.017199

Rental yield is 0.017199 × 100 = 1.72% (Rounded to 2 decimal places)

Benchmarking your rental yield – comparing your property's investment performance against other properties – depends on many factors, but most landlords would expect to see a yield of about 5 per cent.

For instance, you can find out what rent landlords are receiving for similar properties in the same area from local newspapers or letting agents' windows. If your property is failing to achieve that rent, you need to look at why – is your agent doing a good job or does the property need upgrading?

If you have several letting properties, you can compare key performance indicators (KPI) across your portfolio to look at why some properties perform better than others. Such indicators might be how much is spent on repairs and maintenance, how many void rental periods there are, and how much the property value appreciates each year.

Don't forget that even if the rental yield is disappointing, your property should gain value at least in line with inflation every year.

Financing the project

Financing is an ambiguous indicator of your intention to be a a developer or investor – property investment is long term and often properties are mortgaged by a lender on a buy-to-let mortgage for 15 years or more.

Nevertheless, many investment properties are bought for cash or on short-term funding and remortgaged on a longer term after refurbishment.

Property investors and developers tend to go for the easiest finance available to secure the property, then refinance soon after in line with their long-term objectives.

So having a buy-to-let mortgage may not mean you are an investor, just a developer taking advantage of easier finance terms, and an investor may buy a property with development finance and remortgage to a buy-to-let loan after refurbishment.

Establishing whether the property generates income

If a property generates no rental income, then proving the transaction is an investment is more difficult.

The fact that the property is a second home or a non-commercial let, doesn't exclude investment intention, as personal enjoyment from a holiday home or philanthropic actions by providing cheap accommodation to a relative or friend count as intangible returns from investment.

Keep records of property use, for example, who lived there and when, to rebut any accusation by the taxman that the property was a trade and not an investment. If you let a relative or friend stay there long term at a discounted rent, draw up a document signed and dated by you and her, stating the terms.

See Chapter 6 for more information about uncommercial lets.

Considering how long the property has been owned

No rule exists that defines a period of ownership, however long or short, that constitutes investment or trading. Generally, investment is long term, which means 10 years or more. HMRC often questions the intentions of the sale of an investment property that is less than three years after purchase.

Explaining why the property was sold

A property may fail to generate a sufficient return on the capital invested and be sold shortly after buying, but that doesn't make the property a trade.

An investor may buy a property, find it's difficult to rent, during which time another, more attractive investment opportunity arises elsewhere. Trading up under these circumstances doesn't mean the intention to buy was property development.

Equally, a developer may buy a property and find it difficult to sell because of market conditions, such as rising interest rates or falling prices. Renting to a tenant while waiting for the market to rise doesn't change the intention to buy to an investment.

Putting forward arguments on the above line may counter an intention inquiry if you've sufficient evidence to back them in your property register.

Property business structure

HMRC assumes that a property developer only runs a buy-to-sell business and doesn't buy for long-term investment. In practice, many property people operate investment and trading businesses side by side.

Property investors – and you, if you fancy developing – need to show clear and transparent business separation. The easiest and most tax effective way to show separation is by owning investment property personally, but forming a company to develop property.

Personally owning investment property in your own name or as tenants-in-common with joint owners is a strategy that maximises reliefs and allowances on disposal of an investment property to reduce CGT.

Developers should incorporate a limited company to buy and sell property – especially if they receive a salary from employment. A company helps manipulate and reduce the tax you pay.

Individuals have reliefs and allowances to reduce the tax due on any capital gain. These reliefs aren't available to companies. Companies provide a better tax vehicle for dealing with tax due on development profits.

Builders should consider trading through a company to protect their home and other personal assets, especially if they own investment property as well. Unincorporated trading can leave these assets liable to attack by creditors if the builder is sued

Intention for buying and selling property is more easily proved if you've split your business accordingly for investing and trading.

The accounts for each business also go a long way towards proving intention. On an investor's balance sheet, investments are held as fixed assets whereas on a company balance sheet, trading property is shown as stock-in-trade.

Developing a property

If you buy and refurbish a property that's split into flats, for example, or the subject of planning consent, and you then sell it in the short term, the transaction is viewed as property development.

The same example of refurbishing a building into flats, then letting the flats is property investment.

Keeping up with changes

Once you've developed a strategy for your property business, you must carry out a review every year to ensure that Budget changes or new case law don't undermine your planning.

See Chapter 24 for some online resources, providing a good place to start your research.

Juggling Multiple Businesses

A lot of property people have a property portfolio that covers letting in the UK and overseas, plus property development.

In some cases properties may be solely owned and others jointly owned, or owned through a company. To avoid confusion, keep a property register and accounts for each property.

Setting up a tax strategy for your first property and failing to update as you buy further property is a recipe for disaster.

See Chapters 5 to 7 to find out how to keep proper records for all your property business activities.

Chapter 3

Triggering Tax and Dealing with the Taxman

In This Chapter

▶ Owning property the most tax effective way

▶ Recognising tax triggers

▶ Beating the income-shifting rules

▶ Comparing types of ownership

▶ Dealing with tax: self-assessment, filing tax returns, preparing for investigations

*T*ax bills aren't random events or plain bad luck; they come about because you do something to trigger them. Tax planning involves knowing about tax triggers and spotting them looming in the distance, so you've time to realign your financial affairs to minimise the blow.

To avoid paying more tax than you have to, your first line of defence is to start your property business the right way. This chapter tells you how. You follow your business start-up by buying and owning your property in the most tax advantageous way, according to your circumstances. You also come to recognise and understand the events that trigger your tax bills. From your firm business foundation, you can then file the right returns and pay the correct tax with confidence.

Starting a Property Business

A UK or overseas property business starts on the *date of first letting*, the date from which the first tenant of the first letting property is due to pay rent, not the date the rent is actually paid if that date is different.

You only have one personal UK property business and one overseas property business even if you've several properties, owned on your own or with other people.

If you have a property company, this company is also a separate business from your personally owned property. The tax rules are different, and the rest of this chapter deals with property that you own directly yourself.

A property business is not the same thing as a property company. You can own and let many properties without being a company. See Chapters 18 and 19 for the detail on setting up and running a property company.

You also have one date of first letting for each business regardless of how many properties you add or remove from your portfolio.

Grasping the importance of the first letting date

The first letting date is crucial: Your whole tax timetable depends upon it. The first letting date determines:

- ✔ **The first property business accounting period.** The first accounting period ends on 5 April following the date of first letting, for example, for a date of first letting of 1 May 2008, the first accounting period ends on 5 April 2009.

  The period 6 April to 5 April is called the 'year of assessment'. The current year of assessment (6 April 2008 – 5 April 2009) is 2008–09.

- ✔ **The date of filing your first tax return.** If the amount of tax you owe is less than £2,000, and if you want HMRC to collect your tax through your tax code, your first tax return must be filed on paper by 31 October, or online by 31 December following the end of the year of assessment.

  For example, if your date of first letting is 1 May 2008, your first tax return should be filed online by 31 October 2009 and should include receipts and expenses from 1 May 2008 until 5 April 2009 inclusive.

  If you work the tax out yourself, or need to pay more than £2,000 tax, you've an extension to the end of the following January (31 January 2010, in my example).

  Each owner must file a single return for their business regardless of whether they own one or a hundred letting properties.

✔ **The date of paying any Income Tax on rental profits.** Income Tax payments on account become due on 31 January and 31 July of the year following the year of assessment. For example, for 2008–09, the first payment is due on 31 January 2010 and the second on 31 July 2010.

Payments on account aren't required if at least 80 per cent of the total income of the person paying the tax is subject to deduction of tax at source (for example, from a salary), or where the previous year's tax owed, after tax deducted at source, was £1,000 or less.

Under self-assessment, you pay two tax instalments – one on 31 January and the other on 31 July. These are on account of the following year's tax.

If you pay too much on account, you receive a refund, and if you've not paid enough, you pay a balancing charge to make up the difference.

Knowing when a property is let

You may think that you know when your property is let: when someone is living in it and paying you rent, right? Actually, your property let whenever the following conditions have been met:

✔ The property is let to residential tenants.

✔ The property is available to let but vacant between tenancies.

✔ The property is being prepared for letting.

✔ The property is undergoing work between lettings with the intention of letting the property when the work is completed.

Before the first letting date, there's no rental income so there's no rental business. For more on business expenses incurred before the first letting date, see Chapter 7.

Telling the taxman

When you receive income from a new source, and if you've not received a tax return for that tax year, you should advise your tax office by 5 October following the tax year in which you received the income.

The term *new source* refers to a newly started property business rather than new property added to an existing business.

If you run a UK property business and then receive rent from a UK furnished holiday letting or an overseas letting, you're starting a new property business and should inform your tax office. The same applies if you've an overseas property business and receive rent in the UK. See Chapter 16 for more on this subject.

For a date of first letting of 1 May 2008, report the new source of income by 4 October 2009.

Recognising Tax Triggers

The events in your business and personal life create the tax triggers that result in you paying tax. The tax triggers include:

- ✔ **Changes in property status:** When you buy, sell, or change the ownership or use of a property.

- ✔ **Major changes in personal circumstances:** Marriage, separation, divorce, job changes, pay rises, and inheritances can alter your tax status.

- ✔ **The Chancellor's annual budget:** The budget can generate changes in law and change tax rates that may upset your strategy.

- ✔ **Changes in the law:** New acts of parliament and notable court cases can add or amend existing tax law.

So, recognise when a tax trigger is about to be pulled, then step back and review the implications of what you're doing before you trigger the event. That way you can:

- ✔ Decide what type of property business or businesses you run.

- ✔ Own the property in the most tax effective way before any contract becomes unconditional.

- ✔ Keep the appropriate financial records.

- ✔ Minimise your tax by knowing the rules and applying them to your circumstances.

- ✔ Work out an exit strategy that minimises the tax paid before you intend to dispose of a property.

Beating Income-Shifting Rules

Income shifting is nothing new. Accountants have quietly shuffled client's assets around in the background to avoid tax for years.

The principle of income shifting is based on splitting property ownership in such a way that if the property has two or more owners, the ones who pay basic rate Income Tax (at 20 per cent) own a larger share of the property than those who pay higher rate tax (at 40 per cent).

Income shifting is a perfectly legal tax strategy and can save some landlords thousands of pounds of income tax (payable on rental income) and Capital Gains Tax (CGT) (payable on the profits of property sales). So there has to be a catch, right? Right. The government has realised that a hole exists in the rules big enough to take an entire gravy train, and is taking belated action to close it. Income-shifting rules were announced in the 2008 Budget but put on the back burner and may return.

If you're a joint owner, you can gain from income shifting, as long as you own the property in your own right, and not as part of a company. Bear in mind that:

- ✔ Providing the joint owners don't own the property through a business partnership or a company, HMRC can't apply the income-shifting rules to joint property investors.
- ✔ Property investors who are higher-rate taxpayers can continue to avoid Income Tax and CGT by transferring their share in a property to a co-owner who's a lower rate taxpayer.

Check out this step-by-step example detailing how income shifting can save you tax:

Mike is married to Debbie and they own a letting property that returns a £5,000 rental profit for a tax year. Mike is a higher-rate taxpayer, earning £50,000 a year from his job, and Debbie is a basic-rate taxpayer earning ££15,000 a year from hers. For joint tenants, the £5,000 rental profits are split 50:50 and added to each of their incomes for calculating Income Tax.

Mike already pays higher rate tax. Tax on his £2,500 profit share is £1,000 (40 per cent of £2,500).

Tax on Debbie's £2,500 profit is ££500 (20 per cent of £2,500).

The total Income Tax due on their rental profit is £1,500.

If Mike and Debbie jointly owned the property as tenants-in-common, they could make a written declaration to their tax office stating their actual beneficial ownership as a specific percentage. By increasing Debbie's share of ownership, her share of rental profits increases and Mike's share decreases. See the section 'Taking

Note of Tax Efficient Property Ownership' later in this chapter for more on the advantages of owning property as tenants-in-common.

Say Mike and Debbie decided to declare beneficial ownership 80:20 in Debbie's favour. Mike would receive 20 per cent (£1,000) of the rental profits and Debbie 80 per cent (£4,000).

Because Debbie can still earn more than £4,000 in addition to her salary for the tax year without paying higher rate tax, her profit share is taxed at 20 per cent of £4,000, or £800.

Mike's remaining profit share is still taxed at the highest rate: 40 per cent of £1,000 ×, or ££400.

Total rental Income Tax has reduced to £1,200, saving £300.

Joint ownership as tenants-in-common does the same trick for those paying CGT at 40 per cent as it does in saving Income Tax. CGT, which I cover in detail in Chapters 9 and 10, is payable on sales of assets.

For example, Mike and Debbie sell a letting property they bought two years ago. The cost was £75,000 and they sold for £180,000 as joint tenants.

The chargeable gain is £180,000 – £75,000 = £105,000. Subtract £5,000 for incidental buying and selling costs, and you get a final profit of £100,000.

As joint tenants, assume a 50:50 split of the chargeable gain with Mike and Debbie receiving £50,000 each. For simplicity, ignore other reliefs in calculating the Capital Gains Tax, as follows:

Mike, as a higher-rate taxpayer, pays 40 per cent of his share of the profits less his personal CGT exemption, which is £8,800. The calculation goes (£50,000 – £8,800 annual personal exemption) × 40 per cent = £16,480.

Debbie, as a lower rate taxpayer, pays 20 per cent of her share less personal exemption (£50,000 – £8,800) × 20 per cent = £8,240.

Total CGT for the couple = £24,720.

If Mike and Debbie had bought the letting property as tenants-in-common with beneficial ownership 20:80 in Debbie's favour, the CGT bill on the ££100,000 gain would be:

Mike paying 40 per cent of (£20,000 – £8,800) × 40 per cent = £4,480.

Debbie paying 20 per cent of (£80,000 – £8,800) × 20% = £14,240.

Total CGT = £18,720, a tax saving of £6,000.

Mike and Debbie stay outside the income-shifting net as they are joint owners and not a business partnership.

Taking Note of Tax Efficient Property Ownership

To take advantage of income shifting, landlords need to know how to own the property in the most tax effective way for them.

If you own property as an individual, this section doesn't apply to you. If you own property with joint owners, then your ownership may take two forms: *joint tenancy* or *tenancy-in-common*.

Joint tenancy

A *joint tenancy* is one in which multiple owners have equal shares of the property. For example, two owners share a property, with 50 per cent each. Three own 33 per cent each, or four 25 per cent each. Joint tenancy has one big drawback: the percentage of the property owned cannot change. Four joint tenancy owners always have a 25 per cent share each under such an agreement.

Tenancy-in-common

In a *tenancy-in-common*, owners usually have a specific, unequal, percentage share of the property, although two owners can still hold a 50:50 share if they wish. For example, you can split a tenancy-in-common 70:30, 60:40 or 25:25:50. The key point is that tenancy-in-common gives joint owners flexibility to shift income as and when their financial circumstances change.

For instance, a husband and wife may both work and pay higher rate Income Tax, so owning the property 50:50 or in another ratio makes no difference because the tax is the same whether one owner owned the property or two owners share it. But if one partner gives up work – to look after children, for example – and becomes a basic-rate taxpayer, then as tenants-in-common, the couple can change the share of ownership so the lower rate payer pays basic rate tax on rental income profits up to £36,000.

As joint tenants, the same couple do not have this flexibility without paying a solicitor to convert the tenancy into a tenancy-in-common. The solution is to jointly own property as tenants-in-common, and I show you how it works in the following sections:

If no evidence is available of how joint owners intended to share a property, the assumption is that they're equal.

Equal shares are fine for basic-rate taxpayers paying tax at 20 per cent, but mean that joint owners with one partner paying tax at the highest rate (40 per cent) and the other paying tax at the basic rate may be paying too much tax.

Stamp Duty may be due on the transfer of a property. See Chapter 8, for more on Stamp Duty.

Spouses and civil partners

Spouses can pass property between each other as a no-gain/no-loss transaction without incurring CGT.

When a spouse passes a 25 per cent share of a property to the other spouse, increasing the second share of ownership to 75 per cent, no CGT is due. Instead of paying higher rate tax on one half of the profits and basic rate tax on the other, they now pay higher rate tax on 25 per cent of the profits and basic rate tax on 75 per cent of the profits.

The couple can continue to manipulate their percentage shareholding to decrease the higher rate tax for one spouse and increase the basic rate tax paid by the other partner.

Overall, passing property on a no-gain/no-loss basis provides a positive and simple tax saving strategy for joint owners where one is a higher rate taxpayer and the other earns less than the maximum allowed at basic rate.

Where both spouses pay higher-rate taxpayer, the solution doesn't work as there's no tax advantage for either owner. Spouses in this situation should consider incorporating as a property trading company rather than owning the property in their joint names.

Take a look at Chapters 18 and 19 to see why property traders are better off owning property through a company, rather than as private individuals.

Joint owners who aren't married

When buying property, joint owners can set up a tenancy-in-common from the purchase date and enjoy the same tax savings as married couples.

If you already own a property with someone you're not married to, the tenancy-in-common solution won't work because the transfer of ownership triggers a CGT event.

To avoid CGT, transfer a share soon after you've bought the property and before the price rises, as you pay CGT on any gain and the transfer introduces another personal annual exemption that reduces the tax paid if and when you dispose of the property in the future.

Where the joint owners are both higher rate taxpayers, the share-transfer method of avoiding CGT doesn't work, as there's no tax advantage for either owner.

If you're a property developer, the tax situation is currently the same for unmarried partners as for married joint owners – see the previous section, 'Spouses and civil partners'.

 Property developers working as a company or business partnership will have to review their tax status if the income shifting rules come into force, as they won't be exempt from the tax change.

Sole owners

Sole owners who are landlords need to make a business decision to let property as individuals or as a company.

As individuals they benefit from CGT allowances unavailable to a company. However, if they make exceptional rental profits and pay higher rate tax, sheltering income in a company may be advantageous.

Property owning companies

Generally, a limited company isn't a good vehicle for owning residential investment property because of tax disadvantages it has against individuals. Individuals have tax allowances that companies don't – like the CGT personal annual exemption.

The CGT personal annual exemption is a tax-free amount available to each individual every year. For 2008–09, this exemption is £9,600 per person.

Companies provide a useful means of manipulating tax on income, which is why property traders should consider buying and selling through a company.

Business partnerships

Think long and hard before owning property with a business partnership, now that the 2008 introduction of income-shifting rules has come into play.

In tax, joint investors owning letting property are not the same as two builders in business as a partnership to develop property. The first is an investment, the second a business.

In a business partnership, the property is not jointly owned, but owned by the partnership in the name of a nominated partner.

The nominated partner has the rights over the property as ownership is in his name if the relationship should break down.

How Tax Self-Assessment Works

When you trigger a tax event, you must complete and file a personal self-assessment return – your tax return – for the relevant tax year.

HMRC sends you a return that you're obliged by law to complete and file. If for any reason they don't send you one, you have to ask for a return to report the tax event. Some taxpayers complete short returns rather than the full-blown return. The short self-assessment tax return is for people with simple tax affairs, like employees, pensioners, and the self-employed with property turnovers below £30,000.

You cannot elect to fill in a short return yourself. HMRC send a copy to selected people based on information in the previous year's return.

If you receive a short tax return, you can only complete the return if you still meet the qualifying criteria, otherwise you have to fill in the normal return.

The full tax return

The full self-assessment tax return is the one most property owners receive, because it contains the main tax return pages for income and savings plus additional pages for:

- ✔ Land and property, which record information about UK letting property and furnished holiday lets
- ✔ Capital gains, for people who have sold investment property
- ✔ Foreign income, for dealing with letting property outside the UK
- ✔ Self-employment, for property developers

Tax returns for sole traders

If you're a sole owner, you need to work out your property rental profits or losses and put the figures in the land and property section of your tax return. If the property you own is overseas, you need to enter the amounts in the foreign income section.

Tax returns for joint owners

The tax return is a little more complicated for joint property owners than for sole owners.

Investors have to divide any rental profits or losses pro rata their percentage of ownership. If you own a property 50:50 that's straight down the middle; 60:40 is 60 per cent to you and 40 per cent to the other owner, and so on.

You then add all your UK property business profits and deduct any losses brought forward or arising in the tax year to reach your rental profit or loss figure. You do the same for your overseas property business and any UK furnished holiday-letting business.

Keep the three figures separate and complete the appropriate sections of the land and property section of your tax return for your UK property business and any UK furnished holiday lettings. Overseas property income goes on the foreign income section of the tax return.

If you've sold an investment property, you should also complete the capital gains section of the tax return.

Property developers consolidate their accounts by taking all the earnings from property sales for the tax year, deducting costs of sale and general business expenses, to arrive at a profit or loss, which is entered on the self-employment section of the tax return.

Filing Your Tax Return

Self-assessment is a *pay now, check later* process. You complete the return and pay your tax, then HMRC checks the forms to make sure that you've paid the right amount.

You have to keep all your financial records for a year after the filing date following the end of the tax year, so that HMRC can check the originals if it wants to.

Paying your tax

Tax payment dates remain the same from 2008–09, even though the filing dates come earlier.

The first payment on account is due on 31 January 2010, and the second on 31 July 2010. If the tax you owe is more than £1,000, you may have to make payments on account for the following tax year as well.

Key dates

For the 2007–08 tax year, which ran from 6 April 2007 until 5 April 2008, property investors should save any supporting tax return documentation for a minimum of 22 months from the end of the tax year to which they relate, that is, until at least 30 November 2010. If you're a property developer, you should save them for five years – until 31 March 2015.

From 2008, the deadlines for filing tax returns have moved back from 31 January to 31 October for paper returns. The 31 January filing date is retained for filing online.

Failing to File a Tax Return

Filing late or failing to file at all attracts fines and surcharges. If you file online after 31 January, you face a £100 fine and another one six months later if you still haven't filed. You also pick up surcharges of 5 per cent of the tax you owe at regular periods.

If you file late and owe little tax, or should have a rebate but the fines and surcharges amount to more than the tax you owe, write to your tax office requesting they waive the penalties on these grounds.

Dealing with Tax Inquiries

If you're up for an inquiry, the first you know about it is when you receive a letter from the tax man. Don't panic – seek the help of a tax adviser right away.

You're not alone. Every year HMRC selects roughly 1 in 20 taxpayers for an inquiry by various methods:

- ✔ **Random computer picks**: Much like coming up on the bad-luck premium bonds.

- ✔ **Tip-offs:** Often from former tenants, employees, or partners.

- ✔ **HMRC analysis of your tax returns and accounts:** For instance, where your expenses don't match the expected amounts for the sales you've made.

The tax man also has newly introduced powers to bug telephones, intercept mail and even use spy satellites to check current aerial photographs of your property with previous ones to see whether you've enlarged the building and not reported the improvement.

What to do if you're investigated

The first thing to do is check the date. The taxman has 12 months from the previous 31 January to open an inquiry. If he is out of time, then he can't conduct an inquiry.

The next thing to do is to contact a professional tax adviser with experience of dealing with tax investigations. The adviser can't make the inquiry go away, but guides you through the process and helps to negotiate a settlement.

If the taxman is within the time limits, he can undertake one of two kinds of investigation:

- ✔ **Aspect inquiries:** Questions you can answer quickly and simply in a few days about a particular point in your tax return. For instance, the tax inspector may want to confirm how much building society interest you've earned in the tax year.

- ✔ **Full investigations:** These long, lingering post-mortems, involve a tax inspector picking through the bones of your financial records in detail.

Both of these inquiries look into discrepancies in your tax return.

Knowing what the taxman is looking for

Tax inspectors receive performance-related pay based on the amount of understated or undeclared tax they recover. They examine your tax returns and accounts for discrepancies where they believe they can claw back cash you should have paid but have not.

The taxman is not your friend. Every question, telephone call, and conversation is an evidence-gathering exercise for the tax inspector to prove that you've fraudulently, or negligently, failed to complete your tax return properly and to recover lost tax.

HMRC can fine you £60 a day for failing to provide any relevant documents or information.

You may be asked to an interview by HMRC. However, you don't have to attend an interview and can deal with the inquiry by post instead.

Avoid an interview if you can, and respond by post, because that way questions are limited to those in the letter and you've a record of what you said in reply. No inference can be drawn from not attending an interview, as long as you're cooperating with the inquiry in every other way.

In serious cases involving considerable amounts of unpaid tax, you may have no choice about meeting the tax inspector because he may come looking for you with a warrant to search your home, but these cases are few and far between.

If you choose to attend an interview, have an idea of what it's about before you go, and take your tax adviser with you. The interview is not a polite chat but an interrogation.

Watch what you say in writing, on the phone, or in person. Answer questions politely – 'Yes' and 'No' is good enough without offering explanations – and don't volunteer information or documents.

Finalising the inquiry

If you can't negotiate a settlement with HMRC, the tax inspector demands that you pay an estimated figure. You have to grin and bear it unless you can show that the estimated figure is wrong.

HMRC rewards you for cooperating – you get 20 per cent off the penalty by admitting your mistakes and another 40 per cent discount for acting promptly to resolve the inquiry.

Depending on the seriousness of your offence and the money involved, you may receive a further discount.

To avoid tax investigations, you must have a tax strategy and keep accurate records. See Chapters 5 and 6 to find out what records to keep and how to maintain a property register.

COP9 inquiries

If HMRC sends you a COP9 investigation notice, tell your tax adviser straight away. COP9 is like a code to tax professionals – COP9 stands for the Code of Practice 9 leaflet that deals with serious tax inquiries.

With a COP9 letter the taxman is telling you that he knows that you've committed fraud and is giving you a chance to sort matters out.

Failing to act on a COP9 letter leads to serious consequences, as in such cases, tax inspectors can raid your home or workplace with a warrant to seek evidence.

Chapter 4

Playing as Part of a Tax Team

*T*hink of tax advisers like doctors. To diagnose your initial problem you go to your GP – the equivalent of your high street accountant.

Your GP assesses your symptoms and treats you at the surgery with the help of the nurse – the medical equivalent of a book-keeper – or the GP sends you to a consultant. A consultant is a specialist in a particular medical field, like heart disease or cancer. Similarly, tax consultants specialise in areas like property tax, VAT, or estate planning.

Your local accountant probably doesn't have sufficient property tax clients to make her an expert, so you need to know who does what in the accountancy world to make the best of your tax health.

Understanding What a Tax Adviser Does

A tax adviser saves you from yourself by showing you how to organise your financial affairs to your best advantage.

Chapter 2 explains why you should have a tax strategy, and how your intention with a property sets the tax treatment of income from that property, while Chapter 3 covers the events that trigger tax.

A good tax adviser can guide you through this maze and help you set up a management system, including a property register and accounting records. She should also remind you of key dates, work out the tax you owe, and complete the forms for you to sign and file.

A tax adviser helps remove a lot of the administrative burden from you and leaves you to concentrate on running your property business.

Do You Need a Tax Adviser?

Okay, so you're a typical property investor. You're probably.

✔ Aged about 40

✔ A professional person

✔ Married with a couple of children

✔ A homeowner, with maybe a holiday home as well

✔ The owner of three or four letting properties

✔ Employed, and a higher rate taxpayer (your spouse may be a lower rate taxpayer)

Do you need a tax advice team? The answer is probably 'Yes'. You've several issues to address and really need specialist advice to make sure that you don't inadvertently make a mistake. You need to work out how to.

✔ **Own your properties' tax effectively:** Your solicitor should advise on this matter when you buy a property and your accountant or tax adviser should review ownership to manipulate tax on any rental income or property disposals to the spouse paying tax at the lowest rate.

✔ **Do all you can to minimise any tax on rental profits:** Your accountant should make sure that you're claiming all allowable expenses and not claiming any to which you're not entitled.

✔ **Take measures to avoid Inheritance Tax (IHT):** With four or five properties, you're probably a paper millionaire and need to look out for IHT. This possibility is for your solicitor or estate planner to look at in conjunction with your tax adviser.

However, deciding whether you need a tax adviser is a personal decision for you. Any sensible, organised individual running a multi-property portfolio is quite capable of keeping the right records, calculating tax, and filling in forms. But if that ain't you, employing a tax adviser may be a shrewd move.

Plenty of specialist advice and software exists out there on the Internet. Some of it's good, some indifferent, and the rest down-right poor. At the end of the day, you get the standard of advice you pay for. Try starting your search for an adviser at a website like LandlordZONE (www.landlordzone.co.uk) or Taxation Web (www.taxationweb.co.uk).

The question is not so much 'Do I need an adviser?' as 'Is it cost-efficient to employ one?'. You may employ a gardener at several letting properties rather than mow the lawns yourself, even though you're quite capable of doing it, because having someone else do the donkey work frees up your time for something more profitable.

 Repeat after me: The excuse 'My accountant said I can. . . ' just won't wash. In the tax world, the buck stops with the taxpayer. That's you, and that buck ends up in your lap even if you employ an accountant to complete your tax returns for you.

 You've a personal responsibility to make sure that the figures are correct, to file the returns on time, and to pay your tax as and when it's due.

Tax Advisers and Their Roles

You can view tax advisers in a similar way to those baked beans that come in 57 varieties. Hopefully, the following can help you sort the good from the not-so-good as you look at the bewildering array of letters and qualifications that follow your prospective adviser's name.

Accountants

Here's a shock for you: Anyone can set up a business and call her-self an accountant. No legal requirement to hold a qualification is required for an accountant. Be warned.

Accountants handle the nuts and bolts of financial work. Many offer bookkeeping services, accounts preparations, tax calculation, and advice.

Good accountants are an asset to your business because they give guidance and advice to help you avoid obstacles you may not have spotted. An appropriately qualified accountant can also act as an agent with HMRC and Companies House.

In my medical analogy, an accountant is a GP rather than a consultant.

Qualifications

Although anyone can call themselves an accountant, calling themselves *chartered* or *certified* is a different matter.

- ✔ **Chartered accountant:** A member of the Institute of Chartered Accountants In England and Wales (ICAEW) or the Institute of Chartered Accountants of Scotland (ICAS). These professional bodies set standards and regulate their members. Qualification is by passing a series of exams set by the institute and work experience.

- ✔ **Certified accountant:** A member of the Association of Chartered Certified Accountants (ACCA). Again, qualification is by passing a number of exams and work experience.

  Although they may argue among themselves that one qualification is better than another, you can't really tell the difference between a chartered or certified accountant – the services they provide are similar but they way they qualify makes the difference.

- ✔ **Accounting technician**: A member of the Association of Accounting Technicians (AAT). Qualification is by passing exams and work experience. An accounting technician is considered slightly less qualified than a chartered or certified accountant.

  Many technicians have the skills and knowledge of accountants, but the qualification process is less rigorous, and technicians often take on the actual number crunching in an accountant's office by acting as bookkeepers and preparing accounts and tax returns.

Many accountants, though unqualified, have had extensive experience as tax inspectors, bankers, and other financial jobs. Don't think that you shouldn't use an unqualified accountant – just because you've a qualification does not make you good at your job. Check them out like you would any other business (getting references from former clients if possible) and as long as you're happy, go-ahead.

Buyer beware. The drawback with unqualified accountants is that they are not regulated by a professional body, so you've no redress if things go wrong.

Costs

Costs vary enormously. City-centre accountants charge £100 plus an hour whereas small-town accountants charge a great deal less for property accounts, a tax review, and the preparation of tax returns.

What you really want is a property accountant who reviews your tax status while preparing your accounts and tax returns. Expect to pay about £500–£750 a year for these services. The cheaper tax services merely process the numbers and produce the forms; the best also give advice on arranging your financial affairs to save tax.

Tax consultants

Tax consultants generally follow a specific discipline of tax matters. Other practices may have several consultants who work in different tax areas.

A tax consultant advises on detailed tax areas, like property tax, IHT, or VAT. Many tax consultants handle tax investigations as troubleshooters for accountants. Tax consultants prepare accounts, tax computations, and tax returns as well. They can also act as your agent with the HMRC and Companies House.

Qualifications

As with accountants, anyone can trade as a tax consultant. Not everyone can do it well however, so look out for appropriate qualifications.

- **Chartered Tax Adviser:** Otherwise known as a CTA, a chartered tax adviser has passed the Chartered Institute of Taxation (CIOT) qualifying exams.

- **Taxation Technician**: A member of the Association of Taxation Technicians, an ATT has a similar standing in the profession as an AAT (check out the earlier section on accountants).

The professional bodies set standards and regulate members.

Like accountants, retired tax and VAT inspectors often set up as tax consultants without studying for any qualification.

Costs

Tax consultants often come at more of a price than accountants. They charge around 50 per cent more than an accountant for the same work – but their specialist input should be worth the extra money.

Solicitors, legal executives, and conveyancers

As members of the legal profession, solicitors' work includes dealing with property conveyancing, leases, and drawing up wills, among many other things.

What a solicitor does

For property people, a solicitor handles the buying and selling of property, which includes advising and calculating stamp duty land tax (SDLT) and filing the relevant returns. See Chapter 8 for more on Stamp Duty.

As part of the property transfer service, solicitors should advise on the pros and cons of buying as joint tenants and tenants-in-common. Check out Chapter 3 for more on these types of tenancy.

Qualifications

Unlike accountants and tax consultants, solicitors can only set up in business if they're qualified to practise, that is, they've an LLB degree and have completed the necessary practical training.

Legal executives are members of the Institute of Legal Executives (ILEX) and play similar roles in the legal profession to accounting and tax technicians in accountancy. They undertake much of the day-to-day work on legal cases managed by a solicitor.

The Council for Licensed Conveyancers regulates licensed conveyancers, who specialise in property matters, where a legal executive has a broader knowledge base covering, for instance, contract and matrimonial issues.

Costs

Legal charges vary greatly, with a typical conveyance costing about £750–£1,000, although many cost less.

Estate planners

The Society of Trust and Estate Practitioners (STEP) is the body that administers qualified estate planners. Check out their website at www.step.org.

What do estate planners do?

Estate planning deals with reducing tax by writing a will, establishing trusts, and minimising inheritance tax.

If you're a portfolio investor with more than a home and a single investment property, you should take estate planning advice as part of your property tax strategy.

Qualifications

Most members of STEP are accountants, tax consultants, solicitors, or barristers who've obtained the additional trust and estate planning qualification through STEP.

Costs to expect

A STEP member is generally a consultant who freelances for several legal firms when matters arise that a solicitor may consider outside her experience. Costs therefore include those of the legal firm plus those of the STEP consultant.

Will writers

Take note of this warning: If you want to make a will, go to a solicitor, not a will writer. Will writers often operate as fronts for financial services organisations whose estate planning solution is usually to sell you life assurance to cover an inheritance tax bill. See Chapter 11 for wise words on writing wills.

In most cases, such assurance policies are unnecessary as an estate planner can often wipe out any inheritance tax liability in a will or with a trust.

That doesn't mean that all will writers should be considered souped-up life assurance salesman: many are dedicated and professional. Just watch out for the sharks in the water.

Qualified versus unqualified

About 100,000 or so accountants and tax consultants practise in the UK. About a third of them are unqualified, or unregulated by a professional body.

When it comes to choosing between qualified and unqualified advisers, you pays your money and takes your choice.

Because an adviser is not qualified or regulated by a professional body doesn't mean her work is necessarily poor. In fact, despite lots of grumbling from the professional institutions, no evidence exists that you receive better advice from a qualified adviser than from an unqualified one. HMRC treats both qualified and unqualified advisers the same, and doesn't differentiate between their work because of qualification.

Asking Your Tax Office to Help

HMRC policy is not to advise on tax matters prior to submission of a tax return. They don't discuss hypothetical situations, and fine you if you get a real one wrong.

If you're lucky enough to get through, tax telephone help lines can help you with what forms to fill in and when to file them, but they don't help you complete tax calculations, or offer advice.

Despite the HMRC's user-friendly face, as I said before, the tax buck stops with you and it's up to you to get your tax affairs right.

Why HMRC won't help you

Don't expect too much help. This reluctance is because an Appeal Court ruling in October 2007 found for a taxpayer who sued HMRC after a tax worker 'helped out' and got it wrong.

Neil Martin, a builder, suffered severe business disruption and losses because of errors made by HMRC when processing his Construction Industry Scheme application. Among the errors were delays in processing his application following introduction of the new rules, and his company application was muddled with someone else's application for a registration certificate and sent out to the wrong address.

Mr Martin claimed £250,000 damages from HMRC for a breach of a statutory duty under the CIS legislation, or under a common law duty of care owed to the taxpayer. The Court did not agree with the former, but found unanimously in favour of the common law argument.

The court heard that an HMRC employee took it upon himself to complete Mr Martin's declaration for a sub-contractors registration card, instead of a company exemption.

Lord Justice Chadwick, presiding at the Court of Appeal put it that the HMRC employee was: 'Not processing an application which had been made: he was assuming an authority to make an application which had not been made'.

As a result, the judge thought it was fair, just, and reasonable that common law should recognise that a duty of care exists. The decision was unanimous.

The case has huge ramifications as prior to the ruling, HMRC staff regularly assisted taxpayers in making various returns, applications, and claims.

Online Advice

As the Internet expands, so does the amount of property tax advice out there. But beware: the Internet is the modern-day version of the know-it-all bloke in the pub who dispenses advice on every subject under the sun. Like his advice, much of the wealth of information on the Internet is well meaning but often misleading and at worst inaccurate.

Even government bodies, like HMRC, post huge amounts of information, but much of it is out of date.

Updated information on tax law, case law, and advice in this book is available from the Property Tax Plus website at www.property taxplus.co.uk.

Finding an Adviser

Many tax, law, and accountancy professionals advertise locally in newspapers and the telephone directories.

This list of websites for UK professional bodies should help you find a qualified adviser:

- ✔ Chartered accountants: www.icaew.co.uk
- ✔ Certified accountants: www.accaglobal.com
- ✔ Accounting technicians: www.aat.org.uk
- ✔ Chartered tax advisers: www.tax.org.uk
- ✔ Tax technicians: www.att.org.uk
- ✔ Solicitors: www.lawsociety.org.uk/home.law
- ✔ Legal executives: www.ilex.org.uk
- ✔ Estate planners: www.step.org

Foreign Advisers

If you're buying overseas property, you need to take specialist advice from an accountant, tax adviser, or solicitor based in that country as well as the UK. Your UK advisers may not have the specialist knowledge or experience of overseas tax laws to act for you in other countries. Taxation Web (www.taxationweb.co.uk) is a good place to start looking.

Residency has an impact on tax, so if you live in the UK and own property overseas, this residency may lead to unforeseen tax issues in one or both countries.

Double taxation agreements also exist between the UK and many other countries, especially those in Europe and the former Commonwealth.

Dealing with overseas earnings and investments correctly in your tax returns is also important in order to ensure that you remain within tax laws in both countries and don't pay too much, or too little, tax in either.

Part II
Balancing the Books

'I'm sure it's just a coincidence —
little Sam can't read yet.'

In this part . . .

1 f you're going to run successful property businesses, and pay no more tax than you have to, you absolutely *must* get organised. This part is here to help.

Here I talk you through the mysteries of making accurate records of your properties, keeping tabs on all your income, and – just as importantly – tallying up everything you spend on your property businesses.

In particular this part addresses the stuff the taxman doesn't want you to know: The expenses you can claim in order to reduce your tax bills.

Chapter 5

Keeping the Books Straight

. . . .

In This Chapter

▶ Organising your property paperwork

▶ Understanding which documents you need to keep

▶ Keeping a property register to save tax

▶ Making life simple with cost centres

▶ Picking up accounting basic tips

. . . .

The devil's in the detail. The better the records you keep, the better you control your business and tax strategy. Everyone hates paperwork and property people are no different. The problem isn't really keeping the right paperwork, but keeping it accessible and organised. This means that operating a 'bin bag' filing system, where you rummage around when you need a receipt, is not good enough. You need a simple system for recording the right information. This chapter shows you how to put the system together and just what bits of paper you need to keep, and why.

Why You Need to Keep Records

Don't know what all the fuss is about with keeping records? Okay, let's have a small quiz. As of right now:

✔ How much rental profit or loss have you made so far in the current tax year?

✔ How much are your properties worth and what is the balance of any outstanding mortgages?

✔ What tax provision do you have to make for the year?

If you can answer the questions, then you're probably too clever by half or an accountant, which often amounts to the same thing. Alternatively, you're the one of the few maintaining a regularly updated property register and accounting system.

Shame on the rest of you, because you don't know anything about the current trading status of your property business.

You must keep accurate trading records because:

- ✔ The law says that you must.

- ✔ You need to make effective business decisions based on the latest financial information – such as whether you're making a profit or a loss, and how much your properties are worth.

- ✔ You have to know whether you need to ditch a poorly performing property and transfer the investment elsewhere.

- ✔ You need to know whether you need to put money aside to pay any tax.

- ✔ If you face a tax inquiry, you can't prove how you calculated your spending on all those expenses you've claimed.

If you can't prove that you incurred the costs, you're likely to end up paying tax on money you've invested in the upkeep of your property, and probably get a fine for not keeping the right tax records.

What You Need to Keep

Accountants would have you believe that their job is just too complicated for any normal person to comprehend, but the job is no big deal. Even they find admin boring. We all hate it, but it's so important for tax and you simply must *ACT* on the rules by applying some of the basics accountants assign to their work: **A**ccuracy, **C**onsistency, and **T**iming:

- ✔ **Accuracy**: What's the point in all the hard work if your figures are incorrect?

- ✔ **Consistency**: If you apply a rule, then make sure that you apply the rule every time the same circumstances arise. For example, apportion expenses by the day or by the month, not both.

- ✔ **Timing**: Make sure that the right income and expenses go in the right tax year and that the right tax paperwork is submitted on time.

The knock-on effect of not following the rules is you pay too much or too little tax, in which case the taxman is going to chase you.

Keeping your books

You can easily set up an adequate manual system to keep track of your property business income and expenses, but first you need to know which pieces of paper to keep.

Property investors should retain all documentation used to work out their tax for 22 months after the tax year's filing date.

Invoices

Invoices are the records of the income you receive from your property. Most property people don't invoice. Instead, they receive monthly rent statements from their letting agents, so keep a copy of any invoice you give to someone else and every rental income statement you receive from a letting agent.

Date and consecutively number invoices so that you can spot any missing from the sequence.

Receipts

Receipts are proof that you've paid for goods or services from and/or for the general running of your business, for example, postage and telephone bills.

Chapter 7 goes in to the detail of expenses you can claim, those you can't, and why.

Bank, credit card, and loan statements

Keep all your credit card and loan statements as they come in, in sequential order by account. If you don't, it can end up being expensive: Banks can charge up to £15 to replace a statement.

Most property people pay interest-only mortgages and loans, but if you've a capital and repayment loan – where you pay back some of what you borrowed with the interest – then you need to split the figures for the tax year.

The split needs to show how much capital you've paid off the loan and how much interest you've paid on what you owe.

Solicitor's purchase and completion statements

Purchase and completion statements are really important and so often overlooked. They go in your property register to prove the costs you can deduct against any capital gain you've made on a property when you come to sell.

The purchase statement from your solicitor lists the purchase price and incidental purchase costs of the property, such as legal costs and stamp duty.

The completion statement is another piece of paper from your solicitor that lists the sale price of the property and any incidental disposal costs. These costs include estate agent and legal fees.

If you can't prove your costs you won't be able to claim them, so set up a separate folder in your property register for capital costs and keep the statements in it.

Improvement costs

Improvements are not repairs or renewals to a property but additions that increase the value, such as a porch, extension, or garage. Improvements come under the same category as solicitors' purchase and completion statements — they're capital costs.

You really need to understand the difference between day-to-day repairs and one-off improvement costs in order that you record them properly in your property register.

Your profit and loss computation and tax calculation can't be accurate if you include the wrong data. Doing so can lead to a tax investigation or hefty fines.

Coming to terms with capital and revenue costs

You buy a property, intending to refurbish for letting. You fit a new kitchen and bathroom, replacing the fittings that are already there with others of a similar cost and standard. You also redecorate. You need to do a few repairs, like fixing missing tiles on the roof and putting in a new double-glazed front door to replace a rotten wooden one.

These are all revenue or day-to-day expenses because you're repairing or renewing part of something that's already there. Record revenue expenses in the same way as you any other expense when calculating your profit or loss.

If you had replaced the bathroom with much more expensive fittings than were already there – say you've installed a whirlpool bath or upgraded the kitchen with granite worktops and much more expensive units – these are capital costs.

Capital costs are one-off expenses incurred:

- ✔ When you acquire a property – like solicitors fees and stamp duty
- ✔ When you improve a property – like building an extension, porch, or garage, or replacing existing fittings with more expensive items that add value to a property
- ✔ When you dispose of a property – like estate agents fees

Record capital costs in your property register. However, they're not included in your tax return unless you dispose of all or part of the property. Then they slot in to the Capital Gains Tax (CGT) calculation.

Keep a record of your capital costs for each property with the solicitors' purchase and completion statements. Keep them safe because you may not need them for years, but capital expenses are important because they reduce your CGT in the future.

Considering cost centres

This is the bit that makes your property register zing. *Cost centre* is just accountant speak for the people and properties to which you allocate income and expenditure. You allocate income and expenditure to calculate the profit or loss for each owner of each property according to the owner's percentage of ownership.

Mark up every piece of paper, especially if you've more than one property, so you know which property and which tax year needs to be included in the details.

Keep the records for each property and each tax year separate – a good idea is to have a large envelope for each property for each month in the tax year, with the address and date written on the outside, for example, '1 High Street – April 2008'.

If two or more people run the business, note on the receipt or loan payment who incurred the expense.

If you have a UK property business, UK furnished holiday lets, and an overseas rental business, you need to keep separate property registers for each.

Owner's list

This is a sheet of paper or spreadsheet in the property register with the following columns:

✔ **Name:** the owner's name

✔ **From:** the date from which the owner commenced ownership of the property

✔ **To:** the date the owner finished ownership of the property

✔ **Percentage:** the share of the property the owner possesses

Every time ownership or percentage ownership changes, record the information on the owner's list. This is a terrific aid to allocating profits and losses to people and calculating the right amount of tax.

PPR list

PPR is an abbreviation for *principle private residence* – a CGT term for your main home.

Software for property businesses

This is the bit where you pay your money and take your choice. Search Google or a similar search engine for 'UK property tax software' and quite a few products turn up.

Whether any are right for you depends on the size of your property business and how long you want to spend in front of a computer.

If you've several properties and co-owners, I would suggest that computerising your records is a must.

Here's a surprise: We run hundreds of property accounts for businesses with between 1–100 rental properties on a simple spreadsheet program written in-house several years ago.

You don't have to fork out for expensive branded products – try Open Office (www.openoffice.org) for Windows or Neo Office (www.neooffice.org/neojava/en/index.php) for a Mac for free. They're reliable, robust, and well-supported open source programs and have the same bells and whistles as expensive branded software suites.

Both have excellent spreadsheet applications included.

If you want something more high-end – like the popular QuickBooks or Sage – try TurboCash (www.turbocashuk.com). Again, TurboCash is open source, free and contains most of the same modules as its better-known rivals. TurboCash is for Windows only but a Linux version is in the pipeline.

All I would say is, before buying an office suite or proprietary accounting software that's likely to set you back about £250, consider the open source alternatives first. In most cases, they're just as good as the proprietary software and save you money.

If you've owned and lived in a property you now rent out, this affects the CGT you pay, so you must keep a log of the time for which any owners used a rental property as their main home.

Again, this log a simple one-sheet job:

- ✔ **Name:** the owner's name
- ✔ **Property:** the letting property address
- ✔ **From:** the date the owner started living there
- ✔ **To:** the date the owner stopped living there

That's it, done and dusted. You now know how to keep a property register in a few easy steps.

Basic Accounting Rules

You need to remember a few basic accounting principles to make sure that you keep you records in order.

For a full discussion of bookkeeping and accounts, take a look at *Understanding Business Accounting for Dummies*, by John A. Tracy and Colin Barrow (Wiley).

Keeping to your time lines

Don't forget that the tax year runs from 6 April one year until 5 April the following year.

As a landlord, you must file a tax return every year reporting your rental income and expenses, even if you don't make a profit.

HMRC is waging a campaign against landlords who fail to report their rents, because they see them as easy targets. Technology links, previously unavailable, between HMRC, banks, and the Land Registry can easily track property owners and where they live.

If you show up owning more than one property and have not told HMRC about any rents, they check where you live against the electoral roll and other databases and open an investigation into your financial affairs.

Accounting periods

You don't have to draw up accounts for the year ending 5 April, but you can make your life easier if you do.

However, you do have to draw up accounts and file a tax return every year, but you can choose your tax year to run from a different start date, such as 1 January to 31 December each year, as long as the accounting period is 365 days – or 366 in a leap year.

Following the 6 April – 5 April year is easier because it saves a lot of maths for you and your accountant.

You should have one set of accounts for your UK property business and another for your overseas property business, if you have one.

If you don't follow the 5 April date, you have to *apportion* your accounts on a daily basis over two tax years.

Say you follow our 1 January – 31 December example above. You would have to apportion your figures so your accounts matched the 6 April – 5 April period for your tax return. The section 'Apportioning income and expenses' later in this chapter goes into the nitty gritty of apportionment.

So, you would have to work out your 6 April – 31 December figures for one year and add them to your 1 January – 5 April figures for the next year to come up with the accounts required for your tax return.

In Table 5–1, if you follow the 1 January – 31 December example, your accounts for the portion in italics are those required by HMRC for the 2008–09 tax return.

Those up to 5 April 2008 go into the 2007–08 return and those for 6 April 2009–31 December 2009 go into the 2009–10 return.

Table 5–1	Accounting periods
2008	*2009*
1 January	*1 January*
5 April	*5 April*
6 April	6 April
31 December	31 December

Check out the next section, 'Apportioning income and expenses' for the details on how to do this. You may over pay or under pay tax working accounts in this way, and this may result in you paying unnecessary interest on late tax payments, or with HMRC owing you money that can take an age to claim back.

If you do draw up accounts to 5 April, your first accounting period is from the date you let your first property until the following 5 April. Then your tax years run from 6 April until 5 April the following year, until the last year of trading. In the last year in which you let a property, the accounting period is 6 April until the date the last tenant moves out of your last letting property.

This applies to each property business unless you're trading through a company. So, you've a first letting date and a final letting date for a UK property business, holiday letting business, or an overseas property business.

For details about company accounting dates, see Chapter 20.

Apportioning income and expenses

Apportionment is a way of putting income or expenses that cut across two tax years into the correct accounting period.

If you're apportioning monthly, don't bother to apportion expenses for 1 April–5 April if the amounts are small – that's an odd few pounds, just include them in the April monthly figure. If you pay out £200 for buildings insurance in September for the year, then you need to work out the cost from the date the insurance started (say 15 September), until 5 April for one tax year and the cost from 6 April until 14 September for the next.

You can apportion by days or months unless your property business accounting period cuts across two tax years, in which case you must apportion on a daily basis.

First, work out the cost on a monthly or daily basis:

200/12 = £16.66

Apportioned, the buildings insurance is £16.66 × 7 months = £116.66 for September to March and £16.66 × 5 months = £83.30 for April to August.

Don't worry about part months – just divide the figures by 12 to get a monthly cost.

200/365 = £0.55 Apportioned, the insurance is £0.55 × 197 days = £108.35 and £0.55 × 168 days = £92.40

The slight cost differences are due to rounding.

Calculating your profit and loss

This is where you can see how good or bad your record keeping is. If you followed each step in putting a property register together, then working out your profits and losses is straightforward. If you're still digging around in that bin bag then life's a bit harder, but you can be more organised next year.

You can work out your profits – or losses – by replacing the 'x' with your own figures. In bookkeeping a figure to subtract is represented in brackets, so expenses of £2,000 is (£2,000).

Rents received:	x
Less:	
Property costs and utilities	(x)
Repairs and renewals	(x)
Finance costs	(x)
Legal and professional costs	(x)
Costs of services provided	(x)
Other expenses	(x)
Gross rental profit or (loss):	x
Less:	
10 per cent wear-and-tear allowance	(x)
Net rental profit or (loss)	x

Chapters 6 and 7 discuss in detail what you need to include in your accounts as income and expenses.

Now comes the complicated bit.

If you're a sole owner, then just tot up the figures for each property in each business so that you end up with a separate profit or loss figure for:

- ✔ Your UK property business
- ✔ Your holiday letting business
- ✔ Your overseas property business

Now, if you've three UK letting properties and two make a profit of £1,000 and one makes a loss of £750, your UK rental business profit is £1000 + £1,000 – £750 = £1,250.

If you've multiple holiday lets or overseas properties, you can set off the losses of one property against profits of the others in the same category as well.

You can't set off profits or losses of one property business against those of another. This means that if you have a UK property business profit of £1,250 and an overseas property business loss of £1,500, you can't wipe out the profit.

Joint owners need to divide the profit and loss figures pro rata. In our example above, if a husband and wife owned the properties 75:25 in favour of the wife, then she would have a profit of 75 per cent of £1,250 = £937.50 and her husband would have the remaining 25 per cent or £312.50.

Working out your tax

Income Tax is calculated on your total income for the year, including all your earnings, interest from savings, dividends from investments, and property income. You can't isolate your property tax.

You can find out more about working out your overall Income Tax liability in *Paying Less Tax for Dummies* by Tony Levene (Wiley).

Rental losses are not set off against other income, so they don't reduce the tax you pay on earnings, savings, or other investments.

Separating Your Finances

Separating your finances is a simple matter of common sense and good practice. Separate bank accounts and records dedicated to the separate parts of your property activity make the whole business run more smoothly.

Bank accounts and credit cards

Set up a separate bank account for each of your property businesses as you can keep track of the money going in and out much more easily this way.

Annotate your bank statements every month so that in a year's time you know what each payment was for. Pick a system that's easy to follow and stick to it.

Take special care to tag payments in and out of the bank to the property owners. Money paid in this way can be withdrawn tax-free because the money is repayment of money invested in the business or a reimbursed expense. Money invested is dealt with in Chapter 13 (where I give examples of balance sheets and show how owners can draw tax-free income from their business).

A reimbursed expense is where the owner has paid a bill for the company out of his own pocket and the business reimburses that payment against a receipt, such as a receipt for a bag of cement to do small repairs.

If you buy materials and pay bills with a credit card, try to have a separate card for each property business and again, annotate the payments.

If you pay money out, don't bypass your business account and take the cash out of your own pocket or private account. Always put the cash in your business account and pay the bill from there – you can track money and calculate tax much more easily that way.

Joint owners

Don't fall into the tax trap of letting one owner take responsibility for a property. Make sure that paperwork is in joint names and, if you're personally entitled to a share of income, have that money paid into your personal bank account, not a joint account.

If you don't separate out your payments, the taxman may try and prove that the owner who pays tax at the highest rate never lost control of the cash and that the passive owners gave up their rights to the money.

Keeping personal stuff personal

By keeping property business bank accounts and credit cards separate from your personal affairs, the taxman can only see your property business details from your paperwork and can't go on a fishing expedition into your other financial affairs.

Proving Your Expenses and Inventory

A digital camera is an invaluable piece of equipment for a property business. Not only can you take snaps when you view a property to remind yourself of what that property is like when you're comparing details, but the camera's a great tool for proving expenses and inventories if you have to retain a tenant's deposit owing to damage or extra cleaning.

On your first visit to a new property, take pictures of everything – especially the kitchen and bathroom, and the state of décor. Don't forget the outside: rotten windows and the overgrown garden need to be recorded. If the taxman then questions your repairs or renewals, or argues that you've wrongly claimed a capital cost, you've got the evidence. Don't forget to time and date stamp the photographs so they're dated prior to the repairs!

Investors and traders should both keep extensive photo albums. Not only do they prove your expenses but albums are a good sales tool for tenants or prospective buyers because the album shows them exactly what they're paying for.

Before letting a property, photograph the state of the property inside and out – including the condition of furnishings and décor. Think of it as like one of those check sheets a car hire company completes before letting you drive off in one of their cars.

Check the inventory and pictures with the tenant and ask them to sign a waiver stating that the inventory is correct and the photos are a true and accurate representation of the state of the property.

If damage has occurred at the property, or work is required when tenants move out, ensure that you've got photographic evidence to prove your case. Some letting agents take a video tour of the property before agreeing a let, as evidence of condition.

Chapter 6

Tracking Your Property Income

*Y*our first rent cheque hits the bank. You pay the mortgage and a couple of other bills, and have enough left for a burger and a pint.

Before you go off on a spending spree to celebrate your first profit, take a reality check. Business income is not your money. Only after you've paid all the bills and tax do the profits go in your pocket. Unless you keep track of cash flowing in and out of the business as you go along, you never know where you stand with regard to your tax responsibilities.

This chapter explains exactly what property income is and how to record the details in your accounts.

Knowing What Is (and Isn't) Property Income

Your *property income* is anything you receive from anyone in exchange for them renting or buying your property.

Property income covers what you receive in cash or in kind from buyers, tenants of furnished or unfurnished property, and holiday lets in the UK or overseas. The way you treat your property income depends on whether you're an investor or a trader.

> ✔ **As an investor, treat your property as an asset:** You pay Capital Gains Tax (CGT) when you sell and must not set off any capital expenses against rental income.
>
> ✔ **As a trader, treat your property as stock:** You pay Income Tax on the profits you make when you sell.

Rent is not the only property income you may receive – here's how to account for most types of property income. This section takes you through what counts as property income – and what doesn't.

Payment in kind

If you receive payment in kind – for instance a tenant does a bit of DIY for a rent reduction – then allocate the favour a reasonable and fair cash value.

For example, the tenant may buy the paint and materials to paint the kitchen and in return, you dock £75 from the rent in recognition of their outlay. That £75 is still income you've received, it's just not received as cash but as a payment in kind.

No matter what form the payment takes, it still has a cash value and that cash value goes into the accounts as income.

Remember to keep a note with the accounts of how you arrived at the cash value, so if the taxman asks, you can show him your workings.

One-off payments

A single payment for letting a second home to a friend or relative for a weekend break or holiday is as much a property investment transaction as letting a property on a six-month tenancy agreement.

In tax, just one rent payment in the tax year is considered property income and needs reporting on your tax return.

Furnished lettings

A *furnished letting* is a property where the tenant can live quite happily by just taking in personal effects.

Simply providing *white goods* – basic electrical goods and furnishings, like a cooker or a fridge, carpets, curtains, and lamp shades – is not the same as letting a furnished property. Furnishing a property means that you have to provide a lot more, like beds, tables, chairs, kitchen equipment, and the like.

Dealing with tenants' deposits

An official tenancy protections scheme protects deposits held by landlords or their letting agents for property with a rent payable of up to £25,000 a year in England and Wales.

The scheme puts safeguards in place to protect tenant's deposits from unscrupulous landlords who in the past held on to money, often without good reason.

In Scotland, no deposit protection scheme is in force, but one is planned as part of a new Scottish Housing Act. The rules cover all tenancy agreements except:

- ✔ Properties where the landlord is a resident
- ✔ Properties with rents over £25,000 per year
- ✔ Properties let to companies
- ✔ Student accommodation let by universities or colleges
- ✔ Deposits taken prior to 6 April 2007

Taking a deposit

Landlords can choose which deposit protection scheme to opt for and they must inform the tenant within 14 days of taking a deposit which scheme they're using. The landlord's notice must specify:

- ✔ Contact details of the protection scheme
- ✔ Contact details for the landlord
- ✔ How to apply for the release of the deposit
- ✔ Information explaining why a deposit is required
- ✔ What to do if you have a dispute about the deposit

The protection schemes

The three protection schemes are:

- ✔ **Deposit Protection Scheme (DPS):** A free, online service funded by the interest generated by money on deposit. No membership fees and deposits are accessible 24/7. Disputes are referred to the Alternative Dispute Resolution Service (ADR), run by the Chartered Institute of Arbitrators.

- ✔ **mydeposits.co.uk:** An insurance-backed scheme owned by the National Landlords Association and an insurance company. Landlords or their agents hold the deposits. Landlords pay a joining fee, an annual renewal fee and an insurance premium for each deposit. Disputes go to the ADR.

✔ **Tenancy Deposit Scheme (TDS):** Another insurance-backed deposit protection and resolution service. Landlords or agents hold the deposits. An annual fee per property is paid in to the scheme.

What if a deposit is not protected?

If a landlord fails to protect a deposit or does not inform the tenant of the scheme details within the 14-day period, the tenant can apply to a county court and request one of the following:

✔ Repayment of the deposit with 14 days.

✔ An order for the landlord to pay the deposit to one of the protection schemes.

The court can also order the landlord to pay a penalty of up to three times the deposit within 14 days for failing to meet her legal obligations. Failure to supply the required information or to protect a deposit also restricts the landlord's rights to evict a tenant.

Generally, the tenancy agreement gives landlords power to give a tenant two month's notice to quit. If the tenant fails to quit, then the landlord can apply to a county court for an eviction order.

If the landlord is in breach of the deposit protection rules, they cannot issue the notice to quit.

Ending a tenancy

When a tenancy ends, the landlord should return the deposit in full unless the she has a good reason to retain any of the money, such as reclaiming rent arrears or to pay for damage over and above normal wear and tear.

The tenant is entitled to interest on the deposit if it has been held in an interest-bearing account.

If the tenant disputes the retention, the dispute goes to arbitration, which is binding on both sides. If the landlord is holding the deposit, she should hand the money to a protection scheme for safe-keeping pending resolution of the dispute.

If no resolution is agreed, the matter can be taken to county court by either side. If the landlord fails to return the deposit, the protection scheme repays the tenant and seeks redress from the landlord.

Rent holidays

A rent holiday is an agreement between a landlord and tenant, who pays reduced rent for an agreed period.

The landlord may grant the tenant a rent holiday, for instance, to compensate the tenant for upheaval caused by repairs by reducing or declining to take rent for a period, or use a rent-free period to entice a tenant to move in to a hard-to-let property.

Accounting for rent holidays is simple – just treat the whole rent the tenant pays as the rent received for the property.

For example, you charge £7,500 a year rent at £625 per month for a house and give the tenant a free first month as an incentive.

Calculate the new monthly rent – less the rent holiday deduction – as follows:

1. Record the total annual rent (£7,500).

2. Subtract the free month (£7,500 – £625 = £6875).

3. Divide the amount remaining by 12 to give the monthly rent you need to record (£6875/12 = £572.92).

Interest received

Any interest received on cash in any property business account except a company bank account is not property income but *savings income* for the owners. Deal with it on your tax return the same way as any other interest you receive on other savings accounts. Exclude it from your property business accounts.

Lodgers

Property income doesn't include money from taking in lodgers, running a bed-and-breakfast, or running a hotel. Prepare full business accounts for property income. See Chapter 13 for special rules about income from lodgers.

Calculating Buy-to-Let Income

Apply two general rules to working out your property income depending on whether you receive total rents before expenses of £15,000 or more:

✔ For £15,000 or more, apply the earnings basis rule.

✔ For less than £15,000, apply the 'cash basis rule'.

Earnings basis rule

This rule says that for total rents above £15,000 in a tax year, you allocate property income to the tax year when it's *due*, not when it's *paid*.

For rent paid in advance, apportion the amount received that relates to the use of the property during the tax year. Apply the principle in reverse for rent paid in arrears.

Sometimes rent charged is included in your accounts before you actually receive any cash.

You may collect the rent according to a calendar year, that is, 1 January to the following 31 December but the accounts require you to apportion the amount to the tax year – April 6 – April 5 the following year. Say, for example you let two flats and charge rent annually in advance:

✔ The amount due on 1 January 2008 is £20,000.

✔ The amount due on 1 January 2009 is £22,000.

The annual rent is more than £15,000, so you work out the rent chargeable by splitting the rent due on 1 January 2008 according to tax years, applying the earnings basis:

Rent due on 1 January 2008 falls partly into the tax year ending 5 April 2008 (three months' worth) and partly into the period from 6 April 2008 to 31 December 2008 (nine months' worth). The period 6 April 2008 to 31 December 2008 is part of the tax year ending 5 April 2009.

Apportion the amount received for the tax year 2007–08 on a monthly basis as follows:

Annual rent/Months in year × Number of months that fall in the tax year.

([£20,000/12] × 3 = £5,000)

Alternatively, you can apportion on a daily basis, bearing in mind that the 2007–08 tax year has 366 days, and that the period from 1 January to 6 April 2008 has 96 days:

Annual rent/Days in year × Number of days that fall in the tax year.

(£20,000/366) × 96 = £5,246 on a daily basis.

You then apportion the amount for the 2008–2009 tax year in the same way. You can apportion it on a monthly basis:

(£20,000/12) × 9 = £15,000

or on a daily basis, remembering that 2008 has 366 days:

(£20,000/366) × 270 = £14,754.

Rent due on 1 January 2009 falls partly into the tax year ending 5 April 2009 and partly into the period between 6 April 2009 and 31 December 2009. This period falls into the tax year ending 5 April 2010.

Apportion the amount received for 2008–09 on a monthly basis, as for the previous year:

(£22,000/12) × 3 = £5,000

or on a daily basis:

(£22,000/366) × 95 = £5,710)

Apportion the amount received for 2009–10 on a monthly basis:

(£22,000/12) × 9 = £16,500

or on a daily basis:

(£22,000/365) × 270 = £16,274.

Hey presto: Your total property income for 2008–09 is:

✔ Monthly apportionment: £15,000 + £5,500 = £20,500.

✔ Daily apportionment: £14,754 + £5,710 = £20,464.

The difference is due to the more precise methodology of daily apportionment.

The taxman cannot tell you which method to use to work your accounts, as long as you follow generally accepted accounting principles. If one method works out better for you, use it, but you must apply the formula consistently each year and not just pick and mix to try to evade tax.

Cash basis rule

HMRC guidance instructs tax inspectors to accept *small income cases* on a simplified cash basis.

To qualify:

- ✔ Your rents in any tax year must be less than £15,000 before deducting any expenses.

- ✔ You must work out your income and expenses with a consistent formula.

- ✔ The overall profit or loss result must not differ much from the earnings basis.

The cash basis generally occurs when receiving rent and paying expenses monthly. The cash-basis method allows you to tot up what you've received and paid in the year and deduct one from the other to reach a profit or loss figure without any apportionment.

Overseas property income

The same rules apply to both UK and overseas property businesses. The difference is that overseas property income is treated as foreign income on the tax return instead of land and property income.

You also need to bring any income and expenses from overseas furnished holiday lets into the same set of accounts instead of keeping separate accounts, as you do for UK furnished holiday lets.

Other rental income

Include other monies that you may receive from time to time as rental property income on your accounts:

- ✔ **Grants:** Money received from local councils or other organisations that contribute to revenue expenses – such as repairs and renewals to the property.

- ✔ **Insurance payments:** These are pay-outs from policies giving cover against non-payment of rent.

- ✔ **Sporting rights:** Include cash from issuing permits allowing shooting, fishing, or hunting on your land.

- ✔ **Filming rights:** If you've a character property and make money from filming and photography, include the money on your accounts as property income.

✔ **Static caravans and houseboats:** The same rules apply to static caravans and houseboats as other property – long-term lets count as property income whereas short-term lets count as holiday letting income.

✔ **Service charges and ground rent:** If you receive such payments for leasehold property, include these as property income.

Confusing net and gross rents

A basic accounting error in calculating rental income is misinterpreting gross and net rents. Gross rent is the total amount the tenant pays. Net rent is the amount left after the letting agent (if you have one) has taken her commission.

Say you let a property for £650 a month and the agent deducts a management fee of 10 per cent plus VAT. The landlord receives the net amount in the bank calculated as follows:

Rent agent receives from tenant: £650.00

Less 10 per cent management fee: (£650 – 65.00 = £585.00)

Less VAT on management fee at 17.5 per cent of the fee: (£585.00 – £11.37)

Rent paid net to landlord: £573.63

For the accounts, enter £650.00 in the rent receivable account, with an entry of £76.37 for the letting agent's fee plus VAT on the expense side.

The same applies if the letting agent has paid a bill for you – you still enter the rent charged to the tenant and put the amount of the bill on the expense side with the letting agent's fee.

The rent receivable is what you charge the tenant, not what the letting agent pays you.

Adding Up Development Income

Property developers make their money from buying property, adding value by refurbishment then selling the property on. The broad principles for calculating development income, although similar to those for buy-to-let income, contain important differences.

Here's how developing differs from buy-to-let:

✔ Development properties come under the heading of *stock*, not *assets*. That is, they're to be made available for sale, rather than used to generate long-term income. Any profits from a sale by individuals have Income Tax and Class 4 National Insurance Contributions applied.

The concept of stock and assets can be confusing, because what is stock for one business may be an asset for another. For example, a landlord owns a house that needs refurbishment and decides to sell. As a letting property, the house is the landlord's asset because it's an investment generating rental income.

The landlord sells to a developer who refurbishes the house with the intention of selling as soon as possible to make a profit. The house is her stock, because she is keeping the property in the short-term with a view to generating a quick profit.

If the developer sells the house to another landlord who lets the property long-term, the house is now an asset again.

✔ For companies, profit calculations come under corporation tax rules. See Chapter 20 for the low-down on corporation tax.

✔ Your development business can include property in the UK and overseas.

✔ An accounting period can be *any* 12-month period, you don't have to stick to the tax year.

✔ You may set off trading losses against other income and capital gains in the current and previous trading years.

How Development Accounts Work

Now you have laid your foundations for a development business, you need to look at where the figures slot in to the accounts.

The first and most important point is that no costs relating to refurbishing or maintaining a property can be put in to the accounts until the property is sold. So, you buy a house in December 2008 and spend six months doing it up and sell in June 2009. Your accounting period is 6 April to the following 5 April. You have purchased in the tax year 2008–09 and sold in 2009–10.

Any costs incurred against the property from purchase until sale are held on the 2008–09 accounts on the balance sheet as stock and work-in-progress.

In 2009–10, when the property is sold, they move from the balance sheet to the profit and loss account as costs of sale.

Secondly, property development accounts consist of two sections:

- ✔ Buying, refurbishing, and selling property
- ✔ General costs incurred by any business, like telephone bills, stationery, and postage

As an example, look at a typical property developer's profit and loss account:

Barry bought a run-down house at auction in February 2008 for £100,000, intending to refurbish and sell.

He did the work himself and sold the house for £215,000 on 30 November 2008. His tax year end is 31 December. Barry's accounts look like Table 6-1:

Table 6-1	Calculating Net Profits
Sale proceeds	215,000
Less:	
Costs of sale	
Refurbishment costs	(25,000)
Legal and agents fees	(10,000)
Purchase price	(100,000)
Total costs:	(135,000)
Gross profit/(loss):	80,000
Less:	
General business expenses	
Telephone	150
Stationery	50
Bank charges	50
Motor costs and fuel	950
Accounts	350
Total expenses:	(1,550)
Net profit/(loss):	78,450

As Barry did no other work that year, he pays Income Tax and Class 4 National Insurance Contributions on the £78,450 net profit on his year-ending 5 April 2009 tax return.

Not Losing Out On Your Losses

When you first buy and let a property, the likelihood is that you make a loss for the first couple of years or so because of the initial outlay in refurbishing the property and paying the mortgage interest comes to more than the rent you receive.

Record these losses on your tax return. They save you money in the long term because as your portfolio grows, you can set off the losses against future profits.

Jo owns a letting property and her rental profits and losses for the first six years are shown in Table 6-2:

Table 6-2	Rental Profits and Losses	
Year	*Profit or Loss*	*Running Total*
1	−750	−750
2	−680	−1430
3	−425	−1825
4	195	−1630
5	1800	−170
6	2000	1830

Because Jo has banked her losses by submitting them on a tax return, although she made a profit from Year 4, she does not pay any Income Tax on her rental profits until Year 6, when her profits cancel out the losses accumulated in all the other years.

No rule says that you can only keep the losses banked for a particular length of time – you can carry them forward and accumulate them for any number of years.

You can set off UK property business losses against future UK property business profits and do the same with overseas property business profits and losses – but you can't set off UK losses against overseas profits, or vice versa.

Even if you've no letting property, you can still keep the losses banked for three years, as HMRC guidance to tax inspectors states that they can consider a property business active for that time even though the business may not have any property to let.

Letting and Letting Live . . . For Free

Some investors have property that they let to friends or relatives rent-free or for a nominal amount – a type of letting that's known as *uncommercial letting*, which has a set of special tax rules. Uncommercial lets are tax neutral – they don't make a profit or a loss in tax terms. Of course, catches exists:

✔ You can only claim expenses up to the value of the rent received – expenses include any 10 per cent wear-and-tear allowance for furnished letting.

✔ You cannot set off these costs against rent received from other letting property.

✔ You cannot carry the costs forward to set off against future rents received for the uncommercially let property.

On your accounts or tax returns, you needn't include income or expenses relating to properties let uncommercially until you sell, at which time CGT is due.

A friend or relative may stay in a letting property rent-free between commercial lets – a practice known as house sitting – provided that the property is available for commercial letting and you're actively seeking tenants. HMRC accepts that the property is a letting property under these circumstances. HMRC guidance tells inspectors that they can allow a total of a month's house sitting in any three-year period.

The taxman may consider house sitting a holiday cottage an uncommercial let if he suspects that the time is really a break for family or friends.

Landlords Living Overseas

Landlords who live overseas but let property in the UK have two tax options:

✔ Let their letting agent or tenant deduct the tax from the rent for paying directly to HMRC.

✔ Submit a personal tax return like a landlord living in the UK.

Paying tax under either option is via the Non-Resident Landlord Scheme (NRLS). As a non-resident landlord, you have to follow special rules to ensure that you pay Income Tax on any rental profits.

A letting agent must deduct tax at the basic rate from any rent received less expenses and pay the money to HMRC quarterly. This rule applies even if the rent remains out for collection.

A tenant must do the same if:

✔ The landlord has no agent.

✔ The rent payable is more than £100 per week.

Work out tax as the gross rent, less specified expenses. These expenses include those reasonably allowed under UK property business rules (see Chapter 7 for a full list).

If you don't want your agent or tenant to pay Income Tax for you, filing a tax return is often the best option.

Deduction at source is based on rents received, less expenses, but specified expenses don't include some of the larger deductions a landlord can set off against rental income, for instance:

✔ Mortgage interest

✔ 10 per cent wear-and-tear allowance for furnished lettings

Agents sometimes side with HMRC when deciding whether costs are allowable because agents have a personal liability for any shortfall in tax paid.

Deduction at source is likely to mean an overseas landlord pays too much tax; the best way to save tax is to submit a tax return.

Overseas landlords must apply to HMRC for consent to opt out of the deduction-at-source scheme. Without doing so, overseas landlords may not submit a tax return.

Chapter 7

Counting the Costs of Your Property Business

In This Chapter

▶ Claiming property expenses to help cut your tax

▶ Revealing how to beat the property tax Catch-22

▶ Counting down the Top 20 property expenses

*O*ne of the questions any accountant hears most often is, 'Where's a list of expenses I can claim for my property business?' The answer's always the same – it doesn't exist!

So cue the drum roll and fanfare as I pull back the curtain on the list of expenses most commonly available to a property business.

Before shining the spotlight on the information the taxman would rather you did not know, I consider the benefits of tracking your business expenses. The list is not definitive, but it covers the main costs you face as a landlord or small developer.

How Expenses Cut Your Tax

Work out taxable property business profits by adding up the rental income for the year and deducting any expenses. Every pound you stack up as an expense represents 20 pence or 40 pence off your Income Tax bill and with the costs of maintaining a property, that stack of money can reach quite high.

Technically, you may claim any expense as a business expense as long as:

✔ You spent the money wholly and exclusively for your property business.

✔ The expense is not a *capital expense* (a cost related to buying, improving, and selling investment property.

The above rules apply equally to any individual, joint owner, business partnership, or company that lets property.

Property traders also follow the same rules – but with important differences. See Chapter 14 for more information.

Property expenses Catch-22

Here's the property expenses Catch-22 – if you don't claim a legitimate expense, the taxman won't tell you that you can. You just have to know about it. But if you ask for a list of typical property expenses, he says such a thing doesn't exist: so you don't know, and can't claim the expense.

Well, here's your chance to beat his Catch-22, because I've obtained HMRC guidance to tax inspectors on which expenses they should accept, and compiled a Top 20 countdown of the most popular to help you slash your tax bills.

Grasping the 'wholly and exclusively' rule

The 'wholly and exclusively' principle is one you need to get your head around, because it applies to every penny you spend on your property business. Three important aspects apply to every expense:

- ✔ **The expense you claim must be for business purposes.** If you've spent money for a joint private and business purpose, you must identify a definite part of the expense as business spending and apportion only that part of the expense in the accounts.

- ✔ **Incidental benefit doesn't mean an expense is disallowed.** HMRC guidance for tax inspectors quotes the example of a self-employed engineer who may travel to exotic locations to advise on projects. As long as there's no private purpose for the trip, the whole expense is allowed.

- ✔ **The business purpose of the expense must be measurable.** If an expense is for a dual purpose – for example, the same engineer takes his wife and children to an exotic location for a fortnight on the basis that he's looking for work – then he can't claim the expense because no business purpose is measurable.

Keep evidence to back up your decision to include an expense in the accounts – evidence includes receipts, documents, notes, and agreements. The list of expenses in this chapter includes hints on proving these expenses as legitimate to the taxman.

Expenses For All: Claims for Investors and Developers

As promised, this section provides you with the inside track on property tax business expenses you need to consider claiming, whether you're an investor claiming rents from tenants or a developer buying and selling property on a short-term basis.

Travel and meals

Travel costs include air, rail, cab and bus fares, tolls, overnight accommodation, and meals. The key to claiming accurate expenses is to keep accurate records of every cost you incur.

Assessing your vehicle expenses

If you use your own vehicle, claim a percentage of running costs – fuel, repairs, insurance, excise licence, and so on, appropriate to the business use of the vehicle. Running costs don't include the cost of buying the vehicle, but you can apportion interest on any finance.

To work out business use of a car or van: note the mileage on 5 April each year. Keep a log of business trips including:

- ✔ Date
- ✔ Destination
- ✔ Reason for trip
- ✔ Distance travelled

Tot up the business mileage for the tax year and work out the total as a percentage of all your business and personal mileage for the year.

When noting mileage, take a date-stamped photograph of the odometer for your records.

Claiming for accommodation and meals

Food, drink, and accommodation aren't generally classed as business expenses as everyone needs sustenance and shelter to live and therefore these expenses aren't directly a business cost, says HMRC.

If, however, a business trip means staying away from home for a couple of nights, then the hotel and reasonable meal costs can be claimed as business expenses.

Don't put in bills for meals for other people or children because these bills are evidence of an unallowable dual-purpose expense.

Establishing your business base

If you have letting agents, the business base is their office and you're unlikely to be able to claim any travel expenses as they carry out all your management duties.

If you have an office away from home to run your property business, you may claim business travel costs from your office but not between your office and your home.

If you run your business from home, you may claim business travel costs from your home.

Documenting long-distance trips

If you live in Brighton for work, but let a property in Edinburgh, and you then claim a visit to inspect the property, tax inspectors have instructions to scrutinise your claim to ensure that you haven't really disguised a personal trip to visit friends or relatives as a business trip.

Home office costs

Owing to a special twist that HMRC allows on the 'wholly and exclusively' rule, property people may use their homes for business. According to the taxman's internal guidance relating to home and office purposes, 'wholly and exclusively' means:

- ✔ When part of the home is used for business, you can claim costs if the business is the sole use of that part of your home at that time.

    This applies when you use the dining room to write up business records for a couple of hours and shut the door so no one else has use of the room while you do.

- ✔ You do not have to bill business costs separately from your normal domestic bills, like electricity or Council Tax.

- ✔ You do not have to put part of your home permanently aside for business and not use the space for any other purpose at any other time.

Claiming minor business use

Instructions to tax inspectors tell them not to question claims for minor use. In financial terms, minor use translates into £2 per week for 52 weeks a year.

Minor use is writing up your business records on the dining table for a couple of hours a week. It doesn't matter what the costs are – the tax inspector accepts this as a minimum claim from every property tax payer.

You may therefore claim up to £104 a year minor business use on your tax return as an expense without showing bills or receipts – and the tax man won't question the deduction.

The minor use expense is £104. If you paid Income Tax on that £104 as part of your profits, you would pay 20 per cent at basic rate, or 40 per cent at higher rate. Because 20 per cent of £104 is £20.80 and 40 per cent is £41.60, you've already recouped the cost of this book without implementing any of my other advice!

Major business use

Tax inspectors are required only to make inquiries when the amount you claim is inconsistent with the size of the business. Inconsistency is when your claim eats into a significant part of the business turnover.

A significant part of turnover varies from business to business. HMRC keeps template accounts for every type of business by comparing accounts and tax returns submitted by other businesses in the same sector. This data shows HMRC what percentage of your turnover your general business costs should be, and that breaks down into how much as a percentage of turnover may be spent on travel, telephone, stationery, and so on.

If your business spending falls outside these expectations, then the HMRC computer can pick you out for a tax inquiry to check why you're making a claim.

The system never picks out anyone spending less than expected!

You can claim two basic sorts of business cost: *Fixed costs* and *running costs*.

> ✔ **Fixed costs:** Costs that stay the same over a given period of time. They include:
>
> • Insurance
>
> • Council tax
>
> • Mortgage interest
>
> • Rent (if your rent your home and part is used for business)
>
> • Repairs and renewals – only for the exterior and rooms used for business

✔ **Running costs:** Costs which vary according to circumstances. They include:

- Cleaning (only the rooms used for business)

- Heat, light and power

- Telephone and broadband (business calls and a proportion of the line rental pro rata the amount of telephone business usage)

  Ask your telephone provider to itemise outgoing calls and annotate the bill so you can prove business usage.

- Metered water charges – apportion according to use

Calculating your claim

Apportionment plays a big part in claiming business expenses. The factors taken in to account here include:

✔ **Area:** how much of the home does the business use?

✔ **Usage:** what proportion does the business consume of any measurable supplies?

✔ **Time:** how long is an area used by the business and how long is it used for other purposes?

Amanda writes up business records at her kitchen table, using the room solely for business for a short time each week and estimates her costs at ££104. Tax inspectors accept such a claim as minor, so don't need to make inquiries.

Every property investor should claim at least £104 a year home as office costs as HMRC would have problems disallowing a claim from any taxpayer after citing a similar example in their own guidance.

Carl is a landlord with several properties. He uses the smallest bedroom at home exclusively for business. The room is 5 per cent of the property's floor space. Carl claims 5 per cent of his annual council tax, buildings insurance, mortgage interest, and electricity bill as home-office costs. He also claims part of his telephone and broadband bills apportioned *pro rata* his itemised telephone bill.

Carl's total claim is about £250. Tax inspectors can accept his claim but Carl should keep the bills to back his claim.

Kate works from home in the dining room between 2 p.m. and 6 p.m. every week day. Her family uses the room between 6 p.m. and 10 p.m.. The room represents 12 per cent of the floor area of the house and business use is for 4/24 of the day.

Kate's fixed business costs total £5,500 for the year.

12 per cent of the fixed costs by floor space amounts to £660 – but as she uses the room for 4 hours or 1/6 of a day, she claims £660 × 1/6 = £110.

Kate's running costs total £1,850 per year.

12 per cent of the running costs by floor space amount to £222 – the room is in use eight hours a day (9 a.m. to 1 p.m. and 6 p.m. to 10 p.m.) but only half that time is for business, so she claims half the running costs – £111. Her itemised telephone bill shows a third of outgoing calls are for business, so she claims the cost of these calls plus a third of the line rental.

Financial interest

The source of the money you claim as expenses doesn't matter, so you can claim interest on business spending from a range of financial arrangements. These include:

✔ Mortgages

✔ Bank loans

✔ Overdrafts

✔ Credit cards

✔ Hire purchase and other finance agreements

If you sell a property, any interest on loans you've taken out to purchase or refurbish that property isn't allowed as an expense from the date of disposal onwards, even if you've secured the loans against a different property from the one you've sold.

Conversely, interest is allowed from the first day a property is transferred into the property business.

You must show that you spent the money on:

✔ Buying land, property, or assets for your rental business

✔ Funding repairs, improvements, or alterations to your rental business property

If you've borrowed against your own home, bank account, or credit cards to raise money to spend on your property business, apportion the interest and claim the cost back through your property business.

You can withdraw tax-free money from your property business to spend on whatever you like under special circumstances – and reclaim the interest on the borrowing against the business. See Chapter 13 for a step-by-step-guide.

It makes sense if you have property profits, to pay off the mortgage on your home first because you can set off all your rental business interest against profits or losses, but only a small amount of your own mortgage receives tax relief if you've borrowed against it to raise funds for your property business.

Repairs and improvements

Replacing a few roof tiles after a storm is a *repair*. Converting the roof space into bedrooms, storage, or a study is an *improvement*.

The difference between repairs and improvements is important because they're taxed in different ways:

- ✓ **Repairs**: Day-to-day costs to maintain your property at a particular standard, which can be set off against rental income to reduce your Income Tax.

- ✓ **Improvements**: One-off costs that add value to your property, like extensions, loft conversions, porches, and garages. Improvements can include replacing part of the property with a more expensive item – like installing a granite kitchen worktop instead of a standard wooden one.

Improvements and upgrades can be set off against Capital Gains Tax (CGT) when you sell the property. See Chapters 9 and 10 for more on reducing your CGT.

You must account for repairs and improvements separately. If you refurbish a house and some of the costs include improvements, then you must record them in your property register and your repairs in your rental accounts. Refer to Chapter 5 for more on maintaining a property register.

Tax inspectors are instructed to allow a special concession for repairs that involve replacing old parts with new ones made from modern materials. Good examples include replacing rotten wooden windows with PVC windows, or replacing copper or lead piping with plastic.

These types of replacement can be allowed as repairs and not classed as an improvement, in recognition of the fact that technology moves on and sometimes it's just not possible to replace like with like.

Salaries and wages

Whether or not salaries can be claimed as a business expense depends on what sort of property business you're running.

Property investors

Property investors owning properties let for rent can't draw any wages for any time spent working in their property rental business. Profits from the business aren't subject to National Insurance Contributions nor regarded as pensionable income.

You can pay anyone who's not an owner – but if you employ permanent staff, you should set up a payroll scheme. Any payments made under a payroll scheme count as pensionable income for that employee and become subject to tax deduction and National Insurance Contributions.

Property developers

Property development – buying property, refurbishing it and selling it on – is treated the same as any other business: Income is taxed in the same way as that of any tradesman or shopkeeper. All profits are treated as earnings and subject to Income Tax and National Insurance Contributions.

Refer to Chapter 2 for more on the differences between property investors and property developers.

As a property developer, you're self-employed, so you must pay Class 2 National Insurance Contributions unless you've already reached retirement age or your profits fall below the Class 2 NIC threshold of £4,825 for 2008–2009. You need to apply to HMRC for an exemption if your profits are below £4,825.

Tax inspectors scrutinise cash paid to close friends or relatives:

You have to show the inspector that the salary package, which may include benefits like a car, health insurance, and pension contributions, is in line with that of an employee not related to you who would do the same job.

You must relinquish control of the cash by showing that you transferred the money to the employee's bank, and the person receiving must declare the income his tax return. If neither of you performs his part, the cash is considered yours and you pay the extra tax.

Training and seminars

Deducting the costs of training is an issue even tax inspectors dis-agree on! The rules say:

- ✔ If attending a course gives business owners new expertise, knowledge, or skills, the cost is an 'intangible capital asset' and because capital costs can't be set off against rental income, the expense is disallowed.

- ✔ If attending a course updates expertise that business owners already possess, the cost is deductible if it satisfies the 'wholly and exclusively' test. (See 'Grasping the "Wholly and Exclusively" rule' earlier in this chapter.)

Tax inspectors must allow the costs of updating existing knowl-edge but disallow costs that provide new expertise or knowledge, particularly that involving a recognised qualification, such as a Master of Business Administration.

Attending courses and seminars for novice property investors suggests that you're gaining knowledge you didn't have previ-ously, so you may have difficulty in shuffling the cost past your tax inspector.

Companies often pay for training that reinforces employees' skills, but won't pay for them to gain new knowledge that has nothing to do with their jobs.

Apply the same rule to your property business. Books – like this one, for instance – constitute an allowable cost because books reinforce existing knowledge as a reference.

Abortive property costs

Not all property transactions reach completion, for one reason or another, perhaps leaving you out-of-pocket with legal and valuation fees. Whether or not you can claw anything back depends on the nature of your business:

- ✔ Property developers can recoup these costs as part of their business.

- ✔ Property investors can't set off these costs against their prop-erty business. Many investors and their accountants argue that this is unfair, but tax law is a matter of fact, not opinion. In this case, lawyers' and agents' costs count as capital costs. As no asset is attached to them, there's nothing to claim.

Professional fees

Professional fees include payments to accountants, surveyors, solicitors, architects, and so on.

Professional fees are deductible if they're incurred for the rental business, but not if they're *capital,* or not wholly and exclusively for the rental business. Fees are capital if they relate to the purchase or sale of property. You can reclaim expenses relating to the first letting of a property for up to a year but not those relating to a lease for more than a year because they're capital costs.

Allowable legal and professional expenses include:

- ✔ Insurance valuation costs
- ✔ Accountancy costs for drafting rental accounts and negotiating property tax
- ✔ Landlord association subscriptions
- ✔ Costs for evicting bad tenants

Legal and professional expenses that cannot be claimed include:

- ✔ Legal costs incurred in acquiring, selling, or adding to a property (as they're capital costs)
- ✔ Costs in connection with planning issues
- ✔ Personal accountancy fees, such as preparing your tax return or CGT computation

Bad and doubtful debts

If you're a property investor, renting out your property as a long-term investment, bad debts consist of rent arrears. If you're a property developer buying property to sell on, they can be any money owed by customers.

Bring in as receipts any rents that were earned in the year, even if they weren't paid until after the year ended. Then enter as an expense:

- ✔ Any debt that is irrecoverable.
- ✔ Any doubtful debt to the extent that you estimate it to be irrecoverable. The debt is all the money owed to you less any amount you expect to recover. This accounting technique moves the debt from income to expenses, so you don't pay tax on money owed to you. Only record the debt as an

expense when you've taken all reasonable steps to recover the debt. Gather evidence of the debt by writing to the debtor, issuing a summons, or employing a solicitor or debt collection agency to recover the loss.

If you've waived rent for a relative or friend, then you can't include the unpaid money in your rental accounts as a debt.

Cashback on loans

Cashbacks on loans from a mortgage lender are not business income unless the loan is taken in the name of a business.

Investors can pocket the money as a tax-free bonus and have no need to tell HMRC. Developers may do the same provided the loan is not company finance. If the loan is company finance, the cash belongs to the company, not you.

Fees for loan finance

Costs relating to setting up loan finance for a rental business can be allowable expenses providing that they relate wholly and exclusively to property let out on a commercial basis.

'Let on a commercial basis' does not refer to commercial premises but that the rental agreement, whether for residential or commercial property, is for a fair full-market rent.

These expenses include:

- ✔ Loan fees
- ✔ Commissions
- ✔ Guarantee fees
- ✔ Fees involving the security of a loan

As with all spending, HMRC needs to see invoices, bills, or statements.

Fines for law breaking

Fines you incur during the course of your business activities (parking tickets, for example) aren't allowed as expenses.

However, a payment to settle a civil action arising out of a rental business is allowed as an expense where the allegations weren't admitted by you or proved against you.

If they were admitted or proved:

✔ Allow any payment for damages

✔ Disallow any fines

Investors Only: Expenses Tips for Property Investors

If you're a property investor owning property for the long-term returns that letting can bring you, you've a special set of expenses that you can set off against tax. This section walks you through them.

Pre-letting expenses

When you buy your first letting property, repairs may be required to bring it up to standard so that you can command the best rent possible. Landlords often get confused over whether to reclaim these expenses, but the rules are quite straightforward.

You can't reclaim any improvement costs, so these go on to your property register as capital costs. Any refurbishment costs that are repairs but not improvements can go to your rental accounts providing:

✔ You spent the money no more than seven years before the first letting date of your rental business.

✔ You haven't already claimed the expense for tax purposes.

✔ You would've been able to claim the expense in the past if your rental business had already started.

All costs that pass these three tests go in the accounts as if they were spent on the day of first letting.

For your second and subsequent letting properties, these expenses go in to the accounts on the dates they were incurred.

Wear and tear

If you let furnished property in the UK – but not holiday lets – you can't claim the original purchase costs of the furnishings, nor make a claim later for adding furnishings that were not there when you first let the property furnished.

You *can* claim for wear-and-tear on the furnishings, by claiming either of the following allowances:

- ✔ A *10 per cent allowance*, which is, unsurprisingly, 10 per cent of the net rent for wear-and-tear, to cover the depreciation of furniture, fridges, and other items supplied with the accommodation.

- ✔ A *renewals allowance* of the net cost of replacing a particular item of furniture, but not the cost of the original purchase. The renewals allowance covers such items as:

  - Furniture or furnishings, such as beds, tables, chairs, and sofas
  - Televisions and audio equipment
  - Fridges and freezers
  - Carpets and floor-coverings
  - Curtains
  - Bed linen
  - Crockery or cutlery
  - Pictures and mirrors

You may claim the 10 per cent allowance or the renewal allowance, but not both, nor a mixture for different properties. Once you've chosen your allowance, you must stick with it for all your furnished UK lettings.

Calculating the 10 per cent allowance

You may let both furnished and unfurnished property. If so, you must ensure that the 10 per cent allowance is calculated only on the net rent from the furnished let.

The net rent is the total rent receivable in a tax year, less the following:

- ✔ Any costs the landlord pays on behalf of tenants, like Council Tax, water rates, or electricity bills
- ✔ Less any costs of additional services, like cleaning or gardening paid by the landlord, which the tenant would normally pay

Calculate 10 per cent of the net rent and enter the figure in the land and property section of your tax return.

You can claim the 10 per cent allowance each year even if you haven't replaced any furnishings.

Calculating the renewals allowance

To calculate the renewals allowance, simply include the receipts for replacing or repairing furnishings in your letting accounts. You need to prove the following points:

- ✔ The property is furnished. Photograph each room before each let.
- ✔ The property is in the UK.
- ✔ You've paid costs on behalf of a tenant – not when the property is vacant.

  For instance, you can still claim the cost of electricity as a property cost when the house is vacant, but can't deduct the money as part of the net rent calculation unless the property is tenanted and you pay the bill for the tenant.

- ✔ The property isn't a holiday let.

Advertising

You can deduct advertising costs for new tenants, like the bill for placing adverts in newspapers. However, you can't deduct the cost if it's a capital cost, for example, a permanent sign displaying vacancies.

Capital costs also include estate agent fees for buying or selling letting property and you need to deal with them on your CGT return when you sell a property.

Cost of common parts

In a block of flats, some parts of the building aren't let but are used communally by tenants, like hallways and landings.

You can include any money spent on the upkeep of the common parts in your rental accounts. Apportion the costs if you use part of the property privately or for uncommercial lets.

Insurance premiums

Premiums may be allowed as expenses if they cover:

- ✔ Damage to the building
- ✔ Damage to the contents
- ✔ Loss of rents

Each expense is allowed if the property is vacant between lets.

To prove that a property was tenanted or vacant at a particular time, keep the tenancy agreements.

Insulation allowance

Insulation allowance is available for loft and cavity wall insulation costs incurred between 6 April 2004 and 5 April 2009.

The allowance was extended to solid wall insulation from 7 April 2005 and draught proofing and insulation for hot water systems from 6 April 2006.

The allowance is aimed at encouraging landlords to make their rental property greener for tenants. Before the insulation allowance was introduced, landlords were unable to reclaim these costs.

The maximum claim is £1,500 per let property.

Restrictions

You're not able to claim the allowance if:

✔ You're claiming rent-a-room relief for the same property.

✔ The property is a furnished holiday let.

✔ The expense is incurred when:

  • The building is under construction.

  • You don't own the building.

  • For pre-trading expenses, the cost was more than six months before the start of your property business.

Joint owners

For jointly owned property, divide the allowance by the number of owners so each claims the same amount relative to their percentage of ownership of the property.

Part III

Property Taxes and How to Slash Them

'Oh, no! — it's the 5th, 6th 7th, 8th
and 9th Horsemen of the Apocalypse! .'

In this part . . .

*T*his part is where you get down and dirty with the different sorts of tax you have to deal with in your property business. Stamp Duty, Capital Gains Tax, Income Tax, Inheritance Tax: The gang's all here, and they've brought a few friends along too.

I focus throughout this part on what you need to do to reduce your tax liabilities, in whatever circumstance you find yourself during – even after – your property business lifetime.

Chapter 8

Licking Stamp Duty

· ·

In This Chapter

▶ Working out and paying stamp duty

▶ Saving money by sidestepping stamp duty

▶ Switching on to swapping property

▶ Staying on the right side of authority

· ·

Stamp Duty Land Tax is the modern rebranding of the centuries-old stamp tax. Stamp tax is paid on property transactions, by property buyers. The new version, introduced in 2003, is relatively bug free and has few tax-saving loopholes to exploit.

To save stamp duty, you need to focus on structuring transactions in the most favourable way, rather than relying on big money, tax-slashing solutions.

This chapter looks at the key rules you need to know that apply to residential property, so that you can apply them to save money as and when the opportunity becomes available.

You also need to spot the stamp duty tax traps you can fall into if you:

✔ Transfer land to a company

✔ Gift or shift a share in mortgaged property

✔ Split a property transaction into a chain of linked deals

If you're not aware of potential pitfalls, you may end up stumping up for a huge, unexpected tax bill.

Grasping Stamp Duty Basics

Stamp Duty Land Tax is paid by the buyer when taking over land or property in the UK for a *consideration*.

Taking over is when the property is yours and you receive the keys, or the date from when you start receiving the rent if the property already has a tenant at the time you buy it.

Consideration includes:

- ✔ Any cash payment
- ✔ Taking on a share of a mortgage

You also have to bear in mind *substantial performance*, which means occupying a property before paying, or paying about 90 per cent of the price but deferring the balance. Stamp duty is due in both cases as if you'd completed the purchase and received the keys.

Understanding who pays stamp duty

The taxpayer is anyone who would have the right to the proceeds of the sale of the property or to any rent received. It doesn't matter whether the buyer is an individual, company, partnership, or trust – the same stamp duty rules and rates apply.

If the property you're buying is in the UK, you pay stamp duty even if you live overseas. If you're one of two or more joint buyers, remember that each buyer has *joint and several liability*, which is legal jargon meaning that if one of you doesn't pay, the other is liable for the whole debt.

Working out how much you pay

By working out how much you pay you can turn disadvantage to your advantage. Stamp duty rates depend on two factors:

- ✔ **The value of the property:** The more expensive the purchase price of the house or flat, the more stamp duty you pay.
- ✔ **Where the property is:** If the house or flat is in a *disadvantaged area,* the tax rates are lower.

The UK has more than 2,000 disadvantaged areas, designated by the Government because they perform poorly in league tables showing economic indicators such as employment rates and average earnings.

Just because an area is listed as disadvantaged doesn't mean that you shouldn't buy property there. Many disadvantaged areas are spruced up with European and Government grants, and as the area improves, so do the house prices.

Find out if a property is in a disadvantaged area by checking the postcode at `www.hmrc.gov.uk/so/dar/dar-search.htm`, the HMRC web site.

Many solicitors dealing with property conveyancing outside their locality may not know or check if the property you're buying is in a disadvantaged area.

Make sure that you or your solicitor look up the postcode and confirms the details, otherwise you may pay thousands more in stamp duty than you need to. Table 8-1 shows you how much. The taxman won't check, because he assumes that you or your solicitor has – and the taxman isn't there to do you any favours.

Table 8-1	Stamp Duty Rates	
Rate	*Residential Property Price – Disadvantaged Areas*	*Residential Property Price – All Other areas Areas*
0%	Up to £150,000	Up to £125,000
1%	£150,001 – £250,000	£125,001 – £250,000
3%	£250,001 – £500,000	
4%	£500,001 or more	

For a handy stamp duty calculator, go to the HMRC website at `sdcalculator.inlandrevenue.gov.uk`.

Income shifting to reduce stamp duty

If a property is mortgaged and the property, or a share in it, is given as a gift to another person, stamp duty rules say that the consideration, or price paid by the person receiving the gift, is the amount of mortgage that they take over.

So, if you have no mortgage, you have no stamp duty.

Say Ian has a letting property worth £500,000 with a mortgage of £375,000, and he gifts his wife, Jenny, 60 per cent of the property.

Jenny's consideration is 60 per cent of the mortgage value of £375,000, which comes to £225,000. Ian has no Capital Gains Tax (CGT) to pay because the gift between spouses is a 'no gain/no loss' transaction), but Jenny must pay stamp duty at a rate of 1 per cent, or £2,250. (Refer to Chapter 9 for more on CGT.)

If Ian and Jenny were unmarried and decided to undertake a similar property transfer, the rules would be slightly different because the disposal may trigger a CGT or Inheritance Tax (IHT) event as well as the stamp duty payment.

The point to bear in mind is that you can save a lot of money by utilising income-shifting strategies to avoid Income Tax, CGT and IHT, but make sure that you always run through the exercise on paper to look for any tax traps.

In your mind, you have to balance the likely tax savings of your tax strategy against the costs. Sometimes the best textbook tax strategies aren't the most ideal real-life business decisions.

In Ian and Jenny's case, as in any other, you need to look at potential costs and weigh them up against potential savings before putting pen to paper.

Going green: zero carbon houses

Providing you can find one in time, if you buy a house with a *zero carbon* energy rating before 30 September 2012, and the house costs £500,000 or less, the purchase is exempt from stamp duty. A stamp duty discount of £15,000 exists for more expensive homes.

Unfortunately, new house builders have plans for zero carbon houses on the drawing board, but that's as far as they've got.

Sidestepping Stamp Duty

You've already seen that buying in a disadvantaged area can reduce your stamp duty bill – but you can cut the bill in other ways.

Staying below the duty threshold

Never offer the asking price for a property that's priced close to the stamp duty thresholds – see Table 8-1 earlier in this chapter for these thresholds. For instance, paying £252,000 for a house means a stamp duty bill of 3 per cent of the purchase price – a whacking £7,560. Paying £249,999 for the same house means a stamp duty bill of 1 per cent – £2,499. That's a massive tax saving of £5,061.

As a result estate agents price many properties just under the stamp duty threshold, but not many in the 'dead band' of £10,000 or so above.

Chewing over chattels

The chattels method of avoiding stamp duty is a tough one to pull off. The taxman scrutinises every return that goes through under the chattels method, but if you get it right it can save you money.

What are chattels?

Chattels are items that aren't fixed to the land or property, but which the seller decides to leave behind. In calculating stamp duty, you don't include chattels as part of the buying price. Chattels don't include fitted kitchens or bathrooms but they do cover moveable items, such as:

- ✔ Furniture
- ✔ Heaters and fires that can be disconnected and moved without causing damage
- ✔ Carpets
- ✔ Curtains and blinds
- ✔ Fridges, freezers, cookers, microwaves, and other white goods
- ✔ Light shades and fittings – but not sunken lights
- ✔ Garden plants in pots, tubs, or troughs

Cutting a deal on chattels

Say the seller of the house in the last example refused to budge from her £252,000 selling price.

You can negotiate £249,999 as the purchase price and offer the balance of £2,001 payable in cash on completion to buy the chattels.

The seller still gets her price, but you manage to save the difference between stamp duty at 3 per cent and the price of the chattels – still a nice pot of £5,559 (stamp duty at £7, 560 less £2,001) left in your pocket.

You need to be careful that the price you pay for chattels is a fair and reasonable one. If not, the taxman comes knocking at your door asking for more stamp duty.

Get the seller to make a list of chattels, but instead of itemising an individual price for each item, just put a total at the bottom of the list. Photographing the items to provide evidence of their value is worthwhile, too.

If the taxman objects to the deal, you can produce evidence of the cost of the chattels. HMRC explains how on its website at www. hmrc.gov.uk/so/mainfaqs.htm#6.

Examining exchange

You and another person own two properties jointly, but for whatever reason, you fall out and decide to swap your share in one property for the other's share in your property so you both end up with one property each. Providing no cash or mortgage is involved, no stamp duty is chargeable.

Assessing alternative finance

The little known and little practised alternative finance method can avoid stamp duty completely.

Under the alternative finance method, a bank or other financial institution buys the property and allows you to live there in return for rent that's equal to a conventional mortgage payment. Over time, you pay off the property price and become the owner.

The above method is mostly put in to action by Islamic banks, because religious rules don't permit them to charge interest – although tax rules don't stop any bank or building society taking part in such arrangements.

To meet the criteria:

- ✔ The bank has to buy the property.
- ✔ You rent the property from the bank.
- ✔ You and the bank have an agreement that the bank transfers the property to you at some time in the future.

If the deal meets all three criteria, then the property purchase and later transfer are exempt from stamp duty.

Combining strategies

Don't forget that you can combine any or all these methods to cut your stamp duty – even in a disadvantaged area with lower stamp duty banding rates.

Changing Your Circumstances

You can switch ownership of property under several exemptions that mean no stamp duty is paid because no consideration or price is paid by the person receiving the property – but beware! The taxman has a nasty tax trap waiting to spring on you.

It doesn't matter whether you're getting married, entering a civil partnership, or just moving in with someone. If one of you transfers a share in the new home to the other, stamp duty may be due where the new joint owner takes on some of the mortgage or pays cash for a share of the property. (See 'Income Shifting to reduce Stamp Duty' earlier in this chapter.)

Ending a marriage

No stamp duty is payable when a property is transferred between spouses or civil partners because of a court order or agreement relating to:

- ✔ Separation
- ✔ Divorce
- ✔ Dissolution or annulment of a marriage or civil partnership

Gifting and inheriting property

If someone gifts you a property, or if you inherit a property after someone's death, you pay no stamp duty unless the property is mortgaged. Stamp duty is due because in taking on a share of the mortgage and again you're paying a price – and whenever a price is paid in cash or kind stamp duty is due.

This tax trap is one to watch for if you're transferring property, especially as part of an income-shifting strategy.

Avoiding Chain Reactions

Linked transactions are a series of transactions between the same buyer and seller, or persons connected with them. For example, if a seller advertises a house with gardens for sale and agrees that the husband buys the house and his wife buys the gardens at separate prices, these are linked transactions involving connected people. Stamp duty charged reflects a percentage of the total purchase price – not separate bills for each transaction.

Linked transaction rules aim specifically at people trying to evade stamp duty by artificially creating purchase prices that reduce the tax due.

Even if the husband and wife went to separate solicitors to complete their purchases, the transactions are still linked – how the agreement is made or documented doesn't matter.

Tackling Transfer Fees

Watch out for stamp duty if you plan to transfer property you own to a company you run – even if there's no market value for the land.

Stamp duty is charged if:

✔ The person transferring the property is connected to the company.

✔ The company issues shares to the person transferring the property in return for the gift.

The transfer price is the sum of:

✔ Any cash paid for the property

✔ The value of any mortgage taken on from the previous owner

✔ The value of any shares received in exchange for the gift

If no transfer price exists, stamp duty is charged on the market value of the property.

Ensuring Timely Payment

The stamp duty regime has a similar set of rules for filing returns and paying any monies due to any other tax. If you fall foul of the rules, you incur penalties to pay.

Protecting against penalties

You must pay stamp duty within 30 days of taking over the property. Generally, the solicitor or licensed conveyancer who handles the property purchase for you completes and files the stamp duty returns, and collects the tax by deducting the amount from the completion monies.

If you submit your return, or any stamp duty due, late but within three months of the 30-day limit, you're charged a £100 penalty automatically. In all other cases, the purchaser automatically receives a £200 penalty. The penalty increases if you submit the return after the three months of the 30-day limit allowed. If you pay late, you also receive an interest charge on the stamp duty owed.

Being aware of investigations

HMRC may write and ask for information about your purchase. If you don't supply the requested information, an inspector has powers to require you to provide it.

Investigations often arise when the purchase price is just under a change in the banding rate, or involves the chattels strategy.

If you think that you've supplied all the necessary information and that the tax inspector is prolonging the investigation, you can appeal to an independent commissioner to ask for closure on the grounds that.

   ✔ The inquiries aren't relevant or are unreasonable.

   ✔ The investigation is taking an unreasonably long time.

Chapter 9

Saving Capital Gains Tax

• •

In This Chapter

▶ Clearing up Capital Gains Tax myths

▶ Understanding Capital Gains Tax

▶ Reducing your Capital Gains Tax bill with capital expenses

▶ Hitching up for special reliefs for married couples

▶ Claiming property reliefs to reduce your Capital Gains Tax

• •

*I*f you invest in property in order to let it for rent, this chapter is for you. Property developers – those of you who buy property to improve and sell on – can give this chapter a miss.

Capital Gains Tax (CGT) is paid by landlords on the profits made when disposing of all or part of an investment property – and sometimes by owners selling part of their home, especially if they have extensive gardens and sell off a parcel of land to a developer.

This chapter is an introduction to how to deal with CGT, and tells you all you need to know about it – as well as clearing up a few myths.

Don't panic! CGT is not as bad as you fear.

Knowing Who Pays CGT

Generally, CGT is charged to UK residents and long-term visitors who're ordinarily resident in the UK.

Ordinary residence is a concept that enables the taxman to establish liability for Income Tax and CGT. Ordinary residence means that someone lives in the UK except for temporary or occasional absences.

Residence is a complex subject, but generally you would have to be out of the UK for a whole tax year before you can start to consider yourself non-resident for tax purpose. So, if you left the UK in

October 2009, you would have to stay away until at least 6 April, 2011 to be non-resident.

If you've property in the UK but live overseas, providing you've stayed away from the UK for five years or more except for occasional short visits, you don't pay CGT when you sell property here. Also, landlords who have never visited the UK but own property here do not pay CGT.

CGT is not payable on all property transactions, so in most cases you do not pay CGT when you sell your own home or for the time you've lived in another property that you let out.

Paying CGT On Time

You pull the CGT trigger on a property deal as soon as the contract to buy becomes unconditional – that's when you exchange contracts, not necessarily the completion date, unless they take place on the same day.

CGT is levied on all your taxable property disposals in the UK and overseas. If you pay a property tax when you sell overseas, check to see whether a double taxation treaty reduces CGT in the UK.

Inheritance

Inheriting a property isn't a CGT trigger – the transfer is exempt – but you may have to pay Inheritance Tax (IHT). Have a look at Chapter 11 for more on IHT.

Selling inherited property is a CGT trigger.

Non-cash transactions

If you don't pay in cash but by some other means, the base cost of the house you buy is the market value of the means of payment.

For instance, if you swop your spanking brand new £220,000 Bentley Azure for a house, the acquisition cost of the house for CGT is £220,000.

The base cost is important because base cost is the price you paid for the property and the price all CGT calculations use.

Telling the taxman

If the taxman sends you a tax return, fill in the capital gains supplement to report your gain or loss.

If you don't have a tax return, you must tell your local tax office that you've a gain to report by 5 October following the tax year when the gain or loss arose. For the 2008–09 tax year, that's 5 October 2010.

Your tax return for 2008–09 should include the details, and any CGT is payable by 31 January 2011.

Understanding CGT: What You Do and Don't Pay

The scary bit for most people is they sit down with a calculator and work out their CGT on the difference between what they paid when they bought the property and what they received when they sold it. If you pay this amount, you're paying way too much tax.

Now is when good tax advice is worth real money because if you follow the advice in other chapters in this book about the tax-effective purchase of a property (Chapter 2), keeping a property register (Chapter 5), and income shifting (Chapter 8), you can see where it all comes together.

To understand the relationship between income and capital, think of a fruit tree:

- ✔ The fruit is the return on your investment as the income generated from your asset.
- ✔ The tree is the asset or capital you've invested to produce the return.

In tax terms, the fruit is your rent and the tree is your property.

You pay income tax on the fruit – the rent – and CGT on the proceeds of disposing of your property.

Calculating CGT

This section includes all the technical terms you need to understand to help you calculate your CGT payments. Once you've grasped all the facts and figures, all you need do is to slot the figures into the right places in Table 9–1, *et voilà* – your CGT payments.

Taking on the technical terms

To understand CGT fully, you need to speak the lingo. A number of technical terms exist, which you need to grasp if you're going to understand your CGT liability:

- ✔ **Base cost or acquisition cost:** Property cost on the day of acquisition.

- ✔ **Acquisition**: Buying, inheriting or receiving gifted property.

- ✔ **Disposal:** Sale, gift, or transfer of property or part of a property to another owner.

- ✔ **Disposal value:** Property cost on the day of disposal.

- ✔ **Annual exempt amount:** Your personal CGT allowance, which is like your personal income tax allowance. Everyone has an annual CGT allowance each tax year, but if you don't use it, you lose it – you can't apply the allowance to other tax years.

  For the 2008–09 tax year, your annual exempt amount is £9,200. For 2009–10, it's £9,600.

- ✔ **Capital gain (or chargeable gain):** The amount that property disposal proceeds exceed acquisition costs, plus expenses.

- ✔ **Taxable gain:** The capital gain less reliefs and your annual exempt amount.

- ✔ **Allowable loss:** The amount by which property acquisition costs plus expenses exceed disposal proceeds.

- ✔ **Reliefs:** Amounts that reduce CGT under special circumstances, like the time you may have lived in a property as your home.

- ✔ **Incidental costs:** These arise on buying and selling a property and include legal costs, stamp duty, and estate agents' fees.

Working CGT out step-by-step

That's the jargon out of the way, now here's a step-by-step example of how a simple CGT calculation works.

Carl and Kate bought a letting property for £145,000 in June 2003. Neither of them has lived in the property.

They paid £4,626 in legal costs, stamp duty, and mortgage fees. After buying the property, they added a double-glazed storm porch for £5,000.

In November 2008, they sold the property for £275,000, incurring legal fees and estate agent's costs of £6,536. Carl and Kate never lived in the property.

Table 9–1	A Simple CGT Calculation
Disposal proceeds:	£275,000
Less	
Base cost	(£145,000)
Incidental disposal costs:	(£6,536)
Improvement costs:	(£5,000.00)
Incidental acquisition costs:	(£4,626)
Total costs:	(16,116)
Taxable gain	**£258,884**

As Carl and Kate are joint tenants, each with a 50 per cent stake in the property, they divide the taxable gain by 2, giving them £129,442 each subject to CGT at 18 per cent after each deducts their annual personal exemption, which is £9,200 for the 2008–09 tax year:

£129,442 – £9,200 = £120,242

CGT payable each is £120,242 × 18 per cent = £21,643

The total CGT Carl and Kate pay is £21,643 × 2 = £43,286.

Hitching Up For a Tax Break

Special CGT rules apply to married couples and people in civil partnerships who transfer property to their partners. Spouses and civil partners are individuals whose tax is worked out separately, a key point in tax planning.

The separate-tax rule gives scope to tax-saving strategies that aren't available to unmarried couples and sole traders.

Gaining from income shifting

No gain/no loss transfer is one of the keystones of tax planning. Spouses and civil partners can transfer shares in property between each other without paying CGT.

This underpins the income-shifting strategy explained in Chapter 8.

A no gain/no loss transfer allows:

- ✔ A spouse paying higher-rate tax to shift ownership of a property producing rental profits to a partner who pays basic-rate tax to reduce Income Tax on the profits from 40 per cent to 20 per cent.

- ✔ Sole owners to transfer part ownership of a property to benefit from two CGT annual personal exemptions instead of just the one – allowing a couple to take another £9,200 tax-free from the gain for the 2008–09 tax year.

Judging joint ownership

It's no good just saying that you've transferred property to your spouse – you have to prove it.

If no factual evidence is available to determine each spouse's or civil partner's beneficial interest in an asset, tax inspectors' instructions say they should:

- ✔ Tax the spouse or civil partner entitled to the income or profits from sale of an investment property.

- ✔ Tax each joint owner as a holder of a half interest in the asset.

You need to prove that:

- ✔ You own the property as tenants-in-common rather than joint tenants and have registered the title at the Land Registry in unequal shares. See Chapter 3 for more on the different sorts of tenancy.

- ✔ You've given up control of the proceeds. If you sell a property, make sure that the proceeds go into individual personal accounts and don't stay in a joint account.

- ✔ You've transferred the share before exchange of contracts on sale of the property.

Comprehending connected persons

A *connected person* isn't (necessarily) a Mafia member, nor does he have to have friends in high places. Connected persons include your:

Marriage guidance

You may be married and not know, according to the law – that rules differ depending on where you live.

A husband and wife who've undergone a legally recognised civil or church marriage ceremony – and have the certificate to prove it – are married in English or Scottish law.

Couples referred to as 'common-law' aren't married for CGT purposes, so they can't pass assets between themselves under the no gain/no loss rules. They aren't even 'connected persons' (check out the section 'Comprehending connected persons' for the implications). However, this rule has recently been abolished in Scotland.

A polygamous marriage is valid in the UK if it's valid in the country in which the ceremony occurred and was between people who were residents in that country. If so, the husband is connected with each wife and any transfer between him and any wife he lives with is a transfer under the no gain/no loss rules.

In each case, where the relationship is accepted under tax law, each individual has his or her own annual exempt amount.

If a marriage breaks down, and one spouse owning or having an interest in the property moves out of the matrimonial home, that spouse is treated as resident for CGT unless he elects another property as his main home. This concession only applies when the remaining spouse stays in the former matrimonial home and one spouse disposes of his interest in the property to the other.

✔ Spouse or civil partner

✔ Your brothers and sisters or your spouse's brothers and sisters

✔ Parents, grandparents, or remoter ancestors

✔ Sons, daughters, grandchildren, or remoter descendants

✔ Husbands and wives of any of these people

✔ Companies under your control or control of any of the above

When disposing of property to a connected person, whatever the price you've agreed is irrelevant as the taxman takes the open market value on the transfer date as the base cost for any CGT calculation. The taxman assumes that because you and the buyer are connected, the special discounts may apply and he therefore substitutes the market value for the price paid.

For example, Alison sells her nephew a house for £150,000. She originally bought the house for £65,000, and it's now really worth £200,000, but she wants to help her nephew jump on the housing ladder. Her capital gain before deducting capital costs, reliefs and allowances is not £85,000 but £135,000 (£200,000 – £65,000).

Phew, What a Relief . . .

Time for a breather after the ins-and-outs of how and when you pay CGT. A number of different ways to reduce CGT exist. This section covers them.

Private Residence Relief

You won't have to pay any CGT if you sell your main home – providing its been your main home all the time you've owned the property – because the gain in value is covered by *Private Residence Relief* (also called PRR for short).

PRR is an important relief for property investors, because if you've lived in a property as your main home and also let the property, the time you lived there plus the last 36 months of ownership are exempt from CGT.

Qualifying for PRR

Tax advisers always get asked how long you need to live in a property to qualify it as your main home. To confuse matters, it's a question with no real answer.

Tax law does not state a length of time and case law says it's the quality of occupation – not the time you're there – that makes a difference.

The onus is on you to prove you've lived in a house. You need to be able to show that:

- ✔ You've actually moved into the property, so your personal possessions are there even if the property is sparsely furnished.
- ✔ Your official post, like bank statements and utility bills, go there.
- ✔ You're registered for council tax and on the voters' list.
- ✔ If you're married, your spouse and family live there too, unless you're legally separated.
- ✔ The property is listed as the address at the DVLC for your driving licence and vehicle registration.

Unless you can prove that the property was your main home for a period, you don't qualify for CGT relief on the sale.

You may not qualify for full PRR if you have:

✔ A garden that covers more than 0.5 hectares – about half a football pitch.

✔ A number of outbuildings.

✔ Had an exclusive business use for part of the property – for example, used a room as an office, or an outbuilding as a workshop.

✔ Bought the property to do up and sell as quickly as possible for a profit – CGT rules say that if you buy a property with the intention of making a profit, then that's property development and is exempt from qualifying as a PRR.

The first time you trade-up the property ladder by buying and doing up a house to move on, you can probably get away with it because the taxman can't prove your intent.

The second time, well the taxman will probably let you off again – but the third time you buy and trade a house you live in quick succession proves a trend and if the taxman can show you're a serial developer, you can be taxed on the profits of all your previous steps up the ladder.

Banking ownership

When ownership or part-ownership of a property passes from one spouse to another, the years of ownership and occupation the transferring partner has stacked up passes to the other spouse.

This means that the base cost for CGT starts from when the first owner took on the property, not when the share of ownership was transferred to the next owner.

Understanding the 'one home' rule

Married couples and civil partners can only have one home for the purposes of PRR. If each partner owned a property prior to marriage, the couple has a two-year time limit to elect which one is their main residence from the start of the marriage.

You can't have PRR relief on more than one property at the same time, even if you've two homes – unless Delay on Moving In Relief applies (see the section 'Delaying Moving Home' later in this chapter). You've two years from the date that you moved into the second property to choose which one is your main residence, and tell your tax office. To make the choice, you have to have lived in both properties at same time. The choice stays in effect until you make a further choice.

Making the choice (called an *election*) means that one property receives PRR relief while the other one doesn't.

PRR Restricted relief

Where the owner has only lived in a property for part of the period of ownership, PRR relief is restricted. The formula for calculating the restricted amount is.

Total gain × (Period of occupation/Period of ownership).

Any ownership prior to 1 April 1982 is ignored.

The last 36 months of ownership are always exempt from CGT whether you lived in the property or not.

Many people try to evade CGT by claiming that a property they've let, or refurbished to sell on, was their main home. Such a claim is tax evasion, not tax avoidance, and tax evasion is illegal.

PRR Lettings relief

Lettings relief reduces your CGT when you've lived in the property as your main home and then moved on, letting your old home. Lettings relief also applies when you live in part of the property but let the rest.

In both cases, the letting must be for residential use.

You can quickly work out lettings relief.

- ✔ If your PRR is up to £40,000, then your lettings relief doubles your PRR.

- ✔ If your PRR is more than £40,000, then your lettings relief is the maximum of £40,000.

Going back to our example with Carl and Kate, say they bought their house in June 2002 and lived there until June 2004, then moved out to another house. They then let their old home until they sold it in January 2009, making a chargeable gain of £212,000.

The first two years of residence qualify for PRR and so do the last three years whether they live there or not.

Carl and Kate both qualify for five years of PRR, calculated as:

Period of residence/period of ownership × chargeable gain or

5 years/10 years × £212,000 = £106,000

As Carl and Kate are joint owners, the PRR is halved, giving them £53,000 each.

The remaining £53,000 gain for each of them is subject to lettings relief of the maximum £40,000, leaving them each with a chargeable gain of £13,000.

Next, Carl and Kate each deduct their annual personal exempt amount to give their taxable gain. For the 2008–09 tax year, the annual personal exempt amount is £9,200, leaving £3,800. This is taxed at 18 per cent, giving Carl and Kate £684 of CGT to pay each. Table 9–2 summarises the situation.

Table 9–2 Carl and Kate's Capital Gains Tax Calculation

Gain	£106,000
Less PRR	(£53,000)
Less lettings relief	(£40,000)
Chargeable gain after relief	£13,000
Less annual exempt amount	(9,200)
Taxable gain	£3,800
Tax on £3,800 at 18 per cent	£684

Because married couples are taxed as individuals, these figures apply to each of them, so the total CGT to pay is £1,368.

If deducting lettings relief leaves a chargeable gain after relief as a negative figure, just enter a zero at step D because you cannot create an artificial loss by deducting lettings relief.

Delaying moving home

If you buy land and build a house, or buy a house but delay moving in for up to a year because you're having work done or still disposing of your old home, the period from actual purchase to moving in counts as residence so long as this period is followed by a period of actual residence.

An extension beyond a year may be available if you can put forward good reasons – such as unforeseen circumstances holding up the building work.

Don't confuse the delay relief with the rules over having more than one home – you don't have to tell the tax office which is your main home.

Moving for work

Where an employer asks an employee to relocate for his job, and the employee sells his house to his employer or a relocation company for a guaranteed value, plus a share in any profits from the subsequent sale of the house. Both the employee's initial gain on selling his house, and the profit from the employer's subsequent sale of the house, are exempt from CGT.

For instance, if the initial gain was 100 per cent exempt from CGT because the property was the employee's PRR and is share in profit, likewise if the CGT exempt gain was a lower percentage, the exemption is equal to that figure.

Job-related accommodation

People live in job-related accommodation when:

- ✔ Living there allows the person to do their job properly or better.
- ✔ It's customary for employers to provide accommodation for that particular job.
- ✔ The property is part of security arrangements when a special threat to the employee's security exists.

People who have job-related accommodation – for example, members of the armed forces, diplomats, and pub landlords – can have a second home in which they intend to live in due course. Such a home qualifies for PRR relief from the date of purchase.

Business use

If part of your home is exclusively used for business, then any gain in value is apportioned and CGT is charged on that portion of the gain in the value of your property.

So, if you exclusively set aside a room as an office and that room is 10 per cent of floor space of your property, then 10 per cent of any gain you've made when selling the property is taxed.

Entrepreneur's relief

Entrepreneur's Relief is a reduced CGT banding of 10 per cent applied to the first £1 million of capital gains relating to the disposal of certain business assets – including UK furnished holiday lets (see Chapter 16).

Before you get your hopes up, residential letting property is specifically excluded from the relief.

Chapter 10

Beating the Taxman on Capital Gains Tax

In This Chapter

▶ Beating the taxman with let-to-buy

▶ Proving your Capital Gains Tax (CGT) status to the taxman

▶ Banking capital costs

▶ Losing can make you a winner

▶ Emigrating – the last resort for tax exiles

*I*n putting together strategies to save Capital Gains Tax (CGT), you first have to know what holes HMRC is trying to punch in your case so they can charge more tax. I discuss CGT – what this tax is and who suffers it – in Chapter 9. This chapter covers the business of going head to head with the taxman.

Her Majesty's Revenue and Customs (HMRC) publishes a checklist for tax inspectors to follow on notification of change of ownership of a property to the Land Registry. HMRC is linked by computer to HM Land Registry and the information they hold is linked to your personal file held at your tax office.

The foundation of your strategy to save CGT is to go through the points that prove your case one by one, so that you can claim the maximum tax savings on disposal of your residential letting property.

This chapter only applies to landlords – not property developers.

The Taxman's Battle Plan

You need to remember that the taxman is not your friend. Any approach by letter or phone is an information gathering exercise to look for possible grounds to squeeze more tax from you.

Be careful what you say, and keep all communication in writing so that no one can misinterpret what you've said.

Many landlords have a *let-and-buy* strategy, which the taxman tries to pick apart. Let-and-buy is when you've lived in a property as your main home and move to a new home, but keep the old property – probably to let.

On his initial approach, the taxman tries to clarify the following points:

- ✔ Does a high sale price indicate that the property includes gardens or grounds exceeding 0.5 hectare? If so, tax relief on the property may be reduced. See Chapter 9 for more on the 0.5 hectare limit.

- ✔ If a business or company was registered at the address, is there evidence showing that the property was not used exclusively as a home?

- ✔ Does letting income from a tax return show that the property was not your main home for a period?

- ✔ Do the tax files show that you've two homes and may not have made any main residence election? See Chapter 9 for more on main residence election.

In each case, the taxman takes the opportunity to look for more CGT because full private residence relief (PRR) and lettings relief may not apply. See Chapter 9 for more on the reliefs available on CGT.

Now you know what the taxman is looking for, you can put together your case to break down his arguments and maximise your tax savings.

Earning Cash with Let-To-Buy

Let-to-buy is the CGT strategy that pulls together many of the best tax-saving strategies. You let-to-buy when you move from your own home to another home – but instead of selling your old property, you keep it and let it to tenants. The strategy gets its name from the practice of mortgaging the original home and letting it in order to finance the purchase of another property.

The basic strategy of let-to-buy is simple – you just apply the CGT rules to your advantage and there's nothing the taxman can do. First, you must have lived in the property as your main home and then moved out to live in another property as your new main home.

Beating the taxman with let-to-buy

Alan and his wife Nicole bought a house in June 2002 for £275,000.

In September 2004, the house was worth £325,000. Alan and Nicole wanted to move to another house they owned and let their former home to tenants.

Their former home was let for 36 months, and during that time, the value rose from £325,000 to £425,000. They held their nerve for another six months, and the house value rose another £15,000 to £440,000. Alan and Nicole then sold and banked the profits.

Compare the profits if they had sold when they moved out with those from the let-to-buy strategy:

	Selling when moving out	*Let-to-buy strategy*
Sale price	£325,000	£440,000
Sale costs	(£7,500)	(£9,500)
Purchase price	(£275,000)	(£275,000)
Purchase costs	(£5,300)	(£5,300)
Profit	£37,200	£147,950
CGT	Nil	Nil

Even if the let-to-buy sale timing wasn't quite right and some profits were made outside the CGT exempt period, Alan and Nicole still have their annual exempt amount of £9,200 each for 2008–09 and lettings relief, so their CGT bill doesn't knock a hole in their profits.

As an added bonus, Alan and Nicole now have another established main home and can go on to repeat the let-to-buy exercise and make even more money.

Meanwhile, move tenants into your former home for three years – because the last 36 months of ownership is always exempt from CGT, even if the owners don't live in the property.

If you live in the property for the last 36 months of ownership, then you miss out on the relief because you qualify for PRR and for tax, you can only claim one relief for the same period under these circumstances.

Sitting tight

The theory is that rent from the tenants pays the mortgage and the bills while you sit tight and wait for the property value to increase over the last 36 months that you own the property.

You don't have to let your old property, but it's worth the effort because the rent covers any mortgage and repairs. Letting also allows you to claim letting relief, which would be unavailable if you had left the property empty. Chapter 9 has the low-down on letting relief.

Don't panic at the end of the 36 months. Hold your nerve and wait for property to go up another £20,000 – *then* sell.

Timing is everything

If your timing is right, you make a nice profit on your old home paid for by your tenants and have a CGT bill of absolutely nothing.

Even if your timing is slightly out, you've letting relief to fall back on, so your CGT liability is negligible. See Chapter 9 for more on letting relief.

Proving Your Points

If you're going to take on the taxman and make big profits, and at the same time pay little or no tax, then you have to know the CGT rules and how to apply them to your circumstances. These points apply to all CGT tax strategies, not only let-to-buy.

To prove these points, you need to:

✔ **Identify that the property is a home:** the property must be a residential property and not business premises. Always consider photographic evidence inside and out because once you've left a property, you can't photograph the furnished interior.

✔ **Prove that the property was your main residence:** a number of criteria exist to define the term 'main residence'. Check out the list in Chapter 9.

✔ **Identify the period that enables main home relief and letting relief to be given:** show the dates that you lived at the premises and provide copy tenancy agreements for any time the property was let.

✔ **Draw up a scale plan of the house and grounds:** this plan proves that the property is covered by the 0.5-hectare rule. Again, consider photographs. You can buy a scale ground plan of your home and grounds from the Land Registry – and your solicitor probably did so during the conveyance.

✔ **Keep documents relating to any exchange of ownership of the property:** Keep everything to do with your original purchase, and any subsequent changes.

✔ **Make your intentions clear:** When you purchase the property, note your intent on your property register (see Chapter 5 for how to maintain a property register). This note helps to prove that you're not a trader buying with intent to sell on for a gain.

✔ **Record your marital status:** Keep any documents relating to any marriage, separation, divorce, or dissolution of a civil partnership.

✔ **Record your capital costs:** Keep invoices for any improvements incurred while you've owned the property. Check out Chapter 7 for more on what makes up capital costs.

With this information to hand, you can easily and accurately calculate any CGT liability and fend off any inquiries from the taxman.

Counting on Capital Costs

Capital costs reduce tax – every pound you've spent out and can't reclaim as a business expense is generally allowed as a capital cost, bearing in mind that:

✔ You can only claim an expense once.

✔ You can't set off day-to-day business expenses as capital costs.

From the day you take over a property, you should start recording capital costs so that you build up a bank of expenses ready to claim when you dispose of the property.

Strict limits govern the capital costs you can claim. When buying a property you may claim:

✔ **The purchase price:** the price you paid for the property not including chattels.

✔ **Professional fees:** fees for any surveyor, valuer, auctioneer, accountant, or agent. Accountant's fees can only be allowed that they relate to the valuing or apportioning of the value of the property.

✔ **Legal fees:** the costs of legal advice relating to the transaction, and the costs of transfer or conveyance, including stamp duty.

Other fees, such as those of building societies, solicitors, and valuers and any other costs of arranging a mortgage or other loan in connection with the buying property can be disallowed as capital costs.

When selling a property, your allowable costs include:

✔ **Advertising:** costs of advertising to find a buyer or seller, including estate agent costs.

✔ **Legal costs:** the fees you pay your solicitor for selling or transferring the title.

✔ **Professional costs:** reasonable fees for any valuation or apportionment required in a CGT calculation.

Any expenses incurred after a valuation or apportionment aren't allowed, as they're not incurred for computing the gain.

Other expenses that can't be claimed include the cost of resolving any disagreement on value between the taxpayer and HMRC. You can't claim these expenses whether the disagreement is resolved by negotiation or by litigation. In the latter instance, all costs of appeals (and contributions to such costs) are disallowed.

When improving a property, the only costs you can claim relate to improvements, not repairs – for example, building an extension, garage, or porch. Grant money or insurance payouts for improvements aren't reclaimable as a capital cost and are deducted from the final bill.

Don't forget that repairs and renewals don't qualify as capital costs and need to be separated out in your accounts.

Winning with losses

You can work out losses in the same way as capital gains, but with a bonus. Stack up your losses and carry them forward to cancel out future gains. The less gain you show, the less tax you pay.

Your strategy should be to keep your losses 'banked' and set them off against the first available capital gains you make.

For instance, if you've a £10,000 allowable loss from a previous property transaction, then you can bookmark that money for reducing your next capital gain. Work it out as follows:

1. **Calculate the capital gain (of, say, £30,000) before reliefs and losses.**

2. **Reduce the gain by £10,000, because the gain is larger than your loss and you have to set off the loss pound for pound with the first available gain you make.**

3. **Reduce the remaining capital gain by your annual exempt amount, say £9,200 for 2008–09, leaving £10,800 to be taxed at the CGT rate of 18 per cent.**

If you're married, you can transfer a share to your spouse and deduct their annual exempt amount as well, the additional £9,200 would leave you a joint taxable gain of £1,600 subject to CGT at 18 per cent.

If the loss is larger than the gain, then you set off the same amount as the gain, making the chargeable capital gain nil for that tax year, and bring the balance forward to the next tax year when you make a chargeable gain.

In successive tax years, you and your spouse or partner make the gains and losses shown in Table 10–1:

Table 10–1   Example Gains and Losses

	2007–2008	*2008–2009*	*2009–2010*
Gains	£10,000	£17,500	£28,000
Losses	£22,500	£7,500	-

Now look at your CGT liability for each year in tables 10–2 to 10–4.

Table 10–2   Carry forward for 2007–2008

2007–2008	
Gain	£10,000
Loss	(£22,500)
Losses to carry forward	(£12,500)

Table 10–3	Carry forward for 2008–2009
2008–09	
Gain	£17,500
Current year losses	(£7,500)
Losses brought forward from 2007–2008	(£12,500)
Losses to carry forward	(£2,500)

Again, losses from the current year are set off first. Table 10-4 shows you the calculation for 2009–2010.

Table 10–4	Carry forward for 2008–2009
2009–10	
Gain	£28,000
Losses brought forward	£2,500
Less annual exempt amount × 2	£21,500 (estimated)
Taxable chargeable gain	£4,000
CGT at 18 per cent	£720 in total for both of you

The overall picture is that banked losses cancel out your gains and save you tax.

Current or previous year's losses

If you buy shares and sell them at a loss, you can hold the loss on the back burner to bring into play later. The rules are simple:

- ✔ You have to set off any losses against the first available gain, so you can't pick and choose when to use them.

- ✔ If you make a loss in a deal with a connected person, you can only set off those losses against gains made in further deals with the same person. Sometimes, these are called *clogged losses* because you can only set them off under these strict rules.

- ✔ Losses arising from an artificial transaction to create a tax advantage aren't allowed.

Building a firm base

When property is transferred between spouses or civil partners and the giving partner is still alive, the transaction is a 'no gain/no loss' transaction for CGT, and the receiving partner takes on her spouse's base costs.

For example, Mick buys a house for £225,000 in 2004 and gives it to Barbara in 2007 when the house is worth £290,000. Barbara sells the house in 2008 for £310,000.

Her base cost for CGT is the £225,000 Sean paid, not the £290,000 it was worth when she took over the house.

Chattel Rustling

The term 'chattels' covers items of furniture in a home that can be removed – so chattels does not include fixtures and fittings like kitchen units or the bath. Typical chattels include carpets, curtains, and moveable white goods (fridges, cookers, freezers, and so on).

In Chapter 8 I explained the chattels strategy for reducing any Stamp Duty bill. It can also be useful in reducing CGT, and benefits both buyer and seller.

For example, assume you want to buy a letting property valued at £252,000, just above the threshold £250,000 at which stamp duty changes from 1 per cent to 3 per cent. You negotiate £249,999 as the purchase price and offer the balance of £2,001 payable in cash on completion to buy the chattels.

The seller still gets her price. You manage to save the difference between stamp duty at 3 per cent (£7,560) and the price of the chattels – still a nice pot of £5,560 left in your pocket.

If the seller has a CGT bill on the property, she also saves tax at 18 per cent on the amount you paid for chattels, as the law says that what you pay for chattels cannot be charged to CGT or stamp duty if the value of the chattels is under £6,000.

Home Thoughts from Abroad

When you think of tax exile, you generally think of the super rich, but becoming a tax exile can be a strategy to avoid CGT. Landlords can't just sell up, take the money and run, because doing so still leaves them liable to CGT in the UK. If you really want to retire in the sunshine on your property profits, then there's a well-trodden path to follow.

If you already own property overseas and plan to retire there, then it affects your tax status in both the UK and the country in which you plan to settle.

If you're resident or ordinarily resident in the UK, the law requires that you report all earnings and capital gains worldwide to HMRC, not only those in the UK.

If you move overseas, after a time, you become ordinarily resident in a different country and can avoid CGT in the UK when selling your property, provided that:

- **The move is permanent:** just popping out of the country for a long holiday doesn't count.

   Permanent means at least five years, although you can come back to the UK for short holidays and visits.

- **You keep your property until you've emigrated:** selling before you go accomplishes nothing because you're still UK resident for tax – you have to be patient and sit out the time abroad to become non-resident.

- **Your property is not owned by a UK-based company:** in this case, where you live makes no difference – the company is UK resident for tax so pays tax in the UK regardless of where you live.

- **You investigate local taxes:** local taxes include the taxes you may pay instead of CGT in the country where you reside after leaving the UK.

Delay selling any property until at least 6 April in the year following your departure from the UK. This delay puts clear water between you and your UK residency, so that you don't pay CGT.

If you come back to the UK before the five-year-away period is up, you pay CGT in the tax year you return.

Take the money and run

If you plan to retire overseas, then the following is the CGT strategy for you.

The first step is getting your foot on the investment ladder by raising cash from your own home as seed money for your portfolio. Have a look at how a typical couple invest.

They take an extra £40,000 on their home mortgage and decide to buy an investment property. Their home is valued at £300,000.

They borrow the maximum 85 per cent loan-to-value on a property valued at £200,000 and spend the remaining £10,000 on refurbishing the property to make it ready for tenants.

After a couple of years, due to the refurbishment and a rising market, the letting property rises in value to £250,000. Sean and Michelle increase the mortgage to the maximum 85 per cent again – raising another £42,500. This sum is the difference between their new mortgage of £212,500 and the old one of £170,000.

Sean and Michelle buy another property with an 85 per cent mortgage for £240,000 and let that as well.

Now they own their main home, worth about £375,000, which as their residence, is exempt from CGT, and two letting properties valued together at £490,000.

After another couple of years with a rising housing market, they remortgage again, and raise an additional £100,000 that they spend on a nice villa in Spain with a pool.

By now, the value of their UK letting properties has risen to more than a million. Sean and Michelle move to Spain and put tenants in their home to cover the bills.

After a year, they sell up for £1.3 million, pay off their mortgages and have a gain of £550,000 cash.

Because Sean and Michelle reside in Spain, they pay no CGT on this gain, pay off the remaining mortgage on their villa, and bank the rest. Bear in mind, though, that this example ignores any taxes that may be due in Spain.

Chapter 11

Inheritance Tax: Where There's a Will ...

*T*hey say that two things are inevitable: Death and taxes. And the bad news is they can come as a job lot. *Inheritance Tax* (IHT), the tax paid on what you leave behind when you die, can make further heartache for your grieving relatives.

Ideally, you want to pass on as much of the wealth you've collected in your life – through your property business, as well as through everything else – to your family and loved ones. To pass your wealth on, you want to pay the least amount of IHT possible.

If you find it any consolation, experts consider IHT one of the most readily avoidable taxes. In this chapter, I give you the low-down on how to minimise the impact of IHT through intelligent planning.

Grasping the Basics of IHT

Inheritance Tax, sometimes referred to as *wealth tax*, is the tax paid on your *estate* after your death. Generally, your estate is the total of your *assets* at the time of your death, less what you owe. Your assets include your property, possessions, money, and investments.

Understanding the IHT threshold

If you're a property investor, you probably have assets exceeding the IHT nil-rate banding of £312,000 (for 2008–09). Your assets valued up to £312,000 are often called *the nil-rate band* because the people who inherit them don't pay any IHT on them.

In most tax years, the nil-rate band changes in line with inflation, much like your personal tax code for Income Tax and annual exempt amount for Capital Gains Tax (CGT).

 Any part of your estate you leave above the nil-rate threshold attracts a 40 per cent tax charge. If your estate is likely to exceed the nil-rate threshold, then you should seek professional advice from an experienced estate planner, not just a solicitor.

An estate planner should come up with strategies to ensure that you've enough income to last your lifetime while at the same time reducing your assets to minimise any IHT due on your estate.

In Chapter 4 I talk about STEP, the Society of Trusts and Estate Planners. Take a step towards their website at www.step.org.

If you've given away assets in your lifetime, like property, possessions, cash, or investments, your estate may face an IHT bill.

Reporting IHT to the taxman

The *personal representative*, a person you nominate to handle your affairs after your death, pays out any IHT. You usually nominate your personal representative in your will as the *executor* of your estate.

If you die without a will, a court can nominate your personal representative. In this case the representative is known as the *administrator*. Trustees can also act as personal representatives.

IHT rates

For the 2008–09 tax year, IHT is charged at 40 per cent on the value of your estate above the nil-rate band of £312,000.

So, if your estate is valued at £450,000, your IHT is calculated as £450,000 – £312,000 = £138,000 × 40 per cent = £55,200 tax.

Deadlines for paying IHT

In most cases, IHT must be paid within six months from the end of the month in which death occurs, otherwise interest is charged on the amount owing.

Tax on some assets, including land and buildings, can be deferred and paid in instalments over ten years.

If someone dies within seven years of gifting assets or transferring them into a company or trust, those assets count as part of that person's estate and IHT may be due on them. If IHT is due, liability to pay the bill generally falls on the person, company, or trust receiving the assets.

Assessing exemption from IHT

No one should really pay IHT, unless they've failed to arrange their financial affairs properly. This section explains the scope for possible exemptions from IHT.

Inheritance Tax is not paid on every estate. Exemptions apply to people with estates valued at less than the nil-rate band threshold, and other exemptions exist that allow people to pass on assets in their lifetimes without leaving any IHT liability on their death:

- ✔ If your estate passes to your husband, wife, or civil partner and you both live permanently in the UK, there's no IHT to pay even if your estate is above the £312,000 nil-rate band threshold.

  If your spouse hasn't used up all his or her nil-rate band, you can add the surplus to your own nil-rate band to pass on – see the section 'Stacking Nil-Rate Bands' later in this chapter.

- ✔ Any gifts made more than seven years before your death are tax exempt. If you make a gift but die within seven years, the person you gave the gift to pays IHT on a sliding scale, as shown in Table 11-1.

- ✔ Some gifts, like wedding gifts up to £5,000, gifts to charity, and £3,000 given away each year, are also exempt.

Table 11-1	IHT Sliding Scale on Gifts
Years after Gift Made	*IHT Rate*
1	40%
2	
3	
4	32%
5	24%
6	16%
7	8%

Working out your net worth

Before you can plan for IHT, you have to know exactly what you're worth, and what your estate is likely to be, by totting up the value of your assets and then deducting your liabilities. In short, take what you owe away from what you've got.

What you've got

To work out the value of your assets, carry out the following calculation:

1. Take the market value of the property assets you own.

2. Add the market value of your share of any property assets you jointly own.

3. Add your other financial assets (cash, investments, jewellery, antiques, cars, and so on.

4. Add to these:

   • The value of any assets held in trust that pay you an income.

   • Assets you've given away, but in which you've an interest. For example, if you've given your house to your children and you live there rent free.

   • Assets you've given away within the last seven years that aren't exempt from IHT: have a look at the section 'Taking Care of Your PETS' later in this chapter.

What you owe

Now add up all the money you owe – any outstanding mortgages, credit cards, loans, and so on.

What you're worth

Take what you owe from what you've got – hopefully what you've got is a bigger figure than what you owe – and this calculation leaves you with your net worth.

The value of all the assets, less the deductible debts, is your estate. The threshold above which the value of estates is taxed – at 40 per cent – is £312,000 from April 2008. For the tax year 2009–10 it rises to £325,000, and in 2010–2011 to £350,000.

Valuation hints

You should be able to value many assets quite easily, for example, money in bank accounts, or stocks and shares. It won't always be so easy to value some exactly. If you don't know the exact value of an asset, you can put an estimate in the calculation, but try to work from accurate figures if you can. Use the open market value (OMV) of the asset, which is the realistic selling price, not an insurance valuation or replacement value.

For jewellery or property, use the services of a professional valuer.

Net worth calculators can be downloaded for free from the Internet. Try the Microsoft template site for a selection of free spreadsheets at `office.microsoft.com/en-us/templates/TC010183081033.aspx?pid=CT101444811033`.

Stacking Nil-Rate Bands

Stacking nil-rate bands allows you to save up to a massive £124,800 in IHT, providing you qualify to stack your nil-rate bands. This section explains what you need to do.

Everyone is entitled to a nil-rate band for IHT and assets that pass from one spouse or civil partner to the other are exempt from tax. If your spouse or civil partner leaves you all his assets when he dies, then his nil-rate band is unused and passes to you.

When you die, you can pass on £624,000 of assets (your £312,000 nil-rate band plus your deceased spouse's) before the 40 per cent tax band kicks in, saving tax at 40 per cent on £312,000, which is £124,800.

If your spouse or civil partner has eaten into his nil-rate band, you can still pick up the slack and stack it on to your own nil-rate band.

For example, your spouse dies and leaves £125,000 of assets to someone else and the rest pass to you.

For IHT purposes, your nil-rate band is now your nil-rate band plus your spouse's unused nil-rate band:

£312,000 + (£312,000 – £125,000) = £499,000.

In this case, the tax saved by stacking is:

£312,000 – £125,000 = £187,000 × 40 per cent = £74,800.

This strategy applies when the surviving spouse or civil partner dies after 9 October 2007, regardless of when the first partner died.

When first spouse or civil partner dies, that person's personal representative should contact HMRC and agree in writing the amount of available nil-rate banding for transfer.

Talk to your estate planner about stacking or transferring nil-rate bands – you may have to amend your will to take full advantage of these provisions. See the next section 'Using Your Will Power' for more on wills.

Using Your Will Power

A will is a formal document setting out who you wish to benefit from your property and possessions when you die. Making a will is the cornerstone of estate planning, and if you've a net worth or estate valued at £312,000 or above on your death, the people who you wish to benefit from the wealth you've put together during your life can face hefty tax bills.

In addition to your property, you may well have sentimental possessions you wish to leave for particular friends, family, or loved ones.

If you die without making a will, special rules apply that deal with dividing your possessions – see 'Dying without a will' later in the chapter.

The advantages of making a will include:

✔ You make the decisions over who gets what.

✔ You can arrange your financial affairs to pay the least IHT possible.

✔ If you're in a partnership as an unmarried couple, a will is the only way you can make sensible financial provision for your partner and any children.

✔ If you're divorced, you can make sure that your ex gets what you feel he should have. I leave that decision up to you.

Watching out for will rules

When you've made a will, you can't just alter it. To make the will and any changes valid, you have to follow specific rules. A valid will must be:

✔ In writing

✔ Signed by the *testator* (the person making the will)

✔ Signed by two witnesses who cannot benefit from the will (nor can their spouses) unless other independent witnesses are present.

✔ Made and signed by testator who's legally *competent* (that's the bit everyone knows about being of sound mind)

✔ Intended by the testator to be a will

To change a will you must re-write it from scratch, or add an amendment called a *codicil*, made under the same rules as the original will. To revoke a will you can:

✔ Execute a later will that expressly or by implication revokes former wills

✔ Get married

✔ Divorce or have your marriage annulled

✔ Destroy the will

For more on making and updating a will, check out *Wills, Probate, And Inheritance Tax For Dummies*, by Julian Knight (Wiley).

Dying without a will

Dying without leaving a will is called *dying intestate*. If you die intestate, the rules of the Administration of Estates Act 1925 require that your property and possessions be split. Who gets what depends on the relatives that survive you.

If you're married or have a civil partner, the following applies:

- ✔ If you have children, your spouse or civil partner becomes entitled to at least the first £125,000 of the estate and all of your personal possessions. Children or grandchildren can claim some of the estate if it exceeds £125,000.

- ✔ If you've no children, your spouse or civil partner is entitled to at least the first £200,000 and all the personal possessions.

If someone dies without a will, then someone has to deal with their financial affairs.

This person has to apply to the Government's probate service for a Grant of Representation, which is paperwork entitling them to access money and pay bills.

If you're single, your estate goes to your relatives in a pecking order laid down by law, as follows:

- ✔ If you have children, your estate goes to them.

- ✔ If you've no children, your estate goes to your parents.

- ✔ If you've no surviving parents, your estate goes to any brothers or sisters, and so on.

- ✔ If you don't have any relatives, your estate goes to the Crown.

Estate Planning

Sometimes, a better term for estate planning is lifetime planning, because you should try to make decisions about your possessions and assets before you die rather than leave the burden to someone else.

Despite the basic principles of estate planning being simple, the mechanics are complicated. Will writing, setting up trusts and tax-avoidance strategies need a systematic and experienced approach.

1. First, you must work out your net worth and decide who you want to have what.

2. Next, because you've calculated your financial position, you can decide how to arrange your financial affairs to avoid IHT.

3. Most IHT planning consists of gifting or transferring assets to reduce your net worth before you die, which in turn reduces the IHT due on your death.

4. You must decide on the best assets to give away and the best way to make the gift, (for instance, setting up a trust).

The most common mistake in estate planning is holding onto assets for too long rather than giving them away too early.

Your plans should be flexible to allow for changes in law and your personal circumstances. Build in a review schedule at regular intervals to make sure that your plans aren't overtaken by events.

Saving IHT

Saving IHT comes down to manipulating your assets to reduce the value of your estate, which also reduces the amount of any IHT that's due on your death.

Four main strategies, listed below, apply in accomplishing a reduction in IHT. These strategies exclude stacking your nil-rate bands, discussed earlier in the chapter. You need to discuss the strategies in detail with your estate planner before taking any action that may jeopardise your financial security.

Giving is better than receiving

You can reduce your taxable estate while you're alive by taking advantage of IHT exemptions. Some gifts are always tax-free, such as:

- A £3,000 annual exemption under IHT for gifts. The gift can be to one person or divided among several and does not affect your nil-rate band.

- Giving up to £5,000 to someone getting married, if you're a parent of one of the couple, £2,500 if one of the happy couple is a grandchild, or £1,000 for anyone else.

- Maintaining your family or dependent relatives.

- Cash gifts up to £250 out of your normal income so long as they do not reduce your standard of living, for example, a regular life assurance payment in favour of your children.

This list is not exhaustive – and some gifts can be combined, such as giving your daughter a £5,000 wedding gift, plus £3,000 under your annual exemption.

Taking Care of Your PETS

Potentially exempt transfers, otherwise known as PETS, cover gifts or transfers of possessions or assets made while you're alive, that exceed the exempt amounts listed in the previous section, but which may still be exempt from IHT.

The main provision is that you have to live until the seventh anniversary of the date of the gift for the whole amount to be exempt from IHT.

If you die before the seventh anniversary of the gift, on a decreasing sliding scale of IHT, the recipient must pay IHT on the gift, depending on how long you survived during the seven-year period.

No one wants to think about dying, but don't hang onto your assets until it's too late.

Fathoming frozen assets

Freezing assets means to put any capital growth in your estate on hold. A popular way of doing so is to sell property.

Selling is an extremely good way to freeze the value of your estate. For example, if you own a property worth £150,000 that you let uncommercially to your son, that £150,000 (less any mortgage) is contributing value to your estate and is continuing to grow in value every year.

So sell the property to your son or daughter, assuming they've the means to buy it. The sale gives you cash. Spend the cash or give it back to your child as a gift – see the section 'Giving is better than receiving' earlier in this chapter.

This strategy is win-win. You've reduced the value of your estate by disposing of property and then spent or gifted the proceeds. Your estate reduces by the value of the property, and it follows that any IHT reduces pro rata, and as a bonus your offspring enjoy main residence relief on the property, which means that, under capital gains tax rules, any gain in value is exempt from tax.

Shuffling your portfolio

The strategy of shuffling your portfolio takes property and changes it from an IHT liability to an IHT reducer.

Say you've a few un-mortgaged properties that contribute towards a potential IHT bill. You use the rental income to mortgage the properties, immediately reducing your net worth by the amount borrowed.

Outstanding mortgages are deducted from the value of your assets and reduce the value of your estate.

You then have options to dispose of that cash by *skiing* (short for Spending the Kids' Inheritance) or by:

- ✔ Investing the cash in assets qualifying for IHT Business Property Relief.

- ✔ Investing in the Alternative Investment Market (AIM) or in woodland or farmland you work yourself. This shuffle reduces the seven-year gift rule to two years.

Business owners and the self-employed can receive up to 100% IHT relief on the value of their businesses, including business property and equipment they own, provided they've owned it for two years.

Beware that other tax issues may arise by shuffling your assets – for instance, if you have an asset that attracts Business Property Relief but which also produces an income, that income may increase your income tax.

Again, take advice from an estate-planning practitioner before acting on any IHT strategies.

Putting Your Faith in a Trust

Trusts continue to be a useful option to have in the IHT tax-planning toolbox, but recent rule changes render some of the previous advantages less beneficial.

A *trust* is a legal relationship that allows one individual to manage assets for the benefit of another.

Estate planners like to use jargon. A few of the key terms include:

- ✔ **Settlor:** The person putting assets in to a trust

- ✔ **Trust fund:** The settlor's assets

- ✔ **Trustee:** The individual or company managing the trust fund on behalf of the beneficiaries according to the settlor's instructions

✓ **Beneficiaries:** The people the settlor names in their will as the people to receive the assets in the trust fund

Trusts have two main variations on the trust theme for shielding property from tax, namely:

✓ **Discretionary trusts:** Trusts whose constitutions give the trustees discretion over who benefits from any assets.

✓ **Trusts with an interest of possession:** Where someone holds a right to the income or use of property in the trust.

Using your discretion

For many married couples or civil partners, stacking transferable bands is a simple way out of most IHT problems. Discretionary trusts still offer your family extra benefits in your will over and above those of stacking the nil-rate bands:

✓ If the surviving spouse needs long term care from your local council, up to half the value of your home and savings up to £300,000 are locked in the trust so your local council can't reclaim those costs.

✓ You can save your grandchildren tax because the assets passed on in trust can be free of IHT for up to 80 years.

✓ If your beneficiaries are non-taxpayers, they can receive a tax-free income from cash passed on in trust as they can reclaim income tax on any interest earned.

✓ If your beneficiaries are taxpayers, they can set off their tax allowances against trust income to reduce their income tax bills on interest earned by cash in a trust.

Interesting possession

An interest in possession trust is an estate planning strategy leaving the surviving spouse property on trust for their lifetime. This strategy gives the surviving spouse a right to income for life, but on their death, the trust assets pass to the children.

Chapter 12

Managing Extra Property Tax Rules

*T*axes are like buses: you don't see any for ages, then several arrive at once, usually around the end of the tax year. This chapter is for both landlords and developers – but many of the taxes that need to be borne in mind affect the developers.

VAT is a jungle of red tape and rules that are both hard to read and hard to understand, even with the equally complicated 'guidance'. Nevertheless, nuggets can be found buried in the mire, and these can save property developers a lot of money. I show you how to dig these out.

I also explain in detail how landlords and developers can strike gold with the new capital allowance regime that eases your struggles with wear-and-tear and depreciation.

As if VAT and capital allowances aren't complicated enough, I hack a swathe through the jungle of payroll and National Insurance to find, at last, a profitable use for those teenagers you may have lying around at home.

This chapter also considers state benefits and pensions for property business people and the difference between income and earnings from property.

Surviving VAT

Welcome to the area of property tax that has even the experts waking up screaming in the night.

Officially, *Value Added Tax* (VAT) is a tax on the provision of goods and services. So far, so simple. In reality, VAT is a dense tangle of contradictory, poorly written, and confusing rules that even most of the people employed to operate and enforce the system don't understand. For a start, VAT is charged at several different rates:

- **Standard rate VAT**: Charged at 17.5 per cent on top of the goods and services to which it applies.

- **Reduced Rate VAT**: Sometimes charged at 5 per cent on utility bills, like gas and electricity, and on materials and labour for flat conversions over commercial premises.

- **Zero-rated VAT or VAT exempt:** No VAT is charged.

Luckily, most landlords only lightly brush against the VAT thicket, but for developers VAT is a different story.

Registering for VAT

Registration is compulsory when your business turnover breaks the £67,000 threshold or is likely to do so in any 12-month period. You may register voluntarily if your turnover is less than the threshold.

Why register voluntarily?

If you expect to exceed the threshold in your first year of trading, then registration from the start makes accounting and pricing easier, as you can set up for VAT straight away.

Also, if your business invests in a lot of equipment, plant, or machinery as start-up costs, registering early means that you can reclaim the VAT you spend earlier, relieving cash flow.

Pre-registration expenses

If you register for VAT, you can claim pre-registration VAT for spending on goods that you introduce into the business for the 36 months prior to registration and for services up to six months prior to registration – you can only do so if you've kept the VAT receipts, and the goods or services are business related.

You make your claim by writing a letter called a *voluntary disclosure* to your VAT office, explaining why you're making the claim. Add an itemised list with the date of purchase, brief details, the price paid for goods or services including VAT, the VAT amount and price after VAT is deducted.

Keep a copy of any voluntary disclosure with proof of posting as HMRC is notorious for losing them and you may have to prove that you made the disclosure.

VAT and letting property

Rents from residential properties are always exempt from VAT and as a landlord you can't reclaim any VAT that contractors charge you. The exception is if your business involves providing services to tenants, such as cleaning or gardening. If the money you make from these services before expenses is £67,000 or more a year, you must register for VAT. You still don't charge VAT on the rent, but on the extra services you provide at the standard rate.

VAT on UK furnished holiday lets

A UK holiday-letting business must follow the same rules as any other standard VAT rate business.

If the money you receive from letting your holiday flats or cottages exceeds the £67,000 annual threshold, then you must register for VAT and charge the standard rate tax at 17.5 per cent on your rents to guests together with any incidental services you may provide.

VAT for property developers

If you're a landlord refurbishing property held for rental purposes, you can't register for VAT. If you're a developer refurbishing a residential property with a view to selling it on, the position is more complicated, depending on what sort of development you're carrying out.

New builds

Sales of newly built residential property are zero-rated for VAT. The builder can reclaim all VAT incurred on building costs but charges no VAT to the house buyers.

Conversions

All sorts of different rules cover conversions, depending on the property type, its past and intended use, and all sorts of variables.

A straight barn-to-house conversion, for instance, is zero-rated, the same as a new build. So is most work on listed buildings.

This situation means that a VAT-registered developer can reclaim all the standard rate VAT incurred on building and selling costs, but charges the customer or buyer no VAT.

The reduced VAT rate of 5 per cent also applies when converting two or more semi-detached or terraced properties into a single house – but not if the property was one house in the first place.

Flat conversion allowances

The reduced rate 5 per cent VAT can be applied to other types of conversions – like developing space above business premises into flats or converting a house into flats, or back from flats, into a house.

To qualify, properties must:

- ✔ Pre-date 1980

- ✔ Have no more than five floors

- ✔ Have a business use on the ground floor

- ✔ Have been built with residential accommodation on the upper floors

- ✔ Have been vacant, or only used for storage, on the storeys above the ground floor in the year prior to conversion

Restrictions also apply to the type of flat resulting from the conversion. This type of flat generally includes studio or one-bedroom flats limited to a total of four rooms including the bedroom, bathroom, and kitchen.

 Always take professional advice on VAT, and if you contact HMRC VAT departments, do so in writing, not by phone, so you've got written evidence to help you prove your case if necessary. You can stir up all sorts of administrative and financial problems by getting VAT wrong. You won't find VAT easy to reclaim if you've overpaid, and nigh on impossible to claim retrospectively.

Making Allowances for AIA

Every property business – sole trader, partnership, or company – qualifies for an Annual Investment Allowance (AIA) of up to £50,000 for *qualifying expenditure*.

Qualifying expenditure consists of all capital spending on plant and machinery, except for:

- ✔ Cars
- ✔ Spending that qualifies for 100 per cent relief under other rules, for example, enhanced allowances for energy efficient heating and water equipment for small businesses

Now you know what you *can't* include – what *can* you slot in to claim AIA? The list is pretty extensive:

- ✔ **Building and DIY equipment:** Ladders, power tools, and the like.
- ✔ **Garden equipment:** Lawnmowers, power trimmers, and washers can all be included.
- ✔ **Office equipment:** Including computers and printers.
- ✔ **Furniture and white goods:** When your property is for holiday letting.
- ✔ **Vans:** Classed as plant and machinery.

Don't forget that the usual rules apply – wholly and exclusively for business – they have to be capital costs and any private use must be apportioned.

Wholly and exclusively means that the spending is solely for business or that part of the spending can be shown as entirely for business purposes.

A capital expense in this case is a one-off expense on machinery or equipment.

Few property businesses have capital spending of more than £50,000 a year, so they benefit immediately by reclaiming the whole capital spending outlay in the same tax year.

Pooling new features

Don't forget that under AIA landlords can claim tax for installing new building systems, such as:

> ✔ Electrical systems, including lighting
>
> ✔ Cold water systems
>
> ✔ Heating and ventilation systems

Property investors installing these items can claim AIA from 1 April 2008.

Waking up to wear-and-tear

Landlords letting furnished residential property claim the 10 per cent wear-and-tear allowance instead of AIA. You need to make a choice between the two – you can't claim both at the same time.

In practical terms, AIA allows you to claw back the cost of replacing furnishings, and 10 per cent wear-and-tear gives you an annual deduction whether or not you have made any replacement that tax year.

As most landlords do not replace furnishings every year, they find the 10 per cent wear-and-tear route more profitable.

Paying Attention to PAYE

PAYE stands for Pay As You Earn and is a process that places the burden of calculating, deducting, and paying tax on an employer. If you employ any full- or part-time workers in your property business, then you need to operate a PAYE scheme.

A PAYE scheme is registered with HMRC and requires that you keep records of payments to employees and the tax deducted, and to pay that tax to HMRC at monthly or quarterly intervals.

You also have to obey laws relating to sick pay, holiday pay, and maternity leave.

Don't get confused and think that you have to operate a PAYE scheme if you hire tradesmen or contractors – you don't. See the section on the Construction Industry Scheme, 'CIS for Property Traders', later in this chapter.

At last, a use for teenagers!

Property owners can't claim a wage for the time they spend working on their own property, but they can employ family or friends to help out with the business, and pay them a wage instead.

Making a profit from your kids

Mike and Lynne have two children – Tom, 16, and Becky, 14. Being typical teenagers, they both want the latest – and don't care about anything else, as long as they get the latest.

Poor old Mike is working all hours to keep his family and run a property letting business with Lynne. They own properties in several different locations.

Mike gives Tom £12.00 a week and Becky £10.00 a week pocket money.

That's £22 per week × 52 weeks = £1,144 a year.

To pay the teenagers £1,144, Mike has to earn £1,906 (£1,144 + 40 per cent income tax). The kids ought to be helping Lynne around the house, but like most teenagers, they prefer to play music and video games.

Lynne gives Tom and Becky a shock to their systems by politely suggesting they should work for the family property business each Saturday to earn their pocket money.

Grudgingly they agree, and she pays them the same £22 a week as wages for the work they complete.

Now Mike and Lynne can add them to their payroll scheme and deduct the cost of their pocket money from their rental profits as a business expense. Instead of being a drain on Mike and Lynne's resources, Tom and Becky have been transformed into productive members of society.

Now that Tom and Becky are at work, you can redo the maths:

- ✓ The property business pays them £1,144 a year. The status quo for them remains.

- ✓ Mike and Lynne save £1,144 a year extracted from their bank account, because the business is paying the wages. They win.

- ✓ The business sets off £1,144 per year as wages. The business wins, because the wages are an expense that reduces the taxable profits, and thus the tax the business pays.

- ✓ The tax Mike and Lynne pay on those profits reduces by £1,144 × 40 per cent = £457.60. They win.

A good result all round – except perhaps for Tom and Becky who now have to knuckle down to a little hard work now and then.

If you have teenagers lying about not earning their pocket money, you can now put them to work in your property business and pick up tax relief on the money they earn by passing it through your accounts as a business expense.

Of course, you have to keep a record of the work they do for when the taxman asks, as he is sure to do. Having teenagers clear up after tenants, mow grass, and complete other odd jobs, can turn these loss-making assets to profit.

After all, not only can you save on the cash you give your teenagers as pocket money, but you're having work done that you'd otherwise have to do yourself or, even worse, pay for.

If you don't have your own teenagers, you may be able to employ those draining the resources of other family or friends.

Don't forget the tight rules about employing children – they must be aged 14 or over and may only work between five and eight hours on a Saturday.

You can also include your spouse on the payroll, if your spouse is not a property owner. If your spouse isn't in paid employment, he or she can earn up to £5,435 this tax year without paying tax or National Insurance Contributions. To avoid triggering PAYE, pay your spouse less than £104 per week, and keep records of the time worked, the hourly rate, and so on.

Account for the money through the property business accounts in exactly the same way as detailed in the nearby sidebar, 'Making a profit from your kids'.

Again, by increasing your business costs, you reduce tax. Just make sure that your spouse is paid a reasonable rate for the work carried out in relation your spouse's qualification and experience and that the cash is actually transferred to your spouse's bank account and doesn't accrue in the business.

And yes, your worker can have a mobile phone as an allowable expense too!

Lastly, don't forget to take the following precautions:

- ✔ Give out wage slips.
- ✔ Actually transfer the money from your business account to family members that you pay.
- ✔ Keep a record of the work that family members undertake, and the times and dates, in case the taxman asks you to prove your case.
- ✔ Don't forget to include family members on your year-end P35 payroll return.

Contemplating the Construction Industry Scheme (CIS)

The Construction Industry Scheme (CIS) sets out the rules for how payments to sub-contractors for construction work must be handled by contractors in the construction industry. Many property investors and traders who employ plasterers, plumbers, and other builders, worry about whether they should register under CIS and deduct tax before paying the contractors. Don't worry!

Private homeowners employing tradesmen are exempt from CIS, and investors or developers only need to register if they spend at least £1 million per year on construction work.

Your builder may have to pay CIS to his sub-contractors, but this payment is his tax concern and not yours.

 Added bonuses exist. As employees, family members can qualify for benefits in kind, so let the company take out mobile phone contracts for them, because you obviously need to keep in touch while they're out working. If the phone contract's in the company name, the benefit is tax-free, and the cycle goes on because the company can deduct the cost of the phones from expenses, which reduces the taxable profits.

Getting the Knack of NIC

National Insurance Contributions (NIC) are a tax on earnings like your salary or wages, and because rental income is a return on investment, NICs don't apply. In fact, income from letting is exempt from Class 4 NIC.

NICs *do* apply to developers, however. If you develop property for sale, the property is categorised as a trade and the income treated as earnings, so NIC rules apply.

Developers pay *Class 2* and *Class 4* NIC. Class 2 NIC is paid by self-employed developers towards their state pension and benefits. Class 4 NIC is an additional contribution paid as a tax on profits. You don't decide which category you pay – the law does.

Going second class

Self-employed developers pay at the rate for 2008–09, which is £2.30 a week, unless:

✔ You've reached state retirement age 60 or 65.

✔ You're aged less than 16.

✔ Property profits fall below the small-earnings exception – £4,825 for 2008–09.

✔ You already pay Class 2 NIC due to another form of self-employment.

Register your business with HMRC within three months of the end of the month you begin trading unless one of the exceptions apply. You can register online at www.hmrc.gov.uk.

Profits in a class of their own

Class 4 NIC is paid on your trading profits – the same money you pay income tax on. How much you pay depends on a sliding scale starting at £5,435 and with a maximum of £40,040. If you have a job, in addition to being self-employed as a property trader, you may end up paying more Class 4 NIC than the law requires.

If you're employed and already pay NIC, check with your tax office to make sure that you're not overpaying, and if you are, ask your tax office for a refund.

Stating the Benefits

Sorry to keep banging the drum, but property income counts as a return on investment: it isn't classed as earnings. If you try to claim state benefits and show rental profits as your only income, your claim will fail.

When you don't feel the benefit

In 2004, a landlord tried to claim incapacity benefit but had his application refused because he had no earnings. He then tried to claim rental income as earnings to obtain the benefits.

Although the landlord worked full-time for his rental business and was assisted by two employees, the application was refused on the grounds that he had no earnings, only income as a return on his property investment.

The point about landlords' earnings and income comes up regularly before the tax commissioners, and case law always rules that property rental income is investment-based, not earnings-based. As a result, NICs can't be paid on it.

Holiday lettings and property development

Categorised as trading income, not a return on investment, the profits from holiday lettings and property development are earnings and count as pensionable income, and the NICs you pay contribute to state benefits and pensions.

Protecting your state pension

If you don't believe you've paid enough National Insurance Contributions to gain your full state pension rights, then contact the HMRC NIC Office on 0845 302 1479.

They then write to let you know how much Class 3 NIC you need to pay, if anything, to obtain the full state pension.

Private pensions for full-time landlords

If landlords work full-time for their property business and only have rental income, and no other source of earnings to fund a pension, they can still contribute £2,808 a year into a personal pension plan and receive tax relief at 20 per cent. This tax relief boosts the annual pension contribution to £3,510.

Private pensions for developers

For pension purposes, property profits count as earnings, so developers can contribute into personal pensions, subject to the annual allowance and lifetime allowance rules.

The annual allowance for contributions is £235,000 and the lifetime allowance £1,650,000 for the 2008–09 tax year.

The standard lifetime allowance is the amount of lifetime savings you would need to have put aside to return maximum pension benefits, according to HMRC, and is the maximum you can put in to your pension. The figure is due to increase in future years.

Owning (And Owing) Overseas

Many overseas governments don't allow foreign nationals to own property. Others, such as France and Spain, have complex inheritance rules that make it undesirable for foreigners to own property in person.

As a result, many UK residents own property overseas through a company, depending on where the property is located and the particular laws of that land.

If the sole purpose of that company is to hold property for owner occupation and/or letting, and as long as funding is directly by the property owners, this exempts the owners from Income Tax on the *benefit-in-kind* they receive for any personal use of the company property. A benefit-in-kind is a reward other than salary, given to directors and employees. Benefits-in-kind include cars, loans, and medical cover, which as the taxman treats as income.

This important tax exemption only applies to overseas property, not to property in the UK held by a company.

Individuals buying overseas property through a company need to consider the other tax issues involved, for example, accounting for any rental income.

If you're contemplating purchasing overseas property, take advice both in the UK and the country in which you plan to buy, to ensure that your tax arrangements are watertight.

Chapter 13

Taking Tax-Free Cash from Your Property

In This Chapter

▶ Exploiting the cashback loophole

▶ Reaping rent-a-room benefits

*N*ormally if something sounds too good to be true, it is. But if you know how, you really can take money out of your property and spend it on whatever you want without paying a penny in tax.

If you've always wanted a flashy sports car, or longed to treat your loved ones by whisking them away on an exotic holiday, but think you can never afford it, now is the time to look at a tax effective strategy to release cash tied up in your property.

You can even pay off the mortgage on your own home with the money, and gain tax relief for the new borrowing through your property business. Alternatively, take some of the cash and invest in more property to grow your letting portfolio.

In this chapter, I talk you through two strategies you can follow to raise the money to make some of those seemingly impossible dreams come true.

Taking a Look at Tax-Free Property Cashback

Interest payable on mortgages or loans for your property business is allowed as a business expense when calculating profits if the loans are to:

✔ Buy land, houses, or flats

✔ Fund property repairs

If the borrowed money is not spent on property business activities, all or some of the interest is disallowed as a business expense by applying the *wholly and exclusively* test. See Chapter 7 for more on what 'wholly and exclusively' means. If you took a loan out on an investment property to go on holiday or pay your living expenses, you would not be able to claim the interest.

For landlords, your business is the property you let. It doesn't matter if you own the properties yourself or via a company.

Explaining the cashback loophole

The 'wholly and exclusively test' says that you can set off any business expense against rental income, providing the expense is not a capital cost and was incurred wholly and exclusively for the property business. The taxman says that exceptions to the wholly and exclusively test are the following:

✔ You can withdraw all the funds you invested in your property and spend it how you like without paying any tax.

✔ You can claim any interest payable as a business expense on money borrowed by your property business to repay you.

The above just can't be true – the taxman is letting you have your cake, eat it, and is paying for a slice as well! The good news is, the above *is* true, and a strategy that's easy to execute. The strategy is even laid out in HMRC's own internal guidance dealing with business income.

All you have to do is follow these simple steps and work out how to spend the cash:

1. **Take out a loan on your property.**

2. **If you bought the property for cash, keep all the money and spend it how you like without paying a penny of tax.**

3. **If you bought the property with a mortgage, take the difference between the purchase price and the original mortgage, and again, spend it how you like and don't pay a penny in tax.**

4. **Set off all interest payable arising from the business repaying you as a business expense in your property accounts.**

The business can borrow the cash as an overdraft, loan, or mortgage.

Exploiting the loophole

The tax loophole is created when you introduce a property into your business by buying a letting property, or changing the use of another property that you own to make it a letting property. For example, you may move out of your home to a new home and let the property behind you.

When you buy a property, whatever you pay towards the buying price out of your own pocket is your investment in your property business. If you like, you're lending the money to your property business to help buy the property. Similarly, the equity – or loan-free cash – that you transfer in to your property business is your investment.

In both cases, that's your money and you've already paid tax on it, so it's only right that when the business pays you back, you don't pay tax again on the same cash.

The taxman says that if your business repays your investment, then the interest payable on any loan taken on to repay you is allowed as a business expense.

To ensure that the interest payable is allowed, you need to keep a record of the cash you put in to each property.

Cashback step-by-step

The following example is worked through with balance sheets showing exactly how you can exploit this loophole.

You buy a flat for £125,000 and let it out to tenants. You have a mortgage of £80,000 and invest £45,000 cash in the purchase.

You want money to spend on a new car and a holiday but have cleaned out your savings on buying the flat, so, take out a new loan on the flat up to 85 per cent of the market valuation, which is £106,250, and probably the highest amount you can get from most lenders.

Table 13–1 shows the entries in your balance sheet.

Table 13–1   Opening Property Balance Sheet

Description	Debit	Credit
Property valuation	£125,000	
Mortgage		£80,000
Your investment		£45,000
Totals	£125,000	£125,000

You pocket the £26,250 cash raised after the remortgage to reduce the amount the business owes you, so you revise your balance sheet to reflect the changes.

You can see the changes in Table 13–2. Your investment is reduced by £26,250 and the mortgage is increased by the same amount. If you own the property jointly, the investment is split pro rata to each owner's percentage share of ownership.

Make sure that the cash raised goes into each owner's personal account so HMRC can't claim that the money all went to one owner. Paying it into just one account alters the balance sheet and can mean that the owner owes the business money rather than the other way round.

Table 13–2   Revised Property Balance Sheet

Description	Debit	Credit
Property valuation	£125,000	
Mortgage		£106,250
Your investment		£18,750
Totals	£125,000	£125,000

The interest payable on the £106,250 loan is allowed as an expense as the loan is funding the transfer of your flat to the property business at market valuation at the time the business started, and the business still owes you some of your investment.

If the property value has increased, and you draw more cash than you invested when you bought the property, you can only set off the interest payable on the part of the loan which is equivalent to your initial cash input. The business still owes you £18,750, but you can't withdraw that cash until the property value increases enough to remortgage again to take the money out.

You can take your tax-free cashback at any time you own a property providing the business owes you money that you've invested. This situation applies to any property business.

Now, it's a couple of years later and the value of your property has risen to £160,000. You remortgage again to take the remaining investment out of your property.

Over the years, you've withdrawn your initial investment of £45,000 from the business and not paid a penny in tax. Meanwhile, the letting business is paying the interest on the money. Not a bad result.

The new balance sheet looks like Table 13–3:

Table 13–3	Property Balance Sheet	
Description	*Debit*	*Credit*
Property valuation	£160,000	
Loan free cash in the property		£35,000
Mortgage		£125,000
Your investment		£0
Totals	£160,000	£160,000

Back to the beginning

From the balance sheet in Table 13–3, you can see there's still £35,000 equity in the property – that's the money built up by the business in the investment.

The typical scenario for a buy-to-let investor is to keep borrowing to the maximum and reinvesting the cash in more property to expand the portfolio.

If the last scenario was borrowing up to the maximum instead of just withdrawing your capital, you could have taken 85 per cent of the property value, or £29,750.

Why £29,750? Because in the Table 13–3 calculation not all the available mortgage funds were taken from the business. Table 13–4 shows how the total cash is calculated.

Table 13–4   Calculating the cash from the business

Property valuation	£160,000
Available mortgage at 85 per cent property value	£136,000
Less mortgage taken on	£125,000
Balance	£11,000
Plus your remaining investment	£18,750
Total cash from business	£29,750

You then reinvest that cash in another property – and that £29,750 becomes an investment you can draw in the same way as in the examples earlier in this section. Again, the letting business pays the interest on the finance.

This time, the balance sheet looks like Table 13–5.

Table 13–5   New Property Balance Sheet

Description	Debit	Credit
Property valuation	£198,333	
Your investment:		£29,750
Mortgage		£168,583
Totals	£198,333	£198,333

Charging interest on your loan

The taxman says that a business proprietor can charge interest on any loan made to their business. Your initial investment is a loan and you may charge interest at reasonable or commercial rates to your letting business.

The letting business can set the loan interest off as a business expense, but you have to declare the income on your tax return.

In practice, unless the business owes you a substantial amount, accounting for the interest and declaring the income on your tax return is just not worth the hassle.

Reaping Rent-a-Room Rewards

A lodger is someone who pays to live in your home, sometimes with meals provided, and who often shares the family rooms – like the bathroom, sitting room, and kitchen. The lodger can occupy a single room or an entire floor of your home.

If you've a spare room and reckon you can share your home with a lodger, you can earn up to £4,250 in a tax year without paying tax from the rent-a-room scheme.

If you take in a lodger jointly with your wife or partner, the tax-free amount is reduced to £2,125 each.

The scheme does not apply if:

- ✔ Your home is converted into separate flats that you rent out.
- ✔ You let unfurnished rooms in your home.
- ✔ Your home is overseas.
- ✔ The space you let is used as an office or for storage.

Knowing who can benefit

You can take advantage of rent-a-room if you're a homeowner or renting. If you're renting, check whether your lease allows you to take in a lodger.

If you're a mortgage payer, it's best to check whether taking in a lodger is within your mortgage lender's and insurer's terms and conditions.

For the purposes of rent-a-room calculations, *residence* means:

- ✔ A building or part of a building you live in – like a house or flat where you let a room
- ✔ A fixed caravan
- ✔ A houseboat

Generally, a caravan or houseboat is only classed as a residence if connected to mains electricity and water.

Keeping your options open

If your rent-a-room income is more than £4,250 per year, you must pay tax on any surplus amount by one of two routes:

> ✔ **Paying Income Tax on your rental profits.** This way you treat your rent-a-room income the same as any other landlord by setting off business expenses and claiming the 10 per cent wear-and-tear allowance. (See Chapter 7 for more on this allowance.)
>
> ✔ **Paying Income Tax on any rental income over £4,250 only:** You can do this as long as you don't set off any expenses.

If your rent is a lot more than £4,250, the first option is probably better for you. If the rent is only just above £4,250, the second option is a lot less hassle.

The £4,250 allowance includes services provided, so if you're charging the lodger for meals or cleaning on top of rent, you must also include these charges.

Opting in to rent-a-room

If you don't have a tax return to fill in and the rent you charge is below the tax-free threshold for rent-a-room, the tax exemption is automatic so you don't need to do anything.

If you wish to opt in and your rental income is above the tax-free threshold, you must tell your tax office – you can tell them by completing a tax return and claiming the allowance.

Opting out of rent-a-room

To opt out, simply complete a tax return within the usual deadlines and declare the relevant lettings income and expenses on the property pages.

Deciding on division

As long as the property division is temporary, rent-a-room can cover letting a self-contained flat or granny annex in your own home.

Whether such a division is temporary is a question of fact. The taxman uses a checklist for deciding whether partitioned property is permanently or temporarily divided:

✔ Would structural alterations be necessary to undo the division?

✔ How long has the residence been divided?

✔ How long is the division intended to continue?

✔ Can possession of the flat be obtained separately from the property as a whole?

✔ Is the flat separately supplied and metered for mains services?

✔ Does the flat have its own unique postal address?

✔ Does the residence have its own separate entry?

✔ Would a mortgage lender be prepared to lend on the security of the separate flat?

The list is not exhaustive – other factors may be taken into account.

More than one home

Whether a property is your only or main home at any time in the tax year is a question of fact – you live somewhere or you don't and you can have only one main home at any one time. HMRC's internal guidance tells tax inspectors to look critically at any claim for rent-a-room for second homes holiday homes.

The rent-a-room home doesn't have to be the property chosen as the main residence for Capital Gains Tax (CGT). See Chapter 9 for more on private residence relief.

If you rent a room in a furnished holiday let for more than a total of 31 days in one tax year, to the same person, you break the holiday home qualifying rules and automatically lose any tax benefits you may have accrued.

You can move home in the tax year, take in a lodger each time, and still claim rent-a-room relief as long as each property has been your main home at some time in the tax year.

Moving and leaving a lodger

If you move from a property where you had a lodger under the rent-a-room scheme to a new home, leaving the lodger behind in your old home, you can still save tax providing you retain owner-ship of the former property.

Rent can continue to qualify for rent-a-room tax relief until the end of the tax year in which you moved.

If, after the property owner moves, the lodger is allowed the use of the whole house – whether or not extra payment is involved, tax inspectors accept that:

- ✔ The existing rent-a-room scheme continues.
- ✔ The rent-a-room period continues until the end of the tax year.

Moving and taking in a lodger

If you've left a lodger behind in your old home and take on another in your new home, you're entitled to claim rent-a-room relief for both, providing that you satisfy the scheme conditions.

To work out your rent-a-room income, add the rent you receive from both lodgers together. Providing the total does not exceed the £4,250 limit, then no tax is due.

You can't have it both ways – if the combined rent from both lodgers is more than the rent-a-room exempt amount, then you have to submit a tax return.

Rent-a-room: losses

You can only make a profit under the rent-a-room scheme.

If you're making a loss renting to a lodger, contact your tax office and tell them you want to be taxed under Option B (See 'Keeping your options open' earlier in this chapter).

You may make a loss from redecorating or modernising your home, for instance.

Rental losses from letting other property in previous years aren't wasted – you can set them off against rent-a-room profits:

- ✔ If all the money you receive from letting in your own home in the current tax year doesn't exceed the rent-a-room exemption, you don't need to pay tax.
- ✔ The full losses from previous years can be brought forward and set against any other rental profits of the current year.
- ✔ If you've no other rental business profits in the current year, the losses can be carried forward and set against the first rental business profits that arise in later years.

✔ The losses can't be reduced, because rent-a-room exempts or reduces the tax bill for the year.

✔ If gross receipts from letting in their own home exceed the rent-a-room exemption, earlier losses can be set against net rental profits.

For instance, you may make more than £5,750 from letting to a lodger but you've another letting property that racked up a £1,500 loss.

The rent-a-room excess is £5,750 – £4,250 = £1,500 and is cancelled out by the other rental losses, so you pay no tax on your rental income from the tax year.

Part IV
Professional Property Investing

'The only thing worrying me about building
properties in this disadvantaged
area is global warming.'

In this part . . .

*H*ere I take you through the essentials of what to do when your property business becomes more complex. I cover the ins and outs of property development, running a holiday letting business, and the advantages to be gained from investing in property funds.

Throughout, I help you to keep a weather eye open for the taxes you can expect to encounter, and how to manage your responses to them.

Chapter 14

Developing Your Property Skills

* *

* *

*T*his chapter deals with the detail of property development – buying property with a view to selling it on at a profit. It's easy to get confused over the differences between investing (buy-to-let), and development (buy-to-sell). Chapter 2 explains how to establish whether a specific property transaction is an investment or a development.

You have to decide for each property whether you're going to invest or develop, so that you make sure that the right tax rules can be applied to each property in your portfolio. If you've decided to develop, this chapter gets you on the road to understanding your tax obligations, and how to minimise them.

Delving into Development Basics

Forget the term *property refurbishment* – if anything about property tax can confuse you, that term can. You can refurbish any property, but refurbishing doesn't make it an investment or a development. Property refurbishment is simply the preparation of a property prior to letting or selling.

Many property investors refurbish a property before letting to tenants. Equally, many property developers refurbish a property before they sell.

Refurbishment can be as simple as painting and decorating, or as complicated as knocking down an existing structure and building a new house on the plot. Whatever the activity, it's not a tax trigger, but the tax treatment of refurbishment costs differs according to whether you're an investor or a developer. Your intention regarding the use of the property when you acquire it is what counts.

If you intend to hold onto the property long term for capital growth, and generate rent from tenants, the property is called an investment, or a buy-to-let. If you sell the property quickly because someone makes you an offer you can't refuse, or it turns out to be a bad investment, it nevertheless remains a buy-to-let for tax purposes. You pay Income Tax on the rental profits and Capital Gains Tax (CGT) on any gain in the property's value while you owned it.

Even if you decide to let a development property because of a dip in property prices, the property is still a development because your initial intention was to buy and sell quickly at a profit.

If you intend to buy a property to sell on as quickly as possible for a profit, that counts as a buy-to-sell and you're a property developer.

Individual developers pay Income Tax on their profits. Traders who trade through a company pay Corporation Tax.

Taking Stock of Buy-to-Sell

Tax rules say that you cannot decide what a business asset is until you understand the nature of the business. If you're buying and selling property to make a profit, you run a *development* business.

Land or buildings for development constitute *stock* – assets intended for sale. At another time, the same buildings could count as *fixed assets* that generate income for a buy-to-let investor. A property person can run both sorts of business at the same time, so it's important to separate an investment (buy-to-let) business from a development (buy-to sell) business to ensure that each business is run in the most tax-effective way.

Generally, it's tax advantageous for a developer to run that side of the property business through a limited company, and a buy-to-let business as an individual.

Understanding stock

The vital point of stock is that the intention must be to sell the asset to make the profit. For example, the National Trust owns property that's not stock, because the nature of their business is to exhibit the properties – not to sell them. National Trust property is therefore categorised as fixed assets, which generate income.

On the other hand, a builder may put up houses on a site. The first house is a show house that sells after the other homes on the site have all been sold.

The intention is to make a profit from selling the houses and the fact that the builder uses the show house as a display home for marketing purposes does not mean that the show house is not trading stock.

Whipping up stock expenses

In a development business, you need to show the value of a property, which you hold as stock on the balance sheet from the purchase date until you sell it. Similarly, you hold any costs relating to that property in the stock category as *work-in-progress* (WIP).

A balance sheet is a list of the total of everything owned and owed by a business – much like a personal statement of net worth you may draw up for yourself when considering a will. (See Chapter 11 for the inside track on wills.)

The balance sheet differs from the trading, profit and loss statement, which shows the property income and expenses you've had in the accounting period plus your general business expenses, like travel, telephone and postage.

The total stock value on the balance sheet is the value of any buy-to-sell property plus WIP.

When you sell the property, you transfer these figures to the trading, profit and loss account. Fairness is the reason behind this transfer, because if you buy a property in one year, sell in another, and set off the development expenses as you go along, you or the taxman may gain a tax advantage – you may save tax or he may gain tax – because tax rates and rules may change during the period that you own the property.

Valuing your property stock

Tax rules that lay down the acceptable methods of stock valuation are *cost* and *net realisable value*, and the value you use is the lower of the two. The following sections spell out how the two methods work.

Cost valuation

Cost consists of the total expense involved in bringing a property to its current condition. If you find the cost impossible to calculate, then aim for the closest figures that can practically be worked out and keep a record of the calculations in case the taxman asks how you arrived at your valuation.

To work out cost:

1. Take the purchase price and add any expense incidental to its acquisition, for example legal fees, mortgage costs, and stamp duty.

2. Add the price of any materials used in bringing the property to its current condition.

3. If costs have been incurred in your business that indirectly relate to a development property, these can be apportioned and added as well.

Net realisable value

Net realisable value is the expected sale price of the property at open-market value, less any selling costs.

Alan runs a development business with an accounting period ending on 5 April. In November, he buys a development property for £170,000 and spends £3,250 on legal fees and stamp duty.

Before 5 April, he spends another £15,000 on building materials and labour for a new kitchen, bathroom, and general refurbishment costs. The property is not sold by 5 April, so he has to account for the money he has spent on his accounts. He hopes to sell the property for £210,000.

He calculates the cost:

Cost = (Purchase price + Purchase costs + Materials and labour)

(£170,000 + £3,250 + £15,000) = £188,250

Then he compares it with the net realisable value, which is £210,000.

So the stock price entered on the balance sheet is the lower number, £188,250.

The balance sheet shows:

> Property stock = £170,000
>
> Work-in-progress = £18,250 (Purchase costs + Materials and labour to 5 April)

Net realisable value may be less than the cost valuation because of deterioration, or market changes.

Valuing overseas property

If the taxman requests a valuation of any overseas development property you own, you need to provide one that's drawn up by a professionally qualified surveyor, with a translation if necessary.

The valuation should include:

- ✔ The purchase price and date
- ✔ The number of rooms and their uses
- ✔ The floor area
- ✔ Details of any extras – like swimming pools or tennis courts
- ✔ Photographs of the property
- ✔ A plan and details of any additional land, including how that land is used
- ✔ A description of the neighbourhood

Property not acquired as stock

Sometimes a property developer may acquire property other than as part of a buy-to-sell business. *Acquire* in terms of property can mean to inherit, to receive as a gift, or to buy as a buy-to-let investment. Generally, the profits from selling such a property aren't treated as trading profits unless:

- ✔ The property is developed with a view to making a larger profit on the sale.
- ✔ The property is transferred into a new or existing buy-to-sell business.

Tax law says that a property cannot be a buy-to-let asset and development stock at the same time: switching from one to the other may trigger tax because transferring a development property to your investment business is the same as selling the property to someone else.

Living in your buy-to-sell property

If you buy a plot of land, build a house, and move in, the project is not a development and the land is not stock – so it follows that you cannot claim the construction costs against tax in the same way as you can't claim the costs of buying your home.

However, if you develop a house and then move in, the transaction is treated as a sale to you at market value for Income Tax purposes.

Accounting for Development Income

Keeping development accounts is different from keeping buy-to-let accounts. Development is a trade, but buy-to-let is an investment. Depending on the size of your development business, you complete the self-employment section of your tax return or produce company accounts. (See Chapter 20 for more on company accounts.)

Landlords fill in the land and property section of their tax returns, and a few who run companies owning their property produce company accounts.

Developers and landlords fill in different sections of their tax returns because different rules apply to their income and how the taxman can tax it.

If you carry out your development or investment business through a company, the company has its own tax return and you include any money the company has paid you as dividends or salary – depending how you've drawn the money from your company – in your tax return.

Calculating your development income

Property development income consists of the proceeds you receive from selling a property. To arrive at your taxable profits, you carry out the following steps:

1. **Deduct the costs of the sale from the proceeds of the sale.** This calculation leaves the gross profit.

2. **Add up and deduct your general business expenses to leave the net profit or loss.** The net figure is the figure that's taxable.

Check out the sidebar 'Accounting for your taxable profits' for a walk-through of working out your tax obligation.

Accounting for your taxable profits

Mark buys a property for £225,000 as a buy-to-sell and spends £50,000 refurbishing the property and £6,750 on the costs of buying. He has also paid £2,500 in loan interest on finance to buy the property while refurbishing.

Mark's accounting year-end is 5 April and the house is not sold until 30 April for £375,000, incurring £6,000 legal fees and estate agent costs.

Mark's balance sheet entries for the property for the year-end 5 April looks as follows:

Stock:	£225,000
Work-in-progress:	£59,250
Total costs:	£284,250

The following year, Mark transfers the stock costs plus the selling costs to his trading account:

Proceeds from property sales:	**£375,000**	
Less costs of sales	£	
Purchase price of property	225,000	
Refurbishment costs	50,000	
Buying and selling costs	12,750	
Mortgage interest	2,500	
Total costs of sale	(290,250)	
Gross profit:	**£84,750**	(22.76%)*
Less general business expenses	£	
Telephone	250	
Postage	35	
Bank charges	125	
Motor costs	630	
Total expenses	(1,040)	
Net profit	**£83,710**	

*Gross profit is often expressed as a percentage of sales.

Dealing with rent

Rent received from a property held as development stock is excluded from development income. Separate the rent from sales and treat the rent as buy-to-let rental income.

Say you acquire a block of flats for redevelopment, with sitting tenants. You may intend to buy the tenants out so that the property can be sold as a single block, but until you do you need to keep the income and expenses from the let flats separate from those of the empty flats.

You deal with the let flats as buy-to-lets and the costs of any refurbishment of the empty flats as work-in-progress on the trading stock figure for the block of flats.

Buy-to-Sell Business Expenses

Developers can claim expenses relating to the development and dealing with their property stock: they can also claim more wide-ranging general business administration expenses than buy-to-let investors.

The downside is that the purchase and refurbishment costs for a property cannot be reclaimed until the year when the property is sold – so developers do not get tax relief on their spending until the end of their project rather than as it goes along, like investors.

It's not all bad though because, as well as property costs, developers, as traders, can claim far more business expenses than buy-to-let investors can.

The same rules to claiming expenses apply as for buy-to-let investors. The 'wholly and exclusively' test means that the expenditure must be for business purposes, unless the expense can be split into personal and business parts and apportioned in the accounts.

See Chapter 7 for a guide to the expenses that buy-to-sell developers can claim, and for more detail on the 'wholly and exclusively' rule, and Chapter 5 for more on apportionment. In addition, the expenses in the following sections can also be to set off against Income Tax.

Abortive project expenses

Developers can set off project expenses like legal fees and valuations for property purchases that don't complete against their profits. Include these abortive expenses as general business expenses in development accounts.

Capital expenses

Developers do not pay CGT, so do not incur capital costs like investors do. So any improvements, like extensions, go into WIP and then cost-of-sales, for setting off against Income Tax.

Legal, planning, and surveys

Developers can set off legal and professional fees incurred in buying, developing, and selling a property – including finance charges. Account for fees as WIP in valuing your stock, and deduct them as cost-of-sales when the property is sold.

Training

Developers who are plumbers, carpenters, and general builders can set off training and continuing professional development costs that add to their existing skills.

Office premises and yards

The costs of renting or owning office and storage premises for your development business can be set off as business expenses. So can the wages you pay permanent or part-time office staff and tradesmen.

Tools and machinery

Tools of the trade can be put through the accounts, with a different entry in your accounts, depending on whether you buy the tools, or hire them just for a short time:

- **Equipment identified as expenses:** generally small items, such as tools, ladders, and power tools, costing less than £100.

- **Equipment hired:** one-off items that you only require occasionally and which you hire, for example, pneumatic drills and cement mixers.

- **Plant and machinery:** business assets – generally items costing more than £100 and including vans, tools, computers, and office equipment.

Health and safety

The cost of genuine protective clothing worn as a matter of neces-
sity can be set off against income tax through the accounts. Items
covered include hard hats, overalls, protective gloves, and boots.
Ordinary clothing worn underneath protective clothing is excluded,
so caps, jeans, T-shirts, and so on, aren't allowed.

The tax inspector may allow waterproof jackets and the like if you
carry out a lot of outside work in poor weather.

Development finance interest

Funding development of a buy-to-sell property can cause problems
– for instance, where interest is rolled up into a bridging loan, you
can defer setting off the interest until the money is actually paid.

Most tax inspectors expect to see finance interest go into WIP in
the same way as any other cost relating to the buy-to-sell property.
If the finance relates to more than one property, and you sell off
the properties in different tax years, the interest and any other
related costs need to be apportioned.

Capital allowances

The first rule to remember is that capital allowances cannot be
claimed on land or property that's held as stock – tax rules say
they can only be claimed against assets like plant and machinery –
the equipment you need to carry out your business.

For more information about the basics of capital allowances, see
Chapter 12.

A loss incurred by a development business is dealt with in the same
way as holiday-let losses. If you make a trading loss on your buy-to-
sell business, you can choose from three options in the following
sections how best to save Income Tax that you may be paying on
other profits. These are carry back, sideways shuffling, and carry
forward, and I talk about all three in more detail in Chapter 16.

Owning Trading Property

Your trading status can affect the tax you pay on your development
business. For most developers, three means exist by which you
can own property as a business:

✔ As a sole trader

✔ As part of a business partnership

✔ As a limited company

If you're a sole trader, you need to protect your assets. If you own your own home and have significant assets besides your buy-to-sell property, you may lose them if someone sues for poor workmanship.

Avoiding risk by protecting your assets

Sole traders and partnerships are pretty much in the same position as developers, except that in a partnership each partner has *joint and several* liability for business debts.

Both pay income tax on all trading profits, and pay at the higher rate of 40 per cent if those profits exceed £34,600 for the 2008–09 tax year.

The biggest risk for sole traders or partners is if the development business goes under. If that happens, anyone you owe money can sue you, and you may have to sell your assets – including your home – to settle the debt.

This risk is especially important for business partners where one has substantial assets and the other does not – joint and several liability means anyone owed money by the partnership can go after the one with the most assets.

Limited companies

Generally, the best option for property developers is to have a company. It doesn't make any difference if you're a sole share-holder and director or one of several.

With a company, your liability is limited to the money you've invested in shares in the company. For a small developer, this investment is generally no more than a £1,000 and means that your home is not on the line if you have business problems.

Importantly, with limited liability, joint and several liability does not exist, so as a shareholder, you do not have the same risks of losing your assets as a sole trader or partner.

The future of sheltering your income in a company is not quite so clear, as the current government policy is to level the playing field between personal and corporate taxation.

As an sole trading developer you pay Income Tax, but as a company, you pay Income Tax on the money the company pays you and the company pays Corporation Tax on profits.

The complete low-down on forming and running a property company features in Chapters 18 and 19.

Income shifting

If income-shifting rules are made law from 6 April 2009, as they're expected to be, development business partnerships and companies will no longer be able to manipulate Income Tax by shifting income from a higher-rate taxpayer to a basic-rate taxpayer.

If you're currently a buy-to-sell trader in partnership or trading with a company, review your tax options immediately.

Saving Tax with Buy-to-Sell

Two schemes to encourage property developers to bring disused property back into use offer tax breaks that are well worth looking at. They involve converting flats and renovating business premises.

Flat conversions

Developers can reclaim all building costs on flat conversions as a special tax allowance immediately, rather than sitting them in a work-in-progress account to await the sale of the property.

As with all Government schemes, plenty of red tape exists to cut through in order to actually reach the pot of gold at the end of the rainbow. The conditions include the following:

- ✔ The flat must be in a property built before 1980.
- ✔ The property must have a ground-floor business use.
- ✔ The property must be on no more than five floors.
- ✔ The upper floors must have been built for residential use.
- ✔ In the year prior to conversion, the floors that are developed must have been unoccupied or used for storage.
- ✔ The converted flat should have no more than four rooms.
- ✔ The rental value of the flat must be within a range set down by legislation.

This list of conditions isn't comprehensive by any means, and anyone considering a claim under the flat conversion scheme needs to have serious discussions with the local planning department before spending any cash on a development.

 The flat conversion scheme is not well-written legislation and leaves a lot open to uncertainty and interpretation. Make sure that you can claim the allowance before proceeding with the development.

The developer retains the whole flat conversion allowance, providing that she keeps the flats for seven years. If she sells or otherwise disposes of them before the seven-year limit, some or all the allowance is clawed back, depending on how soon within the seven years the disposal occurs.

Renovating business premises

The Business Premises Renovation Allowance (BPRA) is a new allowance aimed at underwriting the costs of bringing disused commercial premises back into business use in disadvantaged areas.

The advantage of the allowance is for developers who also run a buy-to-let business, as development costs can be offset against rental income rather than being carried as capital costs until the building is sold.

Qualifying buildings must be:

✔ In a disadvantaged area: see the list at www.hmrc.gov.uk/so/dar/dar-qualifying.htm

✔ Business premises out of use for at least a year

After redevelopment, the property must have a business use. The scheme has a limited shelf life, so expenditure must be incurred before 11 April 2012 to qualify.

As with the flat conversion scheme, a list of extensive qualifying conditions for the property before and after development stack up against anyone wishing to try and claim the allowance – the same warning applies: speak to your planners before committing yourself to any spending.

Sussing Out Serial Development

Serial developers are homeowners who climb the property ladder by buying, moving in, renovating, and selling houses at a profit and then move on to something bigger and better.

Hoping to exploit the CGT main residence or principle private residence relief (PRR), the typical scenario involves a serial developer buying a house that needs substantial refurbishment, completing the work, and then selling straight away at a profit.

No tax is paid as the developer lives in the house while refurbishing.

The developer then moves on to house two, then three, and so on; making a profit each time.

Unfortunately, this serial development is not allowed as CGT rules specifically state that if a property is bought with the intent of making a profit, the owner cannot claim any CGT reliefs, because the sale is a trade. As a result PRR doesn't apply.

Instead, development tax rules apply and the developer should pay Income Tax on the profit. You may also find developing and then living in the house triggers tax as you're transferring property from business stock to yourself – which is a sale at open market value.

In the real world, property people can buy, refurbish and move once or twice without attracting too much attention from the tax man.

The third time is the one to watch, because you've established a trend in your business activities and the taxman can come back and demand tax on your property profits from all three moves – not just the last deal.

Technically, not paying the right tax on serial developing activity is tax evasion, not tax avoidance. And tax evasion is illegal. Be warned.

Chapter 15

Avoiding Development Tax Traps

. . . .

. . . .

Sometimes developing property is like putting together a jigsaw without a picture. Developers sometimes have to wheel and deal with land and property they don't really want in order to end up with the bits they do.

This wheeling and dealing can trigger tax problems because property can't be for development and an investment at the same time. I explain why not in this chapter.

As with all puzzles, putting the pieces of a development together in the right order is more effective than having a less structured approach. This chapter looks at tax-effective development strategy and how to avoid tax traps hidden along the way.

Structuring Projects

Setting out to structure your property project is the point at which you need to go back to basics. Property can be:

✔ Held as an investment to generate income, in which case it is *buy-to-let*. Buy-to-let incurs Income Tax on rental profits and Capital Gains Tax (CGT) on the sale or disposal of the property.

> ✔ Acquired to trade to generate a quick short-term profit, in which case it is *buy-to-sell*. Buy-to-sell stock incurs Income Tax on the profits of the sale.

Case law states that although property may be either buy-to-let or buy-to-sell, it can't be both at the same time, so how you intend to use the property decides the tax treatment applied to the deal.

The first step of your property strategy should always be to document the purpose to which you are putting your property.

Assembling the jigsaw

Often developments require acquisition and disposal of odd bits of land in order to end up with the site the developer actually wants or needs for the project. This process is called *site assembly*.

Site assembly is not a big problem for a buy-to-sell developer, because site assembly costs can be set off as expenses.

For a landlord, site assembly is a little more complicated. Say, for example, that you own a property with a large garden and want to split the plot to build another property, that itself is split into two or three flats, for letting. It's likely you'd need some grounds, parking space, and vehicle access in order to gain planning permission.

To do this, you may have to buy some tracts of land from your neighbours, and to complete the deal, you may have to swap or trade land you own with them.

Even if you swap a piece of land and no money changes hands, or you swap some land with a small balancing figure of cash, the transaction triggers Stamp Duty for the party acquiring land and CGT for the party disposing of the land. See Chapter 8 for the basics on Stamp Duty, and Chapters 9 and 10 for how to deal with CGT.

The fact that little or no cash is involved does not mean that these taxes can be ignored, as tax rules say the tax is based on the open market value of the land at the time of the swap.

Step two is working out site assembly in the most tax effective way.

In cases involving small pieces of land, the issue can be staggered around the tax year end, so you have annual exempt amounts for capital gains available close together – one for the tax year ending 5 April and one for the tax year starting 6 April.

You can sell one plot in one tax year and another the next and if you have a spouse or business partners involved as joint owners, use their CGT annual exempt amounts as well. This ploy may very well wipe all or most of the CGT.

With larger plots sold in a single transaction, introducing joint owners will reduce the CGT liability.

Building a blueprint for success

Experienced buy-to-sell developers usually have a planning strategy up their sleeves, as they know that the spending involved in making a planning application can easily be set off as a business cost in a buy-to sell business.

Buy-to-let developers need to take a less cavalier attitude to planning, as abortive costs of unsuccessful or abandoned applications can't generally be accounted for as capital costs.

Planning your planning strategies

Buy-to-sell developers can take a different approach to planning proposals than buy-to-let developers, knowing that their costs can be deducted as business expenses. A number of different outcomes are possible for any planning application, and as a buy-to-sell developer, you need to know how to deal with each.

Refusal out-of-hand

Refusal out-of-hand is when a planning application is simply rejected as unsuitable. If a developer knows that the costs can be covered as a business deduction, she's able to put in a planning proposal knowing that, even if the local authority turn down the application out-of-hand, the costs of the application can be set off against tax.

Savvy developers do this when planning officers give unclear indications of what they may or may not allow. A developer can use the ploy to narrow down the options planning officers may invoke when she makes a new application.

 The argument you need to make to the taxman in case of a refusal out-of-hand is that this spending should be allowed as a business expense because it is part of the process to obtain final consent, which may well have failed if the earlier rejected application had not been made.

This ploy produces a win-win situation for you because, even if there's a chance the application may go through first time, if it doesn't, the rejected plan gives valuable intelligence for the next proposal.

Rejected subject to revision

If the planning officer rejects your planning application *subject to revision*, the rejection shows the planning officer's hand by revealing the points of concern that need revision.

The same argument applies as with refusal-out-of-hand. Although the application was rejected, a lot of the work that went into it can contribute to the preparation of the follow-up application.

It follows that this spending is reflected in the value of the developed building. However, the taxman has been known to argue that the first application enhanced the value of the undeveloped site and the subsequent application did the same for the developed site. This would disallow the first batch of planning spending as a business cost because it did not enhance the value of the developed site.

Surviving Section 106

When developers talk about '106' they're referring to Section 106 of the Town and Country Planning Act, 1990. This legislation gives local councils the power to seek a community benefit from a larger development – for instance a big housing estate may have to include provision for social housing to get past the planners. Other conditions may involve road improvements or landscaping.

The tax treatment is dubious. Effectively, a Section 106 condition means that a gift made to the local council by a developer doesn't enhance the development property.

The gift is a business expense for a buy-to-sell developer – but not for a buy-to-let developer. A buy-to-let developer may argue that the cost is enhancement expenditure, but only if the value of the developed property reflects the spending.

Before entering into any Section 106 agreement with a local council, a developer should take expert advice from a solicitor with experience in the field.

Financing the Work

Financing your development as a landlord can cause problems with property tax. The key point is whether the interest you have to pay on any loan can be allowed as a business expense, and if so, when you can claim it.

If a lender finances the project with a loan, generally no problem exists, because the interest is *really* interest.

Sometimes, however, the finance looks like a loan with interest on paper, but it's really a wolf in sheep's clothing when it comes to saving tax. Development agreements sometimes require that interest is calculated on a loan and the lender adds interest to the development costs.

This is not genuine interest and does not qualify for tax relief – the interest is a notional profit for the lender, because it hasn't actually lent any money to anyone but just built a profit into a joint venture.

 Interest is a business expense when you borrow money from a lender. Notional interest is when a lender finances building costs, and is not allowable as an expense because the expenses lie with the lender, not with you as the borrower.

The loan may have interest applied, but if you 'roll up' or defer repayment, the interest can't be reclaimed until the loan is redeemed with the lender.

Keeping to Your Plan

A problem arises when a buy-to-sell developer buys a property to develop and sell on, but then decides to keep the property and put a tenant in. Changing your mind over property use is a key tax trap for buy-to-sell property developers.

The nature of the property changes from trading stock to a fixed asset on the balance sheet. The technical term for moving property from one use to another is *appropriating from trading stock*.

Changing the nature of the property is a tax trigger because the transaction is dealt with as if the property was sold at open market value and purchased at the same value on the same day.

In practice, you're transferring the property from your buy-to-sell business to your buy-to-let business.

If your buy-to-sell business is a company, you pay corporation tax on any chargeable gain in the value of the property. If you're an individual or joint owner, you pay income tax on the transaction.

Plus, because the transaction involves a purchase, Stamp Duty becomes payable. See Chapter 8 for the low-down on Stamp Duty.

Understanding the importance of intention

If, as a developer, you decide to put a tenant in a property pending a sale, this doesn't necessarily mean you've switched the purpose of the property to buy-to-let.

For instance, the market may have dropped and you're waiting for a better selling price, or because your buyers have dropped out you want to defray some costs pending finding a new buyer.

Decisions like these don't mean that you've changed the property from a buy-to-sell into a buy-to-let. They just indicate that you're making sensible business decisions. Plenty of case law supports this.

Keeping property bought as buy-to-sell

If you buy the property as a buy-to-sell and then decide you want to keep it, you need to make sure that you act quickly.

If possible, make your decision before completion of the development, then transfer the property at this stage. You still have to pay tax on the disposal and reacquisition, but as the property is worth less at this stage than when the development is finished, the tax bill is (pro rata) less as well.

Offloading property bought as buy-to-let

Often, a buy-to-let landlord develops a property and prior to letting, or soon after, realises it's a turkey or receives an offer she can't refuse – but neither of these situations makes it a buy-to-sell.

Case law supports the thinking that you can sell poorly performing property and put the money into an investment with a better return.

If you follow my advice in Chapter 5, and keep accurate records, your property register should contain a note that states your intention for the property. The disposal triggers a CGT event whether you sell the property to your buy-to-sell business or to someone else.

Because of the tax issues involved, it's difficult to think of a reason why a landlord would want to transfer a property to a buy-to-sell business.

But if you think that you want to do it, the best time is before or during the actual development, when the property value is lower than on completion of the development.

Splitting the business

Swapping properties between trading stock and fixed assets is a good example of why, if you operate both as a buy-to-let and a buy-to-sell developer, you need to separate out your businesses.

Having separate businesses clearly shows the taxman what is what and takes away any confusion over intent when you buy a property.

Avoiding confusion over intent means that the transaction receives the correct tax treatment, and you cut down confrontation with the taxman.

Claiming Refurbishment Costs

Refurbishment costs fall into different categories depending on whether you're a buy-to-let landlord or a buy-to-sell developer. This section takes you through the differences.

Buy-to-let spending

Buy-to-let refurbishment costs can be revenue or capital, depending on whether they're repairs and renewals, complete replacements, or upgrades or improvements.

These costs should be clearly identified for rental accounts because day-to-day maintenance costs count as revenue costs, which you reclaim in the year in which they're incurred.

You hold capital costs on the property register and reclaim them on disposal of the property.

Buy-to-sell spending

Enter buy-to-sell costs on the balance sheet as work-in-progress until the property is sold, then transfer them to the profit-and-loss account as costs of sale. See Chapter 14 for more on work-in-progress and the profit-and-loss account.

This means that you defer reclaiming the spending until you sell the property and enter the costs in the accounts as a business expense on the day the property is sold. See Chapter 14 for more on development spending.

Considering Council Tax

The local council of the area imposes council tax on your property. Council tax only applies to residential property. The council sets the amount payable, which depends on factors like the size and value of your property. These factors place your bill in an appropriate banding.

Many developers forget that they can save council tax while their property is being refurbished, or empty.

The same council tax treatment applies to both buy-to-sell developers and buy-to-let landlords while a house is under refurbishment.

If the property is no one's main home, then a discount may apply:

- ✔ For furnished second or holiday homes, councils must offer a second homes' discount of between 50 per cent and 10 per cent.
- ✔ Councils can offer an empty homes discount of up to 50 per cent for homes that have been empty and unfurnished for longer than six months.

Some councils charge full rate council tax on unoccupied furnished homes – that is, second homes or holiday homes. Gwynedd in North Wales is an example.

Gwynedd Council argues that so many homes – up to 50 per cent of the housing stock in some places – are second homes or holiday homes from which the council can't raise enough council tax to pay for essential services. So expect to pay full council tax in some places as a fact of life for owning a second home.

Slipping on the Property Ladder

Lots of would-be property developers have been encouraged to take the leap into giving up their jobs to start up a full-time property business – but beware the taxman.

Climbing the ladder

The basic business model for a lot of developers is to buy a house that needs refurbishing and to renovate the property with a view to moving in for a while, then selling on at a profit.

After that, the plan is to move onwards and upwards to bigger and better houses on the back of profits from the previous sale. Fair enough, that's what property development, is all about – making a profit. But it's illegal.

Sliding down the snakes

Serial developers argue that private residence relief (PRR), means they don't have to pay any tax on the profits of selling a house that they've lived in while doing it up. (See Chapter 9 for more about this relief.)

That's just not true, as many of the people who the taxman identifies from their fleeting fifteen minutes of fame on television can confirm, after settling big tax bills for their property profits.

What the programmes don't tell you is that a clause in CGT law says that if you buy a property, no CGT relief can be allowed in either of the following two circumstances:

- ✔ If you bought the property with the intention of wholly or partly disposing of it for a gain.
- ✔ Where you've spent money on the house wholly or partly for the purpose of realising a gain from its disposal.

In practice, first-time developers sell their own home for a profit, and the taxman takes no action.

Depending on the tax office, the developers may escape the second time, but the third time establishes the trend and the taxman comes after them for unpaid Income Tax due on all the profits of all three house sales, plus penalties, and surcharges.

The taxman applies Income Tax and not CGT because the transaction is a buy-to-sell development not buy-to-let investment.

Falling Flat with Flat Conversion

Many property developers make money from buying a large house, moving in, and converting the building into a number of flats. The profits come from the sum of the parts, adding up to more than the value of the original building after the conversion. From here, the developer can sell the flats separately or let them all, or even stay in one flat and sell or let the others.

The same warning applies here as for developers in the previous section – if you buy a house intending to convert it into flats and then to sell for a profit, you get no CGT relief.

It's not all bad news, though. If you qualify for PRR relief on your property – which means proving that you didn't buy the property with the intention of making a gain – then each flat is allowed CGT relief.

Kerry bought a large house for £150,000. She used the house as her only residence. Three years' later, she decided the house was too big for her, so spent £40,000 to convert the it into two flats.

She moved out when the conversion started and the flats were priced at £150,000 each. The value of the unconverted house would have been £245,000.

The part of the gain that's excluded from relief because she spent cash on the property with the intention of making a profit on the sale is worked out in Table 15-1.

Table 15-1	Kerry's CGT Liability
Sale proceeds	£300,000
Less unconverted value	(£245,000)
Sub total	£55,000
Less Kerry's annual CGT exempt amount:	(£9,600)
Less conversion costs	(£40,000)
Gain arising from expenditure	£15,000
Taxable gain	£5,400
CGT at 18 per cent	£972

This calculation shows that Kerry receives CGT relief on the value of her home without the conversion because it was her home, but because she spent the cash on the conversion with the intention of making a profit, the gain resulting from the spending is not subject to CGT relief.

Being Wary of Cheap Finance Deals

Many buy-to-let investors swarm like flies around seminars and property clubs offering new properties with cheap finance deals. The term bandied about by these modern-day snake oil salesmen to landlords is *gifted deposits*.

Gifted deposits

A gifted deposit is a marketing method to encourage you to buy when the seller offers to pay the deposit or discount the purchase price for you.

Legally, gifted deposits are fine – as long as you understand that nothing comes free and somewhere along the line, a price needs to be paid by someone.

No-money-down deals

No-money-down deals take place when the seller offers a 15 per cent gifted deposit and the buyer obtains an 85 per cent mortgage. The problem comes when sellers overvalue properties by the amount of the deposit.

Less scrupulous developers and property clubs price a flat valued at £85,000 up at £100,000 on the market with a 15 per cent gifted deposit. The buyer then has a problem, because in effect the gifted deposit is a sales ploy and doesn't exist.

The valuer bases the property valuation on the completed property price, and often for new-build flats, the valuation is a stab in the dark because of the lack of comparable local properties.

No-money-down deals and tax

If you buy a property with a gifted deposit, the base amount for CGT purposes is the purchase price that goes on the forms that go to the Land Registry.

This figure may not be accurate if your purchase price has been manipulated by a gifted deposit, but it provides the starting point for the calculation.

Many lenders now limit the maximum gifted deposit to 5 per cent of the property value or sales price, whichever is the less.

Off-plan problems

Buying off-plan is buying a property that hasn't yet been built, on the presumption that in a rising market, the property after completion should be worth more than you're paying for it.

Linking property price inflation over recent years with gifted deposits is a strategy used by a lot of buy-to-sell developers who are now having to rethink their strategy as the market has stopped rising.

A problem arises if the property was valued at the completion price – and it's been bought off-plan a year or so before it's finished; and then, in a falling or static market, the value is close to the mortgage borrowed. As a result, the purchaser holds little or no equity.

This scenario is especially likely if you buy a property through a seminar or property club, because you have a developer and a middle man skimming a profit before it reaches you, the end buyer.

Chapter 16

Happy Holidays and Second Home Delights

. . . .

In This Chapter

▶ Running a rule over holiday lets

▶ Taking a tax break with a holiday home

▶ Keeping your profits rolling on

▶ Wrapping a property as a gift

▶ Avoiding holiday let tax traps

▶ Electing to save Capital Gains Tax (CGT)

. . . .

*H*oliday lettings in the UK provide fantastic tax breaks – as long as you stick within the strict rules. Dip in under the tax shelter offered by the holiday lettings umbrella and you can gain from reliefs and allowances that aren't available to buy-to-let landlords.

More than with most property investments, location is crucial. Remember, you don't have to be beside the sea to have a holiday let. A nice flat or cottage in a picturesque inland spot or an historic town or city cuts the mustard as well. You can even enjoy your holiday property yourself if you keep to the rules.

More and more people also buy second homes as holiday homes and need tax strategies to deal with profits made from selling them or passing them on to family or children. This chapter tells you all you need to know about saving tax on your holiday property.

Running a Rule Over Holiday Lets

First and foremost, take a look at the boxes you have to tick to ensure that you save as much tax as you gain by making sure that your property meets all the holiday-let criteria:

- ✔ **The property must be in the UK.** Overseas holiday lets receive the same treatment as overseas buy-to-lets and receive no special tax advantages.

- ✔ **The standard of furnishing is important.** The property must be furnished so the guests can move straight in with just their personal belongings.

- ✔ **You must run your holiday let as a business.** A second home that you let out for the odd week is not a holiday let.

  To qualify as a business you must:

  - Make the property available for commercial letting for at least 140 days in any 12-month trading period.

  - Let the property for at least 70 of those 140 days.

  - Not let the property to the same person for more than 31 days in any seven-month period in the trading year.

The 12-month trading period is generally the tax year – but in the year you start trading, the 12 months start from the day you start the business. The final year ends when the last letting ends.

Understanding the qualifying period

The qualifying period often causes problems. 140 days is roughly five months, and is considered the main holiday season starting at Easter and ending with the children going back to school in September. The remaining seven months count as the out-of-season period.

The qualifying rules really say that your property has to be available to let during the holiday season and that it must be let for half that time. In the tax year, you cannot let to any one person for a period of more than 31 days. If you do, you lose any holiday-let tax advantages that you've accrued.

Proving your points

The taxman is keen to catch second homers who pretend their property is a holiday let so they can reclaim expenses against tax. Proving your property is a holiday let rather than a second home is easy. You need to:

- ✔ **Draw up a business plan and open a separate bank account for holiday-letting income.** The business plan does not have to be anything complicated, just a cash flow projection.

✔ **Advertise your property with an agency.** Not only is an advertisement a good way of getting bookings, but the advertisement is also proof that the property was available for commercial letting.

Averaging without being mean

If you've several holiday-letting properties, and one fails to meet the qualifying rules, but all the others do, then you can apply the 'averaging rule' to lasso the straggler and drag it back into the loop and keep your tax benefits intact.

Averaging is simple: Steve has three holiday lets. One is let for 95 days, one for 73 days and the other for 55 days. The last cottage fails the 70-day letting rule. Steve is allowed to tot up his total letting days: 95 + 73 + 55 = 223.

He then divides the total days let by the number of properties (223/3) giving an average let of 74 days per property. By presenting the information in this way, Steve ensures that each property in his holiday letting portfolio passes the 70-day test and he keeps the tax benefits for each.

Taking a Break From Tax

Big tax advantages make a holiday let a gold-plated investment. These tax reliefs slash the amount of Capital Gains Tax (CGT) you generally pay on selling a residential investment property, and let you *set off* trading losses from your letting business against trading profits from other businesses – though not from a buy-to-let business, if you have one. Check out Chapter 2 for more on buy-to-let businesses.

Combine these tax concessions with other special business reliefs and they add up to a really generous tax regime.

Entrepreneur's relief

Entrepreneur's relief is a brand new tax boost for holiday home owners that only came in to play on 6 April 2008.

Entrepreneur's relief is available to people who are involved in running the business if the holiday property belongs to a company. The relief is available on:

✔ Capital gains made on the disposal of all or part of a holiday letting property

✔ Capital gains made on disposal of a holiday property following the closure of a business

The first £1 million of gains that qualify for entrepreneur's relief is charged to CGT at discount rate of 10 per cent. The normal 18 per cent CGT charge rate applies to gains in excess of £1 million.

Lifetime guarantee

Entrepreneur's Relief is not a one-off relief, because anyone can make a claim more than once, up to a lifetime total of £1 million of capital gains qualifying for relief.

That means that you have to keep a record of prior claims – like a copy of your tax return and CGT calculation as proof of how much of your lifetime allowance you've used. See Chapter 9 for more on CGT calculations.

Combining strategies

If you're married or in a civil partnership, you can transfer a share in your holiday property to your partner under the CGT no gain/no loss rule and double the £1 million lifetime allowance, because each partner has the same right to claiming Entrepreneur's Relief. See Chapter 9 for more on no gain/no loss transactions.

Entrepreneur's Relief applies to chargeable gains made when disposing of property – not to the value of the property.

Contemplating capital allowance

Capital allowance is a special tax relief on furnishing and equipping your property – don't worry, capital allowance is available to holiday lets everywhere, not just in London.

Capital expenses reduce tax – every pound you claim is a pound knocked off your taxable profit. The full low-down on capital allowances would take a book on its own, so rather than go into the nitty-gritty, I'll give you an example. See Chapter 7 for a full run-down on capital expenses.

Sean and Jamila have a second home that they decide to equip and run as a holiday let because they can't find the time to make full use of the place any more.

To charge a top rate, they refurbish the property, spending £7,500 on new furnishings, electrical goods, and so on. Their income from rent in the first year of letting is £5,500.

Their accountant advises them to claim capital allowances, so instead of setting off the costs as a revenue expense, they *write down* the £7,500 they've spent with a first-year capital allowance: This allowance is 40 per cent of their spend – £3,000.

The 40 per cent figure is the current first-year allowance rate laid down by the Government, and is the maximum they can use in the first year they claim.

This amount is deducted from the first-year letting profits of £5,500. Instead of paying income tax on the £5,500, they now only pay it on £5,500 profit less the £3,000 first- year allowance, which leaves a profit of £2,500.

The capital allowances balance of £4,500 (£7,500 initial expenditure, minus the £3,000 write down) carries forward to next year and is again set off against their trading profits – except that for the second and subsequent years, the writing down allowance is 25 per cent of the total brought forward until the £4,500 is completely used.

If you replace any furnishings or equipment, their cost is added to the pool, receiving their own first-year allowance and subsequent annual writing-down allowance.

You can claim capital allowances against any equipment used for your holiday letting business – like vans, ladders, lawnmowers, computers, desks, fax machines, and so on.

Just remember, if you've any private use of such items, apportion the allowance so that you claim only for business use. See Chapter 5 for more on how to apportion costs.

Reviewing reliefs

As if furnished holiday lets didn't have enough tax advantages, a few more exist to throw into the pot under special circumstances. The reliefs covered in this section let you put off paying CGT but don't allow you to avoid the tax completely.

Rollover relief

Any gain made on disposing of a holiday let can be 'rolled over' into buying a new business asset. Any CGT is deferred by deducting the gain on the sale of the old holiday let from the cost of the new holiday let.

The relief is conditional. The hoops you have to jump through include the following provisos:

- ✔ The property sold and the property acquired must be used in your holiday letting business.

- ✔ Reinvestment has a time limit. Reinvestment of the sale proceeds, not just the gain, must happen one year before, or three years after, the disposal date.

- ✔ The new property shouldn't be used for any other purpose. The holiday property must be brought into use in your business as soon as possible after purchase.

- ✔ The time limit for starting the new holiday-let business is three years from the sale of the old property.

- ✔ Putting the money into buy-to-lets is not allowed because they're not business assets. See Chapter 2 for more on buy-to-lets.

You don't have to reinvest in the same business if you run more than one at the same time and can even use the relief to start a new business.

Tim bought a holiday cottage for £35,000 some years ago and wanted to sell it and pay the least CGT possible. Tim discussed his problem with his friend who suggested selling the property and reinvesting the proceeds in a bigger and better holiday let to increase the rental income. Tim considered this advice and looked at the tax calculations. The selling price of the property now would be £175,000.

1. **First, work out the gain on the sale:**

   Disposal proceeds: £175,000

   Less cost: (£35,000)

   Chargeable gain: £140,000

2. **Next, work out the revised base cost of the new holiday cottage:**

   Cost: £175,000

   Less rolled-over chargeable gain: (£140,000)

   Revised base cost: £35,000

If Tim had sold the property and not reinvested the money, the calculation would have been as follows:

Disposal proceeds	£175,000
Less cost	(£35,000)
Chargeable gain	£140,000
Less annual exempt amount	(£9,200)
Chargeable gain	£130,800
CGT at 18 per cent	£23,544

Rollover relief works by deferring the CGT a business is due to pay so that the money can be reinvested to expand. Because Tim reinvested the disposal proceeds from the first cottage in a new one, he paid no CGT at the time of the first sale.

When Tim comes to sell the second cottage, the sale triggers the CGT liability on the first property. For instance, a couple of years later, Tim decides to sell the new cottage for £235,000. The CGT is then:

Sale proceeds	£235,000
Less base cost	(£35,000)
Chargeable gain	£200,000
Less annual exempt amount	(£9,800) – estimated figure for 2011
Chargeable gain	£190,200
CGT at 18 per cent	£34,236

The tax paid here includes the deferred CGT from the sale of the first cottage.

Gift wrapping

Another tactic for delaying CGT comes into action when a holiday let is transferred to another person, effectively transferring the old owner's CGT liability to the new owner. This CGT-saving strategy

Extending relief

All the reliefs available to a furnished holiday let can be stretched to cover any property used in a holiday-letting business, such as property you own that's used as office or storage space.

For instance if you've a lock-up where you store linen, furnishings,all o and equipment for maintaining your holiday let, the same reliefs apply to this lock-up as the holiday let itself, as the building is part of your holiday-letting business.

manipulates various tax reliefs to eliminate any CGT due on the sale of a holiday let. It works like as follows:

1. **You gift the holiday let to someone who is a UK resident.**

2. **You both make a joint election to the taxman saying you want gift relief to apply.**

3. **The person receiving the gift then makes the former holiday home their main residence.**

In tax terms, this means that your CGT is held over, but because the person you gifted the property to has main-home CGT relief, the gain is wiped out along with any gain they've made while owning the property.

If the holiday property had another use, like as a buy-to-let or second home, you can still implement the strategy, but the held-over gain is reduced pro rata on a time basis of the alternate use.

Holiday lets are the only property investments that enable you to take the income as relevant earnings for a pension.

Incorporation relief

Incorporation relief allows you to defer paying CGT when transferring business assets into a company in return for shares. For more details, see Chapter 10.

Shuffling your losses

Holiday letting losses give you a multi-pronged approach to tax saving. If you make a trading loss, you can choose how best to save income tax or CGT that you may be paying on other earnings but not income from investments.

So if you develop property and have a holiday-letting business, under certain circumstances, the losses of one can be set off against the profits of another – but you can't set off the profits or losses of an ordinary property letting business in the same way.

Carry back

Carry back is the practice of using current tax year losses to relieve profits on earnings in previous years. Using carry back gives you three options:

- ✔ **Starting up losses.** Any losses made in the first four years of trading may be set off against earnings from the previous three tax years on the last-in first-out (LIFO) basis.

  LIFO means setting current losses against the most recent tax year's profits and then going back to the previous year and the one before that.

- ✔ **Prior year.** Losses from any year can be set off against profits of the previous tax year, if the loss is more than your earnings. If you've any chargeable gains from the disposal of assets, you can set the remaining losses off against any CGT you paid in the previous year.

- ✔ **Closing down losses.** Any losses in the final 12 months of trading can be set off against profits in the previous three years on the LIFO basis.

Sideways shuffle

You can set the loss against other earnings in the same year. If the loss is more than your profits and you've any chargeable gains, set the balance off against CGT.

Carry forward

Losses can be carried forward indefinitely to set off against the first profits arising from the same business.

Jan runs several holiday cottages, but due to bad weather and the credit crunch stopping people booking holidays, she has made a £18,150 loss this year. Her business made profits in previous years and she knows that she can set off losses made this year against those earnings. Table 16-1 summarises her loss relief.

Table 16-1		Example loss relief	
Loss for 2008–09 tax year:			£18,150
Loss register			
Tax year	*Taxable earnings*	*Loss relief*	*Cumulative loss relief*
2007–08	£6,000	£6,000	£6,000
2006–07	£5,250	£5,250	£11,250
2005–06	£1,000	£1,000	£12,250
2004–05	£3,500	£3,500	£15,750
Totals	£15,750	£15,750	
2008–09 loss less cumulative loss relief			£15,750
Loss brought forward from 2007–08			£0
Losses brought forward used this year			£0
Loss to carry forward against earnings in future tax years			£2,400

So, Jan has carried back her current tax year loss and cancelled out the earnings of previous years, so now she can submit these figures on her tax return and reclaim any tax she has paid in earlier years.

Moving into your holiday home

No rule says that you can't move into your holiday let and make it your main home, or even give it away. Moving in puts the main residence relief protection around the property. See Chapter 9 for more on private residence relief.

You can apply the exemption for all the time you live there – and if you only stay for a short time and sell, the last 36 months of ownership are exempt from CGT.

Nevertheless, although you gain CGT relief, you lose all the other benefits of a holiday home, because as soon as you turn the key in the door to make the property your home, the use changes from business to personal. See the next section 'Holiday Home Tax Traps', for more on the tax distinction between personal and business use.

Holiday Home Tax Traps

One of the key phrases in qualifying for the tax breaks is *commercial letting*, which means hiring the property out at a competitive market rate. Commercial letting is one of the qualifying keys to unlocking the tax benefits of a holiday let. You need to be wary of two factors that bar you from qualifying – personal use and uncommercial letting, and a couple of other circumstances that can catch you out.

Limiting personal use

Commercial letting must be to guests paying the full letting rate – which means that if you're staying in your holiday home, it can't be available to let to guests.

Nothing stops you staying there in the off-season, but you must ensure that you restrain your desire to enjoy time off at your holiday home at the expense of paying guests, because if you do so, the tax advantages fall away.

Restricting uncommercial letting

Uncommercial letting is letting family and friends stay at your holiday let for free or with a discount. By all means, invite your friends and family out-of-season, but explain the tax implications to them if they moan they can't come down for the summer!

If you, your family, or friends spend off-season time at your holiday let, you must apportion the running costs accordingly.

Holding back on leaving the UK

If you use the hold-over or gift-relief strategy, then the person gifting the property must remain a UK resident for six tax years after the end of the tax year in which the gift was made.

If you emigrate before the time is up, any CGT that would have been due becomes immediately assessable on the date you become non-resident.

Benefiting from pre-owned assets

You may have to pay tax if you continue to receive a personal benefit once you've gifted property to someone else.

The point of a gift is that you lose control of the asset, so if you give a gift with conditions, like gifting a second home or holiday let to someone in your family but continuing to use the property without paying rent, you're still receiving a taxable benefit from the gift.

Make sure that when you transfer title, you discuss the pre-owned asset rules with your solicitor. That way, you won't get a nasty tax shock. The rules don't apply if you pay a commercial rent for using the property.

If you sell your property to an equity release company and continue to live there, you're exempt from the pre-owned assets legislation.

If you're caught in the net, the tax is calculated as 5 per cent of the property's open market value, or the rental value of bare land – that's land with no buildings.

The first £5,000 of property value or rent received is exempt from tax.

Electing to Save Tax

You do not pay CGT on selling your home because main-home relief or *private residence relief* (PRR) comes in to play and makes any gain you've made exempt from tax. See Chapter 9 for more on PRR.

Not many people know that if you've a second property in the UK or overseas you can *elect* to use the same rules to save on the CGT paid when you sell – even if the property has not been your main home.

Sizing up a solution for singles

Not many property tax breaks benefit single people over married couples or civil partners, but there's a way you can put tax money in your bank account if you've a partner but you aren't married.

Tax rules say that a married couple can only have one main home, but unmarried couples can have two separate main homes, one for each partner. In this case, PRR applies to both properties and both are exempt from CGT.

Doubling up on main-home relief

The same rule that allows an election to be made can be useful for married couples or civil partners who own more than one home.

The election is valuable when combined with the 36-month CGT exemption rule, as it's possible for PRR to apply to two homes at the same time. See Chapter 9 for the detail on 36-month exemption.

PRR applies to two properties when you actually live in one of the houses as your main home and the other house *was* your main home at some point in the last 36 months that you owned it.

To take advantage of this situation, you have to elect your second home as your main home for a period of time, say six months. To elect a home, you have to file a written notice with your tax office. This election gives a 36-month CGT exemption on both properties.

Take Michelle as an example. She has a house in Glasgow and decides to buy a holiday cottage as a weekend retreat in St Andrew's.

In 2007, Michelle had elected her Glasgow property as her main home, but in 2009, she hears of plans to build a massive marina near St Andrew's, which increases the value of her cottage, so she makes a second election of the cottage as her main home for six months, and then switches it back to her Glasgow home.

In 2010, Michelle sells the cottage and pays no CGT because she had owned it for just 36 months and as it had been her main home for six months, the cottage is exempt from any CGT.

Meanwhile, her main home still has PRR protection for all but six months. Six months is a short period unlikely to produce any capital gain exceeding her annual exempt amount, if and when she comes to sell.

You've two years from when you move into your home to make the election – and don't forget, if you're joint owners, both of you have to make the election.

If you don't make the election, HMRC make the choice for you and you can bet your bottom dollar they'll go for the choice that gives them the most tax.

Overseas elections

Gains on properties overseas can still be liable to CGT in the UK. If you're a resident in the United Kingdom and own a second home overseas, you can still elect your home outside the United Kingdom as your main home.

You need to discuss the issue carefully with your tax advisers in the UK and overseas, as the tax laws in each country may or may not put you at a disadvantage.

Pre-owned assets elections

Rather than paying income tax every year, you can elect to have any property taxed as a pre-owned asset lumped into your estate and have Inheritance Tax (IHT) applied instead.

You need to make the election by 31 January following the end of the tax year for which income tax on the asset becomes payable.

The date would be 31 January 2010 for income tax incurred during the tax year ending 5 April 2009.

Chapter 17

Approaching Investment Alternatives

In This Chapter

▶ Investing in property without the hassle

▶ Funding your savings and pension

▶ Finding out about property funds

▶ Wising up to woodlands

*N*ot everyone who wants to invest in property wants to look at residential property – but you may not have the time, cash, or expertise to play with the big boys in the commercial property market.

Also, whether you're a buy-to-let or buy-to-sell investor, you may want to spread your investment so that you don't have all your eggs in one basket.

This situation is where institutionalised investment comes in. Not buying into prisons, you understand, but into property funds such as unit trusts, pensions, and ISAs. The big attraction here is that armchair investors can often pick up a good return on their investments without getting their hands dirty with dealings relating to their own property.

And if you're really into the idea of alternative investment, I walk you through the wonder of woodlands – and the tax breaks you get from owning them.

Perusing Property Funds

Although tax law only recognises three types of property business – UK buy-to-let, overseas buy-to-let, and buy-to-sell property development – other transactions also masquerade as property businesses.

You may find some of these worth considering as a spread of investments, especially as a way of investing in commercial property that can have a high cost of entry for an individual investor.

Pooling cash in funky funds

Property funds consist of financial products offered by insurance and investment companies. They all work on basically the same principle – a pool of small investors puts cash into the fund and the fund manager and his team then invest that cash in commercial property.

The fund works as follows:

1. **Investors pay in cash to buy 'units' in the fund, which is similar to buying shares in a company.**
2. **The fund management team spends the cash buying high-value commercial property.**
3. **The rents from the commercial property pay for the running of the property.**
4. **The value of the property increases, or if you're unlucky, goes down, and as the value changes, the value of each unit in the fund rises or falls with it.**

The trick is choosing the right time to buy and sell your units – buy when the unit costs are low and sell when they're high – although predicting this right time is sometimes more easily said than done.

Buying low means you can buy more units for your cash, so you are likely to make larger profits when the funds rise and you sell your units.

The difference between property investment funds comes down to the tax breaks and rules applied to the different financial products. All the property funds are basically the same – they invest in commercial property. The difference between the funds is what's called *the wrapper* or the tax rules that govern them.

Think of the funds like burgers – the central ingredient is the same (the bit of meat in the middle) but the wrapper can be a sesame bun or a seeded bun or a plain bun, with or without ketchup.

Now you can cook your own burgers – like a landlord deals directly with his own property – or you can go and buy different sorts of takeaway, which would be the equivalent of different investment groups and insurance companies.

Property funds offer a good way of investing in property without getting your hands dirty. The fund manager does all the work – for a management fee – and you reap the tax benefits. Unlike direct property investment, you don't have to worry about repairs, bad tenants, or void rental periods.

In this chapter, you can see a lot of fancy acronyms: ISA, OEIC, REIT, and SIPP, to name just a few. The acronyms mystify the products, but don't worry about the names – you really want to know about the tax breaks.

ISA, I Say, I Say

If you want to invest in property with no hassle, then consider putting your money into a property fund *wrapped* in an Individual Savings Account, better known as an ISA.

Introducing the ISA

An ISA, or Individual Savings Account, isn't really an investment itself – but rather a way of holding investments, cash, and life assurance in a tax-efficient environment.

Unlike many of the other property fund products, you don't receive tax relief on the money you put into an ISA – but you pay no tax on any dividends, interest or bonuses accrued by the property funds within your ISA. The ISA wrapper is a savings account that includes an option to invest in property funds.

An ISA, therefore, is a tax shelter for your savings. The maximum investment per individual for the 2008–09 tax year is £7,200.

Paying tax on ISA funds

You pay no Income Tax or Capital Gains Tax (CGT) arising on investments held in your ISA, but you can't set off ISA losses against any losses outside your ISA.

You can take your money out at any time without losing tax relief.

You don't have to declare income and capital gains from ISA savings and investments, or tell the taxman that you have an ISA.

Unit Trusts

Unit trusts provide a good way for investors to drip feed small monthly amounts to build a larger fund. If you see the term *OEIC* applied to a property fund, the product is a unit trust. OEIC stands for Open Ended Investment Company. The fund is open-ended because unit trusts cannot borrow money, so if they wish to expand they must open to more investors to raise more cash.

Unit trusts pay no Income Tax on rental income and no CGT on fund growth.

Unit trusts come as two separate beasts:

- ✔ Trusts investing in property company shares.

- ✔ Trusts directly investing in property. When you're comparing unit trust performance, make sure that you compare like with like because recently, returns from trusts investing in property shares have far exceeded many of those that invest strictly in property.

You don't pay tax on income and capital gains from unit trusts in an ISA or in a *self-invested personal pension* (SIPP), which is a pension scheme that you run yourself rather than having a fund manager.

REITs and Wrongs

REITs stands for Real Estate Investment Trusts. Only a handful of these trusts exist for investors to look at.

REITs operate in a similar way to unit trusts, with the same tax benefits, but have a couple more whistles and bells attached. The main extras are that they're stock market listed and can borrow money. So instead of opening the doors to more investors, REITs can expand their property asset base by *gearing up* to borrow 80 per cent of the value of a property already owned or which the management team intends to buy.

Gearing up is borrowing money against existing assets to finance the purchase of new ones.

Paying tax on REITs

REIT investment is taxed like buy-to-let property – Income Tax on rental profits and CGT on any gains on the sale of their shares in the REIT.

So, REITs themselves don't provide tax shelters – only when you buy the shares via your ISA or self-invested personal pensions (see SIPPs later in this chapter) do they become tax efficient.

Investing in a REIT

Investing in a REIT is exactly the same as investing in any company quoted on the stock market. You simply deal through a stockbroker or an online share-dealing service. Check out *Investing For Dummies* by Tony Levene (Wiley) for more on the basics of dealing with stockbrokers.

Are REITs worth the money? That's an investment decision for you to make – the money is yours and you have your own reasons for investing.

REITs have not been around for long and have no track record by which to benchmark performance.

Property Investment Companies

As property investment companies often base themselves offshore (that is, outside the United Kingdom), they have tax advantages unavailable to UK-based companies, although REITs have now levelled the playing field by offering similar tax benefits.

Similar principles operate in each case – you invest savings in a pooled fund with other investors. The fund is professionally managed and the management team makes the investment decisions.

Most of the cash is sunk into business property – property funds own many malls, retail parks, commercial buildings, and industrial estates where you shop and work.

Property Pensions

Pensions come in many flavours, but for property investors, the *self-invested personal pension* (SIPP) is the star performer. SIPPs provide the opportunity for people who want to manage their own pension fund to deal with, and switch, their investments when they choose. Most SIPPs allow you to select from a range of assets for investment, including unit trusts, REITs, and business property.

Unfortunately, because of tax rules, you lose the tax benefits of the SIPP if you hold residential property, but a few workarounds exist relating to REITs or property trusts that bypass these rules, keeping the tax advantages of a SIPP intact.

For technical advice on SIPPs, you need to contact an independent financial adviser.

Pension tax breaks

Pensions offer tax breaks – which is the reason why they're worth their salts as investment vehicles for your old age, but many people don't realise you can invest in property as well as stock and shares inside your pension portfolio.

With regard to tax breaks, pensions resemble an ISA because in themselves they provide a means, rather than an end, of saving tax. A pension is just a set of rules for governing how your investment is managed, and you have to decide whether a pension or some other wrapper provides the best tax shelter for your cash.

When you put money into a pension, remember that:

- ✔ You receive tax relief on your contributions at the highest rate of income tax you pay – 20 per cent or 40 per cent.

- ✔ If you're a basic rate taxpayer, every £80 you put in is topped up to £100 by the Government, which contributes the £20 balance in tax relief.

- ✔ If you're a higher rate taxpayer, the return is even better – for every £60 you put in, the Government tops up the investment by £40 to make the total contribution £100.

- ✔ Pensions are exempt from Income Tax or capital gains on property income.

Doubling up with a SIPP

The real advantage of a SIPP comes about when you link property investment with pension tax breaks. Investors receive tax relief on their contributions, and a SIPP shelters their profits and gains.

Additionally, a SIPP can borrow up to 50 per cent of the value of the fund, so investment can be geared to some extent. See the earlier section in this chapter, 'REITs and Wrongs', for more information on gearing.

Generally, if you borrow money through a SIPP, the lender expects the loan to be paid off from the rental income generated by the property.

Selling property you own to a SIPP

Many companies and partnerships transfer the property where they carry out their business into a SIPP to reap the tax advantages later.

Think very carefully before you sell any of your commercial property to a SIPP. Yes, the SIPP provides a tax shelter designed to maximise the returns from investing in business property. But don't forget, the disposal triggers a CGT bill for your business and purchase costs for the SIPP, including stamp duty.

You need to sit down and work out the return against the costs to ensure that the switch is worthwhile before you go ahead.

Taking cash from your pension

When withdrawing cash from a pension, you have to choose between two main options:

- ✔ Buying a lifetime *annuity* with your pension fund, less any cash lump sum you've taken.

    An annuity is a regular lifetime income payment from a life assurance company received in return for handing over your pension pot.

    The annuity pays you interest as an income for the rest of your life, but your family is likely to receive nothing after your death unless the annuity guarantees a minimum payment.

    For example, you buy an annuity at the age of 65 which is guaranteed to pay out for 10 years, but die when you're 72. The annuity still pays out to your family for three years after your death because of the 10-year guarantee.

- ✔ Alternatively, you can protect your pension pot by leaving your money in the pension and just take out money as you need it – with a few limits. On your death, the family can have any money left in the fund, less 35 per cent tax.

When you reach 75 years of age, you must buy an annuity or draw an income.

Pension Pros and Cons

What you really want to know is whether to consider the tax benefits from ISAs and pensions, or if you should continue to invest in property outside of a pension.

Pensions offer a balance. On the one hand, you receive tax relief on your contributions and shelter your income and gains from tax. On the other hand, you need a sizeable fund to support a decent standard of living when you retire, and low interest rates don't really stretch to this standard unless the pension pot is substantial.

Like any other investment decision, you pay your money and make your choice. Advisers can give you the pros and cons of investing, but no one can predict the state of the economy on the precise day you cash in your investments.

Rental profits aren't treated as earnings for pension purposes whereas profits from a buy-to-sell development business do count as earnings.

Free information about property funds and how they're perform-ing can be found on the Internet and in some newspapers, like the *Financial Times*. Try Google Finance (www.finance.google.co.uk/finance) or the *Financial Times* (www.ft.com).

Wood You Believe It? Investing in Woodlands

If you're a budding entrepreneur looking to branch out into a different type of property investment, try sticking roots down in woodlands.

You may have noticed all those signs offering woodland for sale as you drive around the countryside and wondered who would want to buy them. Traditional property investment may be in bricks and mortar, but root and branch is a fresh approach with excellent tax advantages, providing that you stay within the rules.

Pruning your tax

Income from working woodlands, or from land under preparation for planting woodland, is exempt from Income Tax.

Working woodland means woodland that generates sales from felled and growing timber, underwoods, and thinning.

Special rules constrain buy-to-sell property dealers on buying and selling woodlands. Tax anti-avoidance rules have been set up to prevent dealers buying woodland, stripping out the value by felling and selling the timber, and then selling the land. The rules mean that dealers lose the income tax exemption if they fell or sell timber from the woodland.

You can manage the woodland by felling old trees and clearing fallen trees but not work the land – that changes the deal from investing in woodland to running a timber business. Timber that's growing at the time of purchase and not felled is excluded from any gain you make when you sell the woodland.

You pay CGT on the value of newly planted trees, plus any increase in value of standing timber while the woodland was held as trading stock.

Further tax benefits include:

- After you've owned woodlands for two years, your estate doesn't have to pay Inheritance Tax on the woodlands in the event of your death.

- In the event of the owner's death, any CGT liability is quashed.

- Woodlands count as an asset for the purposes of roll-over relief – so owners can defer any CGT bill as long as the reinvestment is no later than 36 months after selling the original woodland. Any CGT bill is put off until you sell off the woodlands.

Farming trees

Any activity that amounts to farming woodlands constitutes a trade, not an investment. Farming examples include growing Christmas trees and coppicing. And if you're farming, rather than investing in, woodlands, you don't get any tax benefits.

What you do get is free firewood. As a woodland owner, you can take away five cubic metres of timber or thinning every quarter without permission from the Forestry Commission. Five cubic metres equals roughly the contents of a large skip.

From little acorns . . .

Doubling up your investment options by including woodlands in a self-invested personal pension plan (SIPP) may be interesting. Not only do you receive the tax benefits of investing in woodlands, but you also receive tax relief on your pension contributions.

Part V
Keeping the Right Company

'As we three seem to be doing _all_ the work in your company, we've decided you're expendable.'

In this part . . .

*I*f you're considering running your property business as an incorporated company, or maybe if you already are, then this part is for you.

From a tax point of view, many people who should be trading through a company don't, and some who shouldn't touch incorporation with a barge pole seem infatuated with the idea. I make it crystal clear who should and shouldn't be trading through companies, and go on to give you the low-down on the joys of Corporation Tax, the tax companies pay.

I end up with some good news: How best to take money out of a property company. It can be done!

Chapter 18

A Firm Commitment: Becoming a Company

....

In This Chapter

▶ Looking at property companies

▶ Investing in a buy-to-let company

▶ Trading places with a buy-to-sell company

▶ Letting and managing property with a company

....

'Should I put my letting properties in a company?' is one of the most common questions put to a property tax adviser. Landlords often seem to have this latent desire to own a company that just isn't backed up by business sense. Yet the people who should consider trading with a company, buy-to-sell developers, just as often don't seem to give a passing thought to the idea.

The fact of the matter is that when it comes to tax, companies often provide better shelter for buy-to-sell profits than they do for handling investments. Many property people invest and trade in property at the same time – and companies work well in separating business interests.

In this chapter I examine the pros and cons of property companies for letting, trading, and managing property.

Grasping What Property Companies Are

Property companies come in all shapes and sizes, but when it comes down to it, the three basic business models are:

▸ **Property investment companies:** A good idea for buy-to-let businesses

 ✔ **Property trading companies:** The answer for buy-to-sell businesses

 ✔ **Property management companies:** Businesses that don't own property, but act as letting agents

Don't get confused over the term *development* – any of these three types of property company can develop property. Development isn't a property business category.

The same rules apply for incorporating and administering these companies – the nature of their business makes them different, just as the nature of an individual's property business determines how that business is taxed.

Doing Your Homework

Before you can decide your trading status – whether to trade as an individual, joint owner, or a company – you need to establish what sort of business you run: buy-to-let or buy-to-sell.

Once you've done that, you can then look at the implications of continuing to run that business as you are, or switching to a corporate status. The main points to consider include:

 ✔ **Perpetuation:** Passing on your business to your loved ones. Because a company has a separate legal identity from the owners, it does not die with them like a sole tradership or partnership. It outlives the original owners, and their shares can be passed on through a will or trust.

 ✔ **Limited liability:** Protecting your assets with a company. One of the key issues of running a business through a company is that your liability as an individual only extends to the value of your investment, which is generally the value of your shareholding.

 ✔ **Cost-Benefit analysis:** Assessing what you can gain from incorporating and deciding whether the cost outweighs any gain. Companies cost more to run than other businesses because of Government red-tape. You must work out whether your tax benefits are more then the cost of administering a company.

 ✔ **Tax effectiveness:** Deciding whether the corporate structure saves you money. This point ties in with the last one – companies can save tax for the shareholders, but they can also cost more tax.

For instance, companies are good for cutting tax on income a business receives because you can take dividends and avoid paying National Insurance Contributions (NICs). They are not so good at minimising tax when it comes to selling investments, because individuals have CGT allowances that cut tax on selling investments. These allowances are not available to companies.

You need to think through why you want a company and how you intend to use it in order to make sure that you meet your financial objectives.

Identifying your property business

First, you have to look at your reason for buying or acquiring each property in your portfolio, and what you intend to do with that property:

✔ If your intention is to rent the property, then the purpose is probably buy-to-let (an investment, in other words).

✔ If your intention is to sell on as quickly as possible at a profit, then the purpose is probably buy-to-sell or trading.

Now you know the type of property business that your run, you can slot your properties into that business for keeping financial records and producing accounts for your tax returns.

Many people run buy-to-let and buy-to-sell businesses alongside each other. The key is to keep them separate.

Location, location, location

Where you live and where the property is located affects the tax you pay. Buy-to-let companies can run a UK property business in England, Wales, Scotland, or Northern Ireland, and an overseas property business if the property is elsewhere.

If you've property at home and overseas, you may well consider running more than one company.

For buy-to-sell companies, if you're UK registered, the location of the property you develop doesn't matter: You must declare and pay tax in the UK. If you pay tax overseas and the country has a double taxation treaty with a UK, you won't face double jeopardy – the tax you pay overseas is credited against UK tax.

If you're a UK resident, you pay property business tax in the UK regardless of where the property is located – but you may be liable to tax overseas as well if the property is abroad.

Property Investment Companies

A property investment company buys properties to let in the same way that individuals invest in buy-to-let property. The directors plan to sell the properties at some time in the future at a profit, or to pass them on to their families, but these decisions are incidental to the primary intention of collecting rents.

The profits on sale or disposal of property held as capital assets (rather than trading stock) are taxed as a capital gain. Instead of income tax on rental profits and Capital Gains Tax (CGT) on chargeable gains, a property investment company pays Corporation Tax on both.

A company is still taxed under the old Schedule A Income Tax and Corporation Taxes Act 1988 (ICTA 1988) but individual land-lords now come under the Income Tax (Taxation of Other Income) Act 2005.

Although Schedule A ICTA 1988 and the Income Tax (Taxation of Other Income) Act 2005 have subtle differences, the calculation of rental income and expenses is broadly the same.

Totting up the income and expenses

Rents account for the main source of income for a property invest-ment company. Other income includes interest on cash in the bank. A property management company has two types of business expenses:

- ✔ Property expenses arising from rental income. I discuss prop-erty expenses in detail in Chapter 7.

- ✔ Management expenses for administering the company that are deducted from total profits.

Tax law doesn't clearly define management expenses, which some-times overlap with property expenses, but you can only claim them once. These expenses would relate to the running of the company but not the property rental business. Management expenses cover costs like running and equipping an office, for example.

To claim management expenses, a company must show:

- ✔ **UK residence:** A company registered in the UK usually has a registered office at a UK address, and the company is listed at Companies House.

- ✔ **Dedication to property investment:** the company's business wholly or mainly involves property investment and the main income comes from those investments. HMRC generally interprets 'Wholly or mainly' to mean more than 50 per cent.

Dealing with company losses

A property investment company's profits consist of income plus capital gains. If a company's management expenses exceed the profits, the surplus management expenses can be carried forward to set off against future profits, just as a landlord can carry forward rental losses.

No time limit applies to how long surplus management expenses may be carried forward providing that, if the company stops trading as a property investment business, the carried forward surplus management expenses die with the property business.

Financing Your Investments

Property investment companies sometimes find problems in raising finance for expanding their portfolios. Out of the 100 or so buy-to-let lenders in the marketplace, only a few are prepared to lend to companies at the same rates that they lend to individuals.

Problems with raising money

The traditional corporate financiers – banks and finance houses – often want a 20–30 per cent deposit and may charge at least 1 per cent above bank base rate as interest.

Taking this route can severely damage a company's prospects of building a portfolio because the deposit for each property may be twice the amount that an individual has to find.

Mortgage interest payments may be lower – but that's more likely to be due to a lower amount being borrowed rather than to a better interest rate.

A position of trust

A work round that resolves the financing problem is a *deed of trust*. A deed of trust is a legal agreement drawn up between a director and the company that transfers the beneficial ownership of a buy-to-let property from the director to the company.

The deed indemnifies the director against any costs relating to the purchase and running of the property while giving the rights to rent to the company. In simple terms, the deed allows a director to buy the property and finance any mortgage as an individual, transfer the property to the company, and the company pays the mortgage and running costs while collecting the rent.

The deed is not limited to a single purchaser; joint owners or multiple directors can also use the deed to obtain more advantageous borrowing than the company.

So who pays the tax? The company. The deed of trust makes the company the beneficial owner, and the general rule is that tax follows ownership of an asset.

The deed of trust may trigger a stamp duty payment on the transfer of ownership. Check whether it does with your solicitor.

When Investing Doesn't Pay Well

Property investment company directors have a hard time trying to persuade the taxman to let them take a salary from the company. Tax inspectors have instructions to make sure that any salary is apportioned between managing the company's property and directly managing the company. Then, they re-jig your maths.

The tax inspector makes a comparison between a salary claimed for property management and the fees a professional property manager charges. Then she disallows any amount over and above 15 per cent of the gross rent unless you can persuade her that what you do is over and above what a letting agent would do.

If you use a letting agent, forget claiming a salary for managing the property anyway: Why employ an agent if you do the work – which must be reduced if an agent is involved – so why do you need to be paid to do nothing?

The tax inspector can then argue that, because managing the property is the majority of the company's work, only a small payment would be allowed for running the company.

Before you say anything, the tax inspector's heard all the arguments before. She assesses that certain activities you undertake are all part of an investor's research, and not part of company management.

These activities include:

- ✔ Negotiating property sales and purchases
- ✔ Searching for new properties
- ✔ Overseeing the company's business strategy

Think of it as follows: if someone doesn't get paid for selecting their own shares, why should you be paid for choosing your company's houses?

Property Trading Companies

Property trading companies are buy-to-sell businesses. Due to the significant profits that can arise from a single property deal, tax inspectors keep a very close eye on property developers.

Companies provide excellent trading vehicles for development businesses because they can shelter the directors from higher-rate tax by using the income-shifting rules. (Check out Chapter 8 for more on income shifting.)

Working out the profits

Profits are worked out the same way as any for other business. See Chapter 6 for the pro-forma profit-and-loss layout.

You also have to bear in mind that business expenses fall into two categories: *costs of sale* and *management expenses*. I explain these further in the following sections.

Costs of sale

Costs of sale include the direct costs relating to acquiring, refurbishing, and selling a property.

Inclusion of the costs of sale in the profit-and-loss statement only occurs on the sale of the property. Meanwhile, from the purchase date until the property is sold, these costs are held on the balance sheet under one of two headings:

- ✔ **Stock:** the open market value of the property.

- ✔ **Work-in-progress (WIP):** all the costs of finance, materials, and running costs incurred while owning property until the property is is sold.

Management expenses

Management expenses include the day-to-day costs of running your development company, like the phone, stationery and general office costs, rather than spending associated with a particular property.

Calculating the profits

In a development company, you calculate your profits as follows:

- ✔ Work out your total income from property sales.
- ✔ Calculate and deduct the costs of sales.
- ✔ Add any interest received on cash in the company bank accounts.
- ✔ Calculate and deduct management expenses.

Dating rules

Buy-to-sell property acquisition and disposal dates may not necessarily be the dates of contract that apply to investment properties under the CGT regime. No rules lay down the dates that a trading business should use.

Many companies take the exchange of contracts date as the date of acquisition, and the sale date as the date of disposal.

If your tax inspector challenges these dates, politely point out that as long as the policy adopted is generally accepted under accounting principles, and applied consistently, then you can choose which policy to adopt and the tax inspector does not have them power to tell you differently. You can set the accounting policy that gives the most tax effective results for your company.

Trading losses

Development companies can set off trading losses the same as any other business. The three main ways to do so include:

- ✔ Carrying forward to set against future profits
- ✔ Setting off losses against profits in the current trading period
- ✔ Carrying back losses against profits made in the past accounting period

Check out Chapter 16 for the detail on carrying forward and carrying back.

Paying directors

Unlike property investment companies, development company directors can pay themselves a salary without expecting any interference from the tax inspector.

The only times the tax inspector questions salaries is if the director puts in minimal work or is paid a massive salary.

Development earnings also count as pensionable income, so the company can make contributions to directors' pensions as well.

Development companies can't claim capital allowances on stock.

Management Companies

Property management companies don't own any property but act as letting agents. A property letting agency is a trade and is treated in the same way as any other business for the purposes of tax.

Managing your own property

Landlords who want to set up a company to manage their own properties are wasting their time – a company not cost-effective because the cost of running the company is more then the cost of personal accounts, and you can make no tax savings.

Also, if you've a mixture of property owned as an individual and as a company, you cannot set off the losses of one against the profits of another as you and the company are separate legal identities.

Managing other people's property

Best advice – the way to go if you plan to manage property is to set up an agency to let properties for third parties and keep your own properties as a separate, personal business.

Case law says that even if you have a substantial property portfolio that you manage full-time, this portfolio is still an investment, not a bona fide business, like a newsagent or plumber.

Taking the Profits

Whatever type of property company you run, the principles of taking the profits are the same.

The two main methods are:

- ✔ Drawing a salary
- ✔ Taking dividends – the cash returns that shareholders receive for investing in the company

The attraction of dividends versus salary is that you pay no NICs on dividends. If you're a basic-rate taxpayer, the company pays income tax on the dividend and you pay no further tax.

If you're a higher-rate taxpayer, the company still pays your basic-rate income tax– but you make up the difference between basic-rate and higher-rate tax on the dividend bv paying extra tax when you submit your tax return.

Why companies may damage your wealth

Until 5 April 2009, income shifting is the basic principle of saving tax with a company.

Income shifting happens where a company has two or more share-holders/directors – usually spouses or partners. Typically, one is a higher-rate taxpayer and the other a basic-rate taxpayer. To reduce the Income Tax paid on dividends, the lower-rate taxpayer has a larger shareholding and pro rata receives a larger share of the profits. The fact that the lower-rate taxpayer pays tax at 20 per cent instead of 40 per cent reduces the overall tax bill.

The Government intends to bring in new rules affecting companies and partnerships to circumvent these tax avoidance arrangements in the next tax year.

Joint property owners who don't have a company remain unaffected.

Deciding whether property companies are worthwhile

If you're a property investor, with a rental portfolio, and you're not making rental profits, you may find it difficult to see the point in taking on the extra time and costs associated with a company. You can't set off personal losses against company profits anyway.

If you're a property investor making a profit, the question is more complicated. In Chapter 8 I discuss income shifting and the exemption from the proposed income shifting rules for joint property owners, but from April 2009, companies and partnership may have to comply with any new rules.

Perhaps sitting tight is the best bet here because joint ownership allows flexibility for couples, where one is a higher-rate and the other a basic-rate taxpayer.

If all joint owners pay tax at the higher rate, then providing they don't intend to draw down company profits as dividends each year, it may still be worthwhile considering a property investment company.

With reinvestment instead of withdrawal of profits, higher-rate tax-payers face no tax penalties for taking dividends, and the reinvestment pot is larger because the company pays Corporation Tax at a lower rate than a higher rate income tax payer.

If you've other income, and just develop the occasional property, trading as a company makes sense as you can reinvest your profits and avoid higher-rate tax. Higher-rate taxpayers can still withdraw dividends and save on NICs.

Bear in mind that you may lose the income shifting option from April 2009.

If you fit the basic-rate/higher-rate taxpayer model, then buying property as tenants-in-common and reducing the percentage ownership of the higher-rate taxpayer can do no harm, whether you're a buy-to-let investor or a developer. See Chapter 3 for the inside track on creating tenancies-in-common.

Because this arrangement falls outside a company or business partnership, it remains unaffected by the proposed income-shifting rules.

Income shifting to the younger generation won't work. The taxman treats dividends paid to children under 18 years old on shares in a company owned by their parents as dividends paid to the parents, and taxes them accordingly.

Chapter 19

Starting and Running a Property Company

*T*his chapter gives you the low-down on limited companies and limited liability partnerships. If you do intend to form a company, this chapter takes you through the factors you need to bear in mind to meet your legal obligations as a director, and the changes in company law that came into force on 6 April 2008.

Understanding What a Company Is

When most people talk about a *company*, they're talking about a UK registered limited liability company. The shareholders in a limited liability company – that's a business with Limited or 'Ltd.' after its name – are protected from personal loss if the company has debts or fails.

As long as the company has not broken the law, the shareholders are not responsible for more than the value of their shares regardless of how much the company may owe.

For our purposes, *company* also means a small company, which is by law a company that:

  ✔ Has an annual turnover of less than £6.5 million.

  ✔ Has a balance sheet total of less than £3.26 million.

  ✔ Employs an average of 50 or less staff.

Other types of company exist – for instance companies limited by guarantee and public limited companies, better known as PLCs – but these fall outside the scope of this book.

You're not your company

In law, a company has its own legal personality, which means that the company is a separate entity from its owners and managers.

Shareholders own the company and the directors manage the company. From April 2008, small companies no longer need a secretary, even if they only have a single director who's also the only shareholder.

This separate legal personality gives two important advantages to companies that aren't available to individuals: *perpetuity* and *limited liability*.

Perpetuity

Perpetuity in this context means that the life of a company doesn't depend on the lives of the owners.

For a sole trader or partnership, the business dies with the owner, but if a shareholder dies, the shares pass to the beneficiaries of the shareholder's estate. The company can continue trading uninterrupted with just the personnel behind the scenes changing.

Limited liability

Limited liability gives a company responsibility for its own tax, debts, and losses. Generally, limited liability means that once a shareholder has paid for a share, that's the limit of the shareholder's liability if the company fails with bad debts.

Exceptions to this limitation rule include criminal acts carried out by company directors or shareholders, and money owed to the taxman, through Pay As You Earn (PAYE) and Value Added Tax (VAT). See Chapter 12 for more on PAYE and VAT payments.

As a sole trader or partner, you've full liability for your business debts.

The importance of limited liability

One of the key reasons for incorporating a company is the shelter of limited liability, although new regulation is making this shelter a good deal more rickety than it was.

If you're developing property as a buy-to-sell business, limited liability may often be the main reason to consider trading as a company.

Say you're developing a plot to sell, but everything goes wrong and the bills start mounting up. Your creditors can, and no doubt will, stop supplying your company but they can only sue you for the amount you've invested in the company as a shareholder. The amount can be as little as one pound paid for a single share in most small companies.

It doesn't matter that you may have a personal letting property portfolio worth a million pounds – because of limited liability the company creditors can't come after your portfolio and other personal assets.

Registering a company

Companies must register or be incorporated at Companies House – in Edinburgh for companies with a Scottish registered address, or Cardiff for companies with a registered address in England or Wales.

The registered address, or registered office, is the place where:

- ✔ Official documents regarding the company are sent and considered to have been received by the directors.

- ✔ The company register should be open for public inspection. This register is a kind of logbook for the company listing directors, shareholders and other information that the law says has to be available to the public. The process is explained later in the chapter in full detail.

- ✔ A company nameplate should be displayed at the entrance.

The cost of registering a company is about £100 or so, depending on whether you go through an agent, solicitor, or accountant.

Before incorporation

Before incorporating as a company, you need to consider the structure of your company and who makes the key decisions. Strict rules, laid down by law, govern how a company functions. Companies House administers these rules on behalf of the Department of Trade and Industry.

Companies House monitors registered companies to make sure that documents like accounts and information about directors and shareholders are filed on time.

In extreme cases, directors can be disqualified for failure to provide information. This failure is a criminal offence and bars a disqualified director from holding office in a UK company.

Sharing the spoils

Dividends are paid *pro rata* per share and constructive thinking about who should hold shares is an important part of tax planning, especially with the Government's proposed income-shifting, anti tax-avoidance legislation, due to come into force on 6 April 2009.

One person can own all the shares as a *single member company* or many people can own one or more shares. Just because a company is made up of 100 or 1,000 shares doesn't mean they all have to be distributed – a single member holding a single share is sufficient for incorporation.

No restrictions apply to the age or nationality of shareholders and they don't have to be resident in the United Kingdom. However, be careful giving under-18s shares, as the Inland Revenue can dispute who controls their dividends – their parents, for instance – and tax those people accordingly.

A company may own shares in another company.

Directors

A company must have at least one director. No restrictions apply to the age or nationality of directors, nor do they have to be UK residents. Undischarged bankrupts, or persons disqualified by a court judgement, may not act as directors.

Company secretary

From 6 April 2008, appointing a company secretary becomes optional for private companies.

If you're registering a new company, there's no need to do anything other than opt not to appoint a secretary. For existing companies, the secretary can keep their job or, if the directors decide they don't need one, the secretary is required to resign and inform Companies House.

The *articles of association* – the rules that govern the administration of the company – need to specify whether the company should appoint a secretary. If they do, and the company opts not to appoint one, the articles have to be amended.

If the articles only refer to a company secretary, you don't need to take any action.

Naming your company

You may choose any name you wish for your company provided that:

- ✔ The name isn't the same or similar to any other registered name.

- ✔ The name isn't offensive.

- ✔ It doesn't contain the words 'unlimited', 'limited', or 'public limited company' except at the end of the name.

- ✔ It doesn't include words or expressions only allowed by special permission, for example, 'royal', 'bank', or 'international'. The word 'group' can only be used to describe an organisation comprising three or more companies.

You can check whether a company name is already in use by entering the name you want in the search box at the free section of the Companies House website www.companieshouse.gov.uk.

Accounting for the ARD

The *accounting reference date* (ARD), also known as year-end, is the date by which accounts must be prepared each year.

For private companies with accounting periods starting after 6 April 2008, the accounts must be filed nine months after the ARD. For instance, if a company was incorporated on 12 April 2008, the accounts must be made up to 31 March 2009 and should be filed by 31 December 2009.

The ARD can be changed once every five years by up to six months.

The ARD often changes on incorporation, as a company may not start trading for a period while the directors prepare the business, after registration of the papers with Companies House.

For the company that was incorporated on 12 April 2008, even if the ARD was changed to 31 May, the first accounts would prepared up to 31 May 2009, but would still need to be filed 21 months after the date of first incorporation for the first year – 31 January 2010.

Thereafter, they would be prepared to 31 May each year and filed by 28 February of the following year.

Banking

A company has its own identity in law even if there's a single shareholder and director.

Every company should have a bank account that's completely separate from the director's private funds. The bank account doesn't have
to be in the company name, but make it so if you can, as corporate
money can be easily separated from the director's private funds.

Dormant companies

Many companies stop and start trading for various reasons. Buy-
to-sell companies may cease trading for a time if the director can't
find any attractive property deals. These companies go under the
names of *non-trading* or *dormant* companies.

If the company doesn't trade at all in its accounting period, and
the corporate bank account be closed, then special shortened
accounts can be filed. These shortened accounts – effectively *nil
returns* – confirm to HMRC that the company hasn't traded and that
no corporation tax is due.

A company can remain dormant for an unspecified period, although
after 24 months, Companies House may inquire whether the company is still required.

The company can be struck off if documents that should have
been filed haven't been received at Companies House, or if mail is
returned as undelivered from the registered address. If a company
is struck-off, the directors can be disqualified from holding office
with other companies, and if any assets exist, like cash in the bank,
they're seized by the Crown.

To make sure that a dormant company does not get struck off, the
directors must file dormant accounts, corporation tax returns, and
deal with the annual shuttle return. (See the section 'Shuttling information' later in this chapter for more on the annual shuttle return.)

Deregistering a company

In the event of a company ceasing to trade and no longer being
required, special procedures exist for deregistering at Companies
House.

A company can't just shut up shop and disappear, otherwise HMRC
is likely to object: no official returns from a disappearing company
means that HMRC can't assess any tax or VAT that's owed.

Voluntary striking off or dissolution isn't a complicated process, providing that you follow the correct steps. For voluntary dissolution,
the company should be dormant or not have traded or changed in
the past three months, or, if the company is trading, should file

final accounts completed until the date trading ceased with Companies House and HMRC.

The directors then make an application to Companies House on a Form 652 requesting that the company be removed from the Companies House register. A company can't be dissolved if insolvency proceedings are pending or an arrangement has been made with creditors.

Before a company files its application, it must notify shareholders, creditors, directors who haven't signed the dissolution forms, employees, and others, and give them an opportunity to collect any money owed to them.

Red tape by the mile

Okay, so a company gives you limited liability and perpetuity, but now comes the downside – bureaucracy. Tight regulation governs companies, and regulation eats into your time and money with the additional professional and accountancy costs necessary for meeting the extra compliance.

One factor you always need to take into account on incorporation is whether the costs and administration of running a company balance any benefits – like perpetuity, limited liability, and tax savings.

Close companies

Generally, a *close company* satisfies one or more of the following criteria:

- ✔ It has five or fewer shareholders.
- ✔ It has any number of shareholders, but *all* the shareholders are directors.
- ✔ If the company was wound up, more than half the company's assets would be distributed to the people listed above.

Guilty by association

Watch out for the *associated company* tax trap. Associated companies consist of two or more companies under the same ownership or control. Ownership and control means the same people or connected persons are in control.

Unless the associated company is *dormant* – accountant speak for not trading – associated companies can cost you extra Corporation

Tax, which is the corporate equivalent of personal Income Tax. Check out Chapter 20 for the nitty gritty on Corporation Tax.

For instance, your property trading company is due to make a £600,000 profit. The Corporation Tax rate up to £300,000 profit is 21 per cent, and rises to 30 per cent over that. You decide to split the company so both make a £300,000 profit to save tax. Unfortunately, tax doesn't work like that.

Because you've two associated companies, each gets £150,000 of 21 per cent Corporation Tax band and pays 30 per cent on everything over and above that. If you had three associated companies, the 21 per cent band would be £100,000 for each company, and so on.

Don't get connected

Keep an eye on who you're doing business with to avoid the problems of connected persons for associated companies and close companies.

A *connected person* falls into one of the following four categories:

- ✔ Your spouse or civil partner
- ✔ Your blood relatives and in-laws
- ✔ Business partners
- ✔ Companies or trusts under the control of any other party to your transaction and any of the above that are 'connected' with them

Looking at Limited Partnerships

A limited liability partnership (LLP) provides the organisational flexibility of a partnership and, although taxed as a partnership, has the limited liability shield of a company. An LLP must have at least two members. If the number of partners falls to one and the LLP continues to carry on business for more than six months, the LLP loses the benefits of limited liability.

Members cease to be members of an LLP:

- ✔ On their deaths or, if one of the partners is a company, on the dissolution or striking off of the company
- ✔ By agreement with the other members
- ✔ By giving reasonable notice to the other members

Dealing with Companies House

Companies House maintains three policing functions:

- ✔ To incorporate and dissolve limited companies and partnerships and to ensure that they meet their legal obligations.

- ✔ To examine and store company information delivered under the Companies Act and related legislation.

- ✔ To make company information available to the public.

A key difference between a company and an individual's accounts is that, whereas company accounts are open to the public to buy for a small fee, an individual's accounts remain private.

Shuttling information

The main dealings with Companies House, after a company is registered, involve completing a Form 363, otherwise known as the *annual shuttle return*.

This information in this form provides an annual update for the Companies House database of share capital, shareholders, and directors. Each year, the company also files a copy of the annual accounts or financial statements.

Penalties

If the directors fail to discharge their obligations to Companies House, a scale of fines operates for late filing of returns or accounts.

If the directors ignore Companies House and fail to file any documents, after a time, Companies House can disqualify them as directors.

Disqualification can have serious consequences on a director's business standing as banks, business suppliers and other parties can check the public register of disqualified directors.

Logging the details

Directors must keep an up-to-date company register, which needs to include:

- ✔ A list of directors

- ✔ A list of directors' interests

- ✔ A list of charges and securities

- ✔ A list of company secretaries, if applicable

- ✔ A list of registered offices

- ✔ A list of shareholders

- ✔ A list of shares

- ✔ Minutes of meetings

A good place to source company register templates is www. simply-docs.co.uk. This subscription service costs £35 a year, but holds hundreds of template documents for business, residential and commercial property letting, and for managing a company.

Corporate Mortgages

Companies registered in England and Wales must register any mortgages they take out with Companies House within 21 days of completion.

Registration assists the mortgage company in regaining its money if the company goes into liquidation. The company needs not inform Companies House that a mortgage is paid off, but is often worth doing for trading purposes.

Chapter 20

Taxing Company Profits

· ·

In This Chapter

▶ Busting offshore company myths

▶ Clearing up confusion over accounts

▶ Taking a look at loans

▶ Dealing with the taxman as a company

· ·

*R*unning a property company is pretty much the same as running any other property business. The rules about accounting for income and expenses are pretty much the same.

The main difference between running a company and, say, being a sole trader, is the bureaucracy that ties a company up in red tape. Although it all seems over the top for a lot of small companies – perhaps involving a couple of family or friends – the rules are there to protect the interests of the shareholders.

All companies come under the Corporation Tax regime, whether they're property buy-to-let or buy-to-sell companies. This chapter covers the differences between accounting for an unincorporated and an incorporated business.

Most of the information concerns Corporation Tax and keeping company accounts, with little tax-saving information. So, if you just want to get down to business and find out whether a company can save you tax, you can flick through to the next chapter where all is revealed.

Getting to Know the Taxes Companies Pay

Companies registered in the United Kingdom pay Corporation Tax (CT) on their worldwide profits, including chargeable gains, instead of Income Tax or Capital Gains Tax (CGT). The rates are:

- ✔ **Main rate:** 28 per cent of profits.

- ✔ **Small companies rate (SCR):** 21 per cent of profits. SCR is claimed by qualifying companies with annual profits of less than £300,000.

A small company is a company that:

- ✔ Has an annual turnover of less than £6.5million

- ✔ Has a balance sheet total of less than £3.26million

- ✔ Employs an average of 50 or less staff

If you've profits arising from an overseas transaction and you keep them in an overseas bank, the profits still have to be reported in the company's UK accounts.

CT applies to companies registered in the UK and therefore classed as resident. Companies also pay other taxes that individuals pay, like stamp duty, National Insurance Contributions (NICs), and VAT.

Busting the myth of offshore tax saving

If central management and control originate in the UK, even a company incorporated overseas – or *offshore* – is considered UK resident for CT purposes.

A myth exists that central management and control can be exported to, say, Mongolia, by appointing Mongolian nominee directors and holding board meetings in that country. That's simply not true.

Case law emphasises that what matters is not what should happen, but what does – which means that if the directors take any significant decisions in the UK that nominee directors overseas subsequently carry out, control really remains in the UK.

That being the case, a UK resident controlling an offshore property investment company is billed for all the chargeable gains made by the company.

However clever a legal structure a company may implement, the reality remains that if an individual resident in the UK has day-to-day responsibility for a company in another country, the company's residence is the same as the individual's – the UK.

Exactly the same conclusion must be reached where a portfolio investor wants to retain day-to-day control over her investment in deciding what to buy and when to sell.

If she takes the important decisions, her investment company, even if registered offshore and blessed with the services of local nominee directors, resides where the investor resides.

Taking a company abroad

A property investment company can't avoid tax on chargeable gains by moving abroad in the same way an individual can, to avoid CGT.

To do so, the company must pay a penalty, which in reality equates more or less to the same amount of CT that would be due if the company was to dispose of all its property at market value.

Running a UK company from abroad

Running a UK-based company from another country seems a pointless exercise, because the overseas individuals running a UK property investment company would place themselves in the UK tax regime and lose their personal tax advantages – such as not paying CGT on UK chargeable gains.

Instead, the company would pay CT on any chargeable gains arising from selling property.

Counting the Cost

Basically, accounting initially consists of drawing up a database of financial information. This includes financial documents like invoices, bills, and bank statements. Once this information is organised, accountants look at it in two ways:

- ✔ **Financial accounting:** Preparation of financial information held in the accounts for organisations outside the company – for example, the taxman, Companies House, and mortgage lenders.

  These accounts, called financial statements, incorporate the format laid down by the various Companies Acts, accounting standards, and other rules.

  Companies produce financial statements annually, at the end of the accounting period.

✔ **Management accounting:** Preparation of the same information in a custom format for the directors of the company to enable them to make sensible day-to-day business decisions.

For example, management accounts may break down rental income and expenses by property in a portfolio so that you can review which properties make you the most profits, or cause you the most hassle.

Management accounts may be produced often, whenever the business managers consider necessary, but usually at least quarterly.

Accounting Periods

The tax year for an individual runs from 6 April in one year to 5April the following year. Companies don't follow tax years but have *accounting periods*. Generally, the accounting period is 12 months.

Working out accounting periods

For newly registered companies, the first accounting period runs from the registration date until the next month-end after the first anniversary of the registration date.

For example, if you register a company on 15 September, the first accounting period runs from 15 September 2008, until 30 September 2009. Subsequent accounting periods run from 1 October until 30 September.

Exceptions to the rule

Companies can change their accounting periods by up to six months, once every five years. They may change the periods for convenience: a company formed on 12 August 12 may find it easier to keep accounts to the calendar year (1 January to 31 December) or tax year (1 April to 31 March for CT).

Changing accounting periods means a longer or shorter accounting period may occur. Accounting periods may also vary if a company is dissolved during an accounting period.

When a company's accounting period is longer than 12 months for any reason, the period is split into two periods – the first of 12 months and the second of the new accounting period, less 12 months.

Take the example company above, registered on 15 September 2008. The directors decide to change the accounting period from 30 September 2009 to 31 December 2009. The first accounting period ends on 30 September 2009, the next on 31 December 2009 and subsequent periods on 31 December each year.

Because a company has nine months from the end of the accounting period to prepare and file accounts before the CT due date, consider keeping your tax money in the bank until the last minute to earn a bit more interest.

Computing Profits

Tax law is currently undergoing a rewrite to simplify the terms and make them more understandable. CT is still awaiting its rewrite, so the rules laid out in the Income and Corporation Taxes Act 1988, and later amendments, still apply to companies.

Schedules and cases

CT follows the old schedule and case system where different tax rules apply to different types of income, depending on which *schedule* the incomes slot into. A schedule is basically a set of tax rules that lays out how to account for income falling under that category:

- ✔ Schedule A details the rules for dealing with rental income.

- ✔ Schedule D deals with income from a trade like buy-to-sell property development.

So, to work out a company's profits, the income and expenses must be categorised according to the source of the income.

For instance, a company that lets property and develops property has both Schedule A rental income and Schedule D income from buy-to-sell activities.

The pro-forma profits calculation looks like this:

Schedule D income (buy-to-sell)	x
Schedule D loan interest received	x
Schedule A rental income	x
Net chargeable gains (from rental property disposals)	(x)
Total profit chargeable to tax	x

This calculation is simplified and only takes into account the parts of the computation that directly apply to property people.

Rental Income

Calculating rental income and expenses works pretty much the same for a company as for an individual.

As with individuals, a company's income from UK properties and overseas properties is recorded separately as two property businesses and the company can't set off profits and losses from one property business against those of the other.

Looking at loans

Companies can have loan relationships with borrowers and lenders, with interest payable being recorded in the accounts as a debit and interest receivable a credit.

Before you can look at the tax treatment of a loan relationship, you have to consider whether you've a trading or non-trading loan relationship:

- ✔ **A trading relationship**: Money borrowed to fund trading activities, for example, buy-to-sell property.

- ✔ **A non-trading relationship**: Money borrowed to fund investment activities, for example, buy-to-let property.

- ✔ **Bank interest received**: a non-trading loan relationship.

Taxing loan interest

Once you've classified the type of loan interest you're paying or receiving, you can slot it into the right pigeonhole for tax:

- ✔ Trading loan interest can be included in the accounts as an expense. Property developers engaged in a buy-to-sell business need to remember that this interest appears in the accounting period in which they sell their property. Until then, they must hold loan interest on the balance sheet as work-in-progress (WIP) costs.

- ✔ Non-trading loan interest can be added together as one category – payments out are debits and payments in are credits.

Interest payments received are income and slot in to the accounts as Schedule D interest received on the pro forma.

A net debit is treated like a net loss and set off against any profits arising in the current accounting period or non-trading loan interest credits arising in the previous accounting period.

Income received net of tax

Companies generally receive interest gross, that is, without tax deducted. Interest received net of tax should be *grossed up* for the accounts so that tax can be deducted in the calculation.

If interest received is net of tax at 20 per cent, which means that tax has already been deducted at the rate of 20 per cent on the total interest paid – then to gross up the figure, follow this formula:

(Amount received/100) – (tax rate × 100)

So, if you receive £50 net interest and have paid tax at 20 per cent, the formula is:

£50/85 x 100 = £58.82

Chargeable Gains

Companies do not pay CGT. They pay CT on all their profits and gains. Residential investment properties don't qualify as business assets, so they don't attract the chargeable gains reliefs available for business assets.

Development properties are business assets. A company pays CT on any profits from selling development property. UK furnished holiday-letting properties have all the tax advantages of a business asset, but a company still pays CT instead of CGT on any gains arising from disposing of UK holiday lets.

Corporate Losses

Trading losses for buy-to-sell property companies, unlike those of property buy-to-let companies, can be set off against profits in other years.

Setting off losses means that losses from one accounting period can be deducted from profits in another period. This set off is important because deducting the loss reduces the taxable profit £1 for £1 and so cuts the tax you pay.

> ✓ **Carry forward against the next profits arising:** If the loss carried forward is still greater than the next profits, the unrelieved losses can be carried forward again until they're cancelled out by profits.
>
> So, if you carry forward a £10,000 loss from last year and make a £8,000 profit this year, then you match £8,000 of the loss against the £8,000 profits and carry forward the remaining £2,000 to set off against the next available profits.
>
> This means that you pay no CT on £10,000 of profits until the carried forward loss is wiped out against profits.
>
> ✓ **Carry back against past profits:** If the company is trading, losses can be carried back 12 months. If the company is winding up, the carry back can be extended to 36 months.

Losses can only be set off against losses arising from the same trade, so if you changed from trading as a development company to a buy-to-let or property management company, the company would lose the buy-to-sell losses.

Property Depreciation

Fixed assets include letting property owned by a company. Other such assets include plant, machinery, computer equipment, and vans.

To recognise the wear-and-tear on these assets, an accountancy formula called *depreciation* is included in accounts. Depreciation isn't real money, but a calculated amount knocked off the profits to reflect the diminishing value of the business assets as they're used.

Special depreciation rules apply to companies holding letting property:

> ✓ A company can't depreciate or claim depreciation or capital allowances for residential investment property.
>
> ✓ Investment property must be held as land and property on the balance sheet at open-market value.
>
> ✓ The properties must be valued annually by an internal company valuer or by an external qualified professional valuer every five years.
>
> ✓ The name and qualification of the valuer should be noted in the financial statements.

Filing Company Tax Returns

Individuals and companies have their taxes dealt with by different departments within a tax office.

CT has its own self-assessment tax return, called a *CT600*, which must be completed and filed, along with a set of financial statements for the accounting period.

These documents must be filed within 12 months of the end of the accounting period. CT must be paid within nine months and one day of the end of the accounting period. The company has 12 months from the filing date to amend a tax return. If the taxman spots any errors, he must ask for corrections within nine months of the filing date.

Tax rates and dates

The CT year runs from 1 April to 31 March the following year, so profits for company accounting periods straddling 31 March are apportioned to make sure that the correct tax rate is applied to the profits.

That's because the Government can change the CT rate each year and the correct rate has to be applied to the profits allocated to the tax period.

A company formed on 15 September 2008 has a first year accounting period of 15 September 2008 until 30 September 2009. Apportionment is as follows:

- ✔ 15 September 2008–31 March 2009 = 182 days with tax charged at 21 per cent.

- ✔ 1 April–14 September 2008 = 183 days with tax charged at 22 per cent.

- ✔ 15 September–30 September = 16 days with tax charged at 22 per cent.

Under these circumstances, the company would submit one set of financial statements, one CT return and two CT600s – one for 15 September 2008–14 September 2009 and the other for 15 September 2009–30 September 2009.

Tax rates assume that the company pays CT at the small company rate.

Making sense of marginal relief

Marginal relief is available to companies making profits between £300,000 and £1.5 million, when the CT full rate of 28 per cent applies. Basically, marginal relief is a way of saying that if you make profits of £300,001, this profit is a long way short of the £1.5 million threshold, so a formula is applied to reduce the rate of tax.

On profits between £300,000 and £1.5 million, the rate gently scales up from the small company rate to the main rate of CT.

A useful online marginal relief calculator is available at `mrrcalculator.inlandrevenue.gov.uk/MRR0.aspx`.

Eyeing inquiries

From 31 March 2008, the taxman's *inquiry window* – the time HMRC gives notice that they're making inquiries about company accounts – changed. The inquiry date now links to the filing date of the CT600 tax return and accounts to HMRC, even if a company files these accounts early.

The inquiry window closes 12 months from the statutory filing date for tax returns filed early for companies with accounting periods ending on or before 31 March 2008.

The statutory filing date is generally 12 months after the end of the company's accounting period.

The inquiry window for most returns delivered by, or on, the filing date closes 12 months from the day on which HMRC receives the return for companies with accounting periods ending after 31March 2008. For example, a company's accounting period ends on 31 April 2008. HMRC receives the tax return on 26 November 2008, so a notice of inquiry has to be issued by 26 November 2009 to be valid.

If your company files late, the rules don't change. The inquiry window still closes on the final quarter date following the date the return is filed.

Delving into determinations

If a tax return isn't filed, HMRC raises a *determination* of the tax they consider to be due. A determination can only be corrected by filing a CT600 for the accounting period.

A determination is the taxman's estimate of the tax he thinks is a fair amount to pay based on past accounts, if you've filed any, and the sort of tax bill similar companies face.

Perusing penalties and surcharges

Penalties for failing to file returns and interest on unpaid tax may be levied by HMRC if a company misses filing deadlines. The penalties start at £100 for filing a day late and increase at regular periods.

Unpaid tax attracts statutory interest charges – you can find details of the rates on the HMRC website at www.hmrc.gov.uk/ rates/interest-late.htm.

The upside is that if the taxman owes you money, you're entitled to claim interest as well. Go to www.hmrc.gov.uk/rates/interest-repayments.htm for up-to-date information. Individuals and companies both pay interest on unpaid tax and receive interest on overpayment.

Chapter 21

Extracting the Cash from a Company

*T*aking money out of a company is a potential minefield for the unwary. All sorts of checks and brakes are in place to make sure directors and shareholders keep to the rules.

Run the right way, companies are effective tax vehicles, especially for property buy-to-sell traders – but if you fall foul of the rules, the penalties can be harsh.

This chapter is a guide to making your company work for you by minimising tax and maximising your returns.

Duties of a Director

Directors are responsible for the day-to-day running of a company on behalf of the shareholders.

For many large public companies with many thousands of shareholders, the board of directors is elected at the annual general meeting.

Private companies may be a single director and shareholder, or spouses, partners or friends.

The directors' duties are the same whatever the size of the company:

- ✔ To keep accounting records
- ✔ To prepare 'true and fair' annual accounts

Directors generally announce dividends based on the profits in the annual or interim – quarterly or half-yearly – accounts.

Moving the Money

Several tried and tested methods are available for taking money out of a company. These include:

- ✔ Salary and bonus
- ✔ Dividends
- ✔ Loans
- ✔ Petty cash
- ✔ Benefits-in-kind
- ✔ Company cars

This is by no means an exhaustive list, but the methods most people consider. Each method has pros and cons for a director and/or shareholder that I consider in more detail below:

Salary and bonus

A *salary* is a regular payment from the company to an employee or a director in return for the efforts they put in to make the business successful. A *bonus* is a salary top-up for a job well done.

Extras like company cars and medical insurance do not count as salary.

The key here is salary paid to people who work for the company – if you don't put in the hours, you can't draw a salary, and if you do put in the hours, you need to show the taxman how many hours you work and exactly what you do to deserve the money.

Drawing a salary

If you have a buy-to-sell company, you should draw a salary, even if it is not much money. Drawing a salary keeps your National Insurance contributions up-to-date so you qualify for a state pension and other benefits.

The company can also set off your salary, tax and National Insurance as a business expense against income before tax – which means every pound of salary, tax and National Insurance reduces your profits and in turn, the tax your company pays.

You must make sure that if a salary is paid, the cash actually leaves the company account for your private account, and that it is paid within nine months of the end of the company's accounting period.

Earnings for pensions

Salaries are regarded as earnings for pensions and can be used to swell the contributions you make from the minimum £300 per month.

Investment companies may face opposition from the tax man if they pay salaries.

Dividends

A *dividend* is the return on the money a shareholder has invested in a company by purchasing shares. Dividends are paid out of the profits a company makes in the accounting period, and are generally paid as earnings per share.

For instance, if Mike has 100 £1 shares in ABC Ltd and Kelly has 50 £1 shares in the same company and the company announces a dividend of 50p a share, Mike receives 100 × 50p = £50 and Kelly receives £25.

Saving National Insurance

Many companies pay directors a small salary and top up the amount with a quarterly dividend to avoid National Insurance.

This method means the director pays the same amount of tax but neither the director nor the company pays National Insurance contributions on the dividend.

Shielding higher rate Income Tax

If the director or shareholder is already a higher rate taxpayer or the payment of a dividend would push them in to the higher rate tax bracket, this 40 per cent tax can be *deferred* by the company holding the dividend.

By this, instead of declaring a dividend to pay out profits, no dividend or a smaller dividend is declared that keeps the shareholder below the top rate tax threshold.

The dividend can be kept in reserve by the company as retained profits and paid at some time in the future when the shareholder is not a higher rate taxpayer.

Dividends are paid to shareholders regardless of whether they work for the company or not.

Paying attention in class

All shareholders holding the same class of shares receive the same payment per share.

If you want to pay one set of investors different dividends to others, then the company must set up different share classes.

Going back to Mike and Kelly, if Mike was paid 50p a share on 100 Class A ordinary shares; he would still receive £50 in dividends.

Should the directors feel Kelly ought to receive a lesser dividend, they could issue her Class B ordinary shares and pay a penny per share dividend giving her a 50p payment.

If a company has insufficient profits to cover the dividend payment, the tax man can treat the dividend as a loan and charge tax – see the section on loans below for more information.

Dividends are not considered earnings for pensions.

Directors' loans

These are the cause of more grief and unforeseen to directors with lax financial control over a company than anything else.

The problem is mainly is small companies with a single director and shareholder.

The temptation for the director is to pay personal bills from the company account instead of paying a salary and taking dividends by transferring the payments to a personal bank account.

These payments build up as debits to the director's loan account, and if payments come in as credits, tax problems are triggered.

Loan account ins and outs

A director's loan account is not real money – it's a tally kept on the balance sheet of money paid out to the director and money the director pays in to the company.

Most loan accounts would include:

✔ Director's drawings on account of salary and dividends

✔ Personal bills paid by the company for the director

✔ Net salary and dividend due and not transferred to the director

✔ Reimbursed expenses paid personally by the director

If a company has more than one director, tag the accounting entries so each transaction can be debited or credited to the right director. Keeping one account and splitting it is no good – each director needs his or her own loan account.

Director loan tax trap

If a director's loan exceeds $5,000 in an accounting period, the tax man treats it as a benefit in kind and charges Income Tax on the balance.

If your company is a close company, the company must also pay 25 per cent of the loan as tax and submit form CT600A with the company tax return if the loan is not repaid within nine months of the end of the accounting period in which the loan was made. The company also has to pay employer's National Insurance contributions on the loan amount.

The extra Corporation Tax charge is refunded nine months after the end of the accounting period when the loan is repaid. The National Insurance contributions are not refundable.

Solving overdraft problems

If a director has an overdrawn account, ways exist of resolving the issue:

✔ **Declare a dividend for the loan amount but don't withdraw the money:** This creates a credit to the loan account and wipes out the loan.

You would need a $8,889 dividend to clear a $8,000 loan. Income Tax would be $2,000 ($8,000× 25 per cent) with no employer's National Insurance.

✔ **Pay a bonus to cover the loan:** A higher rate taxpayer (paying 40 per cent) would have to take a bonus of $13,333 to clear a $8,000 director's loan.

This would cost $5,333 in Income Tax and $1,706 in employer's National Insurance for 2008/2009.

✔ **Pay cash to cover the loan from your personal bank account in to the company bank account:** Tax and National Insurance would already be paid on this cash, so no more would be due.

In most cases, the most tax-effective method of clearing a director's loan account is to declare a dividend and leave the money on account in the company.

Director loans – good or bad?

If you play the game by the rules you can borrow £5,000 from your company tax and interest free. Borrow more than £5,000 and you and the company end up paying extra tax. This threshold applies to each director.

Charging your company interest

If you have invested a substantial amount of your own cash in to your company, there is absolutely no reason why you cannot consider charging the company a commercial rate of interest on the investment.

After all, if you lent the money to someone else, you would probably charge them interest.

This profit extraction method is a double-edged sword, because:

✔ You have to report any interest received on your tax return and will pay Income Tax.

✔ The company can set off the interest paid as an expense against profits and reduce the amount of Corporation Tax paid.

Getting petty about cash

Keep a track of any expenses you pay for the company – put the receipts in every month with a claim sheet detailing the date, details of the expense and the amount and transfer the money from your company to personal account.

This is really the equivalent of drawing petty cash in reverse for incidental expenses. Instead of keeping the cash in a tin, dipping in to your own pocket and reclaiming the money is quite OK.

No tax or National Insurance is due on the amount you are reimbursed for genuine business expenses.

Benefits-in-kind

Don't forget you are not the company, so it follows that anything the company owns does not belong to you.

If you have private use of those assets, the use is given a taxable value or 'cash equivalent' and you will then pay tax and National Insurance for the benefit you have enjoyed at the company's cost.

Some assets, like mobile phones and computers are tax-free, but most are not. Special rules apply to some assets like company cars and living accommodation.

Beware of gifts

Don't let the company gift you any assets – you will be taxed on the market value of the asset as if it was a bonus.

How is the tax worked out?

The company works out the 'cash equivalent' of your personal use of the asset, which the tax man says is 20 per cent of the assets value. You pay Income Tax on the cash equivalent figure.

So, if the company buys a pool table for £1,000 and lends it to you to use at home, the cash equivalent is £200 (20 per cent of £1,000) for every year you enjoy personal use of the pool table.

If you are a basic rate taxpayer, you pay £40 tax, or £80 if you are a higher rate taxpayer.

The company also pays employers' National Insurance contributions on the cash equivalent of the benefit.

Is there any real benefit?

Benefits in kind are a mixed blessing, for four main reasons:

- ✔ The director doesn't pay employee's National Insurance but the company pays employer's National Insurance on the 'cash equivalent'.

- ✔ The company can set off the cost of the asset against income even if the asset is only ever used privately by the director, but if the director never uses the asset, tax still has to be paid if it was available.

- ✔ As long as the director keeps the asset for four years or less, the taxable 'cash equivalent' of 20 per cent a year is less than the asset's worth.

> ✔ Depending on the type of asset, the company may be able to claim capital allowances.

Company cars

Just a quick word about company cars – the general consensus is not to have a company car as the Government is almost taxing them out of existence.

The solution is to own the car yourself and reclaim business mileage at the HMRC rate – See Chapter 7 for more detail on claiming mileage.

Telling the Taxman

Directors have to tell the tax man about any benefits in kind by filing an Expenses and Benefits form P11d by July 6 following the end of the tax year in which the benefit was received.

Benefits received in the 2008–2009 tax year, must be reported by July 9, 2009 and the details included in the director's personal tax return for filing by January 31, 2010.

Companies also have to complete a form P11d(b) for filing by July 9 following the end of the tax year in which the benefit was received to report any Class 1A National Insurance contributions due on any benefits paid.

National Insurance due must be paid by July 19.

As with all form filing, if you miss the key dates, HMRC will automatically fine you and interest will accrue on any money you owe.

Part VI
The Part of Tens

'Owning property's all very well, but
it can be a tremendous burden.'

In this part . . .

*T*his part contains three vital chapters. First up, I draw back the curtain on ten top tax tips: Follow these to save yourself a *lot* of money. I then talk you through a bunch of the commonest property tax pitfalls, and give you the inside track on avoiding them. Finally, since keeping up to date is so important in the ever-changing world of tax, I introduce you to a few of the best information resources out there.

Chapter 22

Ten Tax Tips to Save You Thousands

*I*f you pick up this book and only thumb through a few pages, the tips in this section include some of the most important information you should read, and can save you thousands of pounds in property tax.

Let-to-Buy Strategy

Let-to-buy is when you move from a house that you've lived in to a new house, but instead of selling your old home, you let it to tenants.

Let-to-buy is one of the most profitable tax strategies for landlords because you can let the house for at least 36 months and then sell without paying any Capital Gains Tax (CGT), should the house increase in value.

For more information on let-to-buy see Chapter 9.

Tax-Free Cashbacks for Landlords

Keep a track of your investments – as property prices rise you can take tax-free cash out of your property business to spend how you like.

For the low-down on getting tax-free cash out of your property business, check out Chapter 13.

Tax-Free Loans for Directors

If you're a director of a property company, you can borrow up to £5,000 tax and interest free from your company.

If you want to know about tax-free loans from property companies, check out Chapter 21.

Income Shifting with Joint Ownership

Income shifting is when a higher-rate taxpayer arranges financial affairs so that some of the tax burden is shifted to a partner or associate who's a basic-rate taxpayer.

Starting 6 April 2009 the government plans new rules to stop companies and partnerships from income shifting. Property investors are to be exempt from the new rules as long as they run their business as sole traders or joint owners.

See Chapter 8 for more on the pros and cons of income shifting.

Furnished Holiday Lets

Running a UK furnished holiday letting business gives you the best of all tax worlds. Because holiday letting is a trade and not an investment, you can benefit from the tax advantages of the new Entrepreneur's Relief.

Doubling Up Strategies

Remember that many tax strategies can be doubled up to increase the tax benefits. For example, if you let-to-buy and then split ownership following the income-shifting strategy, you can reduce income tax on rental profits, and also bring additional allowances into play to save CGT.

Buying in Disadvantaged Areas

For 'disadvantaged' you can often read 'up and coming', because the Government and European Community is pouring grant money into the place to pull it up by its bootstraps.

Buying property in a disadvantaged area reduces the stamp duty you pay for a property of the same value outside a disadvantaged area.

For more information on buying in disadvantaged areas, take a look at Chapter 8.

Scour Your Spending for Expenses

The more you spend on your property business the more you save in tax. Every pound you can put through as a business expense reduces your profits by a pound and saves you tax.

Make sure that you're claiming all the business expenses you can. For the full rundown, see Chapter 7.

Keep to the Taxman's Timetable

There's absolutely no point working hard to arrange your financial affairs so as to minimise your tax and then filing tax returns and official paperwork late.

Filing tax returns and paperwork late triggers fines and penalties that can undo all the tax savings that you've worked hard to achieve.

For individuals, make sure that you file your tax returns on time – paper returns by 31 October and online by 31 January. For companies, remember the filing dates are nine months from the end of your accounting period.

Don't Hide and Hope for the Best

The taxman can use a wealth of technology and access many databases to track people who deliberately evade tax. You're taking huge risks by thinking that you can get away with not filing tax returns and reporting capital gains.

Remember, tax evasion is a crime and tax avoidance is legal.

The law enshrines your right to arrange your financial affairs to pay the least tax you can by using the strategies in this book. However, evasion is deliberately misrepresenting your income to pay less tax and is a crime.

Chapter 23

Ten Tax Disasters to Avoid

. . . .

In This Chapter

▶ Side-stepping tax problems

▶ Resisting cash-in-the-hand discount deals

▶ Reviewing your strategies regularly

▶ Tying up loose ends

▶ Avoiding the money pit of credit – it can cost a fortune

. . . .

*J*ust as you can plan to save tax, you can end up paying too much if you fail to plan.

Tax disasters don't just happen. They generally occur because the property people entering into the transactions have little or no knowledge of how to finance and manage their projects.

Hopefully, if you recognise yourself in one of the following examples, you can catch yourself and get back on track before that disaster hits home.

Mixing Your Property Businesses

Separate your property business affairs if you both let and develop property.

If you don't separate the two, you can't apply the right tax rules to the right transactions. The taxman always goes for the tax treatment that costs you the most money.

Ignoring the Taxman's Deadlines

File your tax returns and accounts on time and pay your tax by the due date. Failing to do so triggers fines and interest on outstanding tax bills. Chapter 3 talks you through dealing with the taxman.

Serial Developing

You may think that you're clever moving house, developing a property, and selling at a profit to climb the property ladder, but it only ends in tears.

A little-known clause in capital gains tax (CGT) rules says that if you spend money on a property with a view to making a gain, the PRR tax exemption doesn't apply. See Chapter 9 for more on this subject.

Paying Cash to Cowboy Builders

It's always tempting to get a discount for cash, but if you do, you won't get an invoice and you miss out on putting the expense through your accounts.

The only winner is the builder, who doesn't declare the cash to the taxman. You lose because that expense can reduce your tax by increasing your business expenses.

It's not illegal to pay cash. However, if the builder evades tax and VAT by not charging you for them, or does not put the cash through his accounts (thus misrepresenting his income), then he's breaking the law.

Of course, if you pay a builder cash and he charges you VAT, if it's applicable, and then declares the income and tax, then that's fine.

Failing to Keep Financial Records

By law, you're obliged to keep financial records of your property business and may face a fine if you don't.

You must keep all original invoices, receipts, bank statements, letting agreements, and any other financial documents relating to your business. See Chapter 5 for more on keeping proper records.

Estimating profits and losses is unacceptable and you end up paying more tax than you should when a taxman launches a tax inquiry.

Getting Stuck in a Rut

Tax law changes and so must your strategies. Use the online resources listed in Chapter 24 to keep up with new rules and make sure that you don't unwittingly fall into a tax trap.

Leaving Loose Ends Behind You

Estate planning is often called the cornerstone of financial planning. Inheritance tax can decimate the value of your estate and leave your family and loved ones in financial turmoil.

Simply sitting down with an adviser and making a will can take away a lot of this heartache at a stroke.

Trusting in Tax Seminars

If something seems too good to be true, that often means that it is. Many seminar providers are genuine types imparting worthwhile information – but beware the sharks.

Look at our list of online resources before handing over your hard-earned cash to salespeople who demand small fortunes for revealing property tax 'secrets'. Most of what you want to know is out there for free, or available from qualified professionals for a modest fee.

Ask yourself – why are these people asking me for money when they say they can make millions from property? Is the answer that they can actually make more from selling seminars?

Grabbing at Gifted Deposits

Failing to tell your mortgage provider that a seller is providing a gifted deposit may be fraud. Take legal advice before signing up to risky deals, and remember: there's no such thing as a free lunch.

Playing Fast and Loose with Your Tax Responsibilities

Don't forget your tax responsibilities. Think of the money you make from letting or developing property as a cake. Unfortunately, not all the cake is yours – a slice belongs to the tax man and he wants his share.

So make sure that you put aside enough money from your profits to pay your tax bills.

Chapter 24

Ten Online Property Resources

● ●

In This Chapter

▶ Finding property tax information on the web

▶ Linking in to communities of property people

▶ Remembering that well-intentioned opinion can make things worse

▶ Taking professional advice is always best

● ●

*F*inding the right answer to your tax questions on the Internet is not as easy as it may seem.

Certainly the World Wide Web is knee-deep in well-intentioned people who want to try to help you out. Beware! Keep the following points in mind when checking out info from the web:

✔ A response on a web forum or message board is the modern day equivalent of the bloke in the pub who's got an answer for everything. Even well-intentioned advice is not necessarily accurate in the fast-changing world of tax and law.

✔ When reading websites, check the date on which articles were posted – if they've not changed for years, the information may be well out-of-date.

✔ Check that you're looking at a UK tax site and not one from overseas – many countries have similar tax laws but their rules don't apply in the UK.

✔ Don't mistake opinion for fact – an opinion is an interpretation of the facts, not the facts themselves.

✔ If you bookmark sites, refresh your browser cache regularly to make sure that you're not reading old news.

Bearing those points in mind, may I present ten top-drawer online tax resources.

HMRC

www.hmrc.gov.uk. The HMRC site offers a comprehensive guide to UK tax law, from the taxman's point of view. Remember that it's just that – the taxman's point of view – and that guidance on the site doesn't have the force of law, it's just the way the taxman interprets the law, and it may not necessarily be right.

Business Link

www.businesslink.gov.uk. Business Link contains lots of useful, practical information about starting and running a business. It's aimed more at property developers or property management businesses than investors but nevertheless, it includes a stack of well-written and easy-to-digest articles.

DirectGov

www.direct.gov.uk/en/index.htm. DirectGov is the government's wide-ranging website stuffed full of consumer information. The site includes a special section on property tax as well as other tax information. Helpfully, the pages link in to more detailed information at the HMRC website.

LandlordZone

www.landlordzone.co.uk. An independent website, LandlordZone offers a wealth of help to landlords. The site is a good jump point for researching any questions that you may have about managing your rental business and dealing with tenants. The forums are active and the topic experts are generally well qualified to answer questions.

Landlord Law

www.landlord-law.co.uk. Landlord Law is another independent website, run by a professional solicitor, specialising in property and tenants. The site includes free information, but the real meat is available by modest subscription. Tessa Shepperson, who runs the site, writes popular legal guides for landlords.

TaxationWeb

www.taxationweb.co.uk. TaxationWeb is one of the old-school sites that has offered tax advice on the web for many years. The site includes active forums on many tax topics and contains a wealth of information for buy-to-let and buy-to-sell property people.

Singing Pig

www.singingpig.co.uk. Made up of an online community of property investors and entrepreneurs, the Singing Pig website includes a vast array of forums where members discuss all sorts of relevant issues for landlords and traders.

News Now

Tax: www.newsnow.co.uk/h/Business+&+Finance/Tax.

Property: www.newsnow.co.uk/h/Business+&+Finance/ Industry+Sectors/Property.

A free, online news service, News Now consists of sections devoted to the latest breaking news about tax and property.

Tax Central

www.taxcentral.co.uk. This useful tax information site includes online tax calculators, help on finding a tax adviser, and a helpful question and answer archive.

Property Tax Plus

www.propertytaxplus.co.uk. This site is my own website where you can find the latest tax news, advice, and updates to information in this book.

As helpful as these online sites may be – and the many others that you can find out there – don't make decisions based solely on what you read.

Tax is complicated and you may be unaware of factors that alter your circumstances. Always consider taking paid-for professional advice.

Index

Notes

FOR DUMMIES

Do Anything. Just Add Dummies

HOME

UK editions

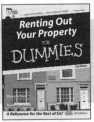

PERSONAL FINANCE

BUSINESS

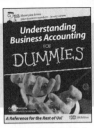

British History For Dummies
(978-0-470-03536-8)

Buying a Property in Eastern Europe For Dummies
(978-0-7645-7047-6)

Cognitive Behavioural Therapy For Dummies
(978-0-470-01838-5)

Cricket For Dummies
(978-0-470-03454-5)

Diabetes For Dummies, 2nd Edition
(978-0-470-05810-7)

Detox For Dummies
(978-0-470-01908-5)

eBay.co.uk For Dummies, 2nd Edition
(978-0-470-51807-6)

Genealogy Online For Dummies
(978-0-7645-7061-2)

Life Coaching For Dummies
(978-0-470-03135-3)

Neuro-linguistic Programming For Dummies
(978-0-7645-7028-5)

Parenting For Dummies
(978-0-470-02714-1)

Rugby Union For Dummies, 2nd Edition
(978-0-470-03537-5)

Self Build and Renovation For Dummies
(978-0-470-02586-4)

Thyroid For Dummies
(978-0-470-03172-8)

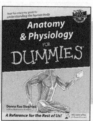
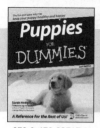

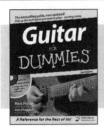

FOR DUMMIES®

Helping you expand your horizons and achieve your potential

SOFTWARE & INTERNET

The Internet For Dummies
978-0-470-12174-0

Starting an Online Business For Dummies
978-0-470-10739-3

Creating Web Pages For Dummies
978-0-470-08030-6

Also available:

Creating Web Pages All-in-One Desk Reference For Dummies (978-0-470-09629-1)

Dreamweaver CS3 For Dummies (978-0-470-11490-2)

Everyday Internet All-in-One Desk Reference For Dummies (978-0-7645-8875-4)

Web Design For Dummies (978-0-471-78117-2)

DIGITAL MEDIA

Digital Photography For Dummies
978-0-7645-9802-9

iPod & iTunes For Dummies
978-0-470-17474-6

Digital SLR Cameras & Photography For Dummies
978-0-470-14927-0

Also available:

Blogging For Dummies (978-0-470-23017-6)

Digital Photography All-in-One Desk Reference For Dummies (978-0-470-03743-0)

Digital Photos, Movies & Music GigaBook For Dummies (978-0-7645-7414-6)

iPhone For Dummies (978-0-470-17469-2)

Photoshop CS3 For Dummies (978-0-470-11193-2)

Podcasting For Dummies (978-0-471-74898-4)

COMPUTER BASICS

PCs For Dummies
978-0-470-13728-4

Laptops For Dummies
978-0-470-05432-1

Windows Vista For Dummies
978-0-471-75421-3

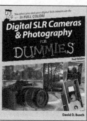

Also available:

Excel 2007 For Dummies (978-0-470-03737-9)

Macs For Dummies (978-0-470-04849-8)

Office 2007 For Dummies (978-0-470-00923-9)

PCs All-in-One Desk Reference For Dummies (978-0-470-22338-3)

Pocket PC For Dummies (978-0-7645-1640-5)

Upgrading & Fixing PCs For Dummies (978-0-470-12102-3)